LIBRARY OF
AND
MONEY BANKING
HISTORY

OBSERVATIONS
ON THE FINANCIAL POSITION AND CREDIT
OF THE NORTH AMERICAN STATES

OBSERVATIONS

ON THE

FINANCIAL POSITION AND CREDIT

OF SUCH OF

THE STATES OF THE NORTH AMERICAN UNION

AS HAVE

CONTRACTED PUBLIC DEBTS

BY

ALEXANDER TROTTER

[1839]

REPRINTS OF ECONOMIC CLASSICS

AUGUSTUS M. KELLEY · PUBLISHERS
NEW YORK 1968

First Edition, 1839

(London: Longman, Orme, Brown, Green &
Longmans, *Paternoster-Row*, 1839)

Reprinted 1968 by

AUGUSTUS M. KELLEY · PUBLISHERS

New York   New York   10010

Library of Congress Catalogue Card Number

67-21885

PRINTED IN THE UNITED STATES OF AMERICA
by SENTRY PRESS, NEW YORK, N. Y. 10019

OBSERVATIONS

ON.

THE FINANCIAL POSITION AND CREDIT

OF SUCH OF

THE STATES

OF

THE NORTH AMERICAN UNION

AS HAVE

CONTRACTED PUBLIC DEBTS :

COMPRISING

AN ACCOUNT OF THE MANNER IN WHICH THE SUMS RAISED BY
EACH STATE HAVE BEEN APPLIED,

AND A CONSIDERATION OF THE PROBABLE EFFECTS OF SUCH APPLICATION
UPON THE GENERAL WEALTH AND PROSPERITY OF
THE COUNTRY.

BY

ALEXANDER TROTTER, ESQ.

LONDON

PRINTED FOR

LONGMAN, ORME, BROWN, GREEN, AND LONGMANS,
PATERNOSTER-ROW.

26TH DECEMBER, 1839.

ERRATA.

Page 446. for " Liabilities" read " Resources,"
447. for " Resources" read " Liabilities ; "
and reverse the sides.

CONTENTS.

CHAPTER I.

CHAP. II.

CHAP. III.

CHAP. IV.

CHAP. V.

APPENDIX.

OBSERVATIONS,

&c. &c.

CHAPTER I.

THE United States of America, in point of national credit, have long held a high place in public estimation ; but that confidence to which the
federal government has acquired a just claim, by
a strict adherence to its pecuniary engagements
often maintained under trying circumstances,
ought not, without further inquiry, to be extended

CHAP.
I.

Credit of
the federal
govern-
ment not
identical
with that
of the
separate
states.

to the separate states of the Union, each of which ought to be judged of by a special reference to its own necessities and resources and to its conduct under the circumstances in which it is placed. It may, nevertheless, be of service, in examining the condition of these different states, to consider shortly the financial history and actual position of the entire confederation, as a sketch of these, by exhibiting the extent of the national resources of the United States generally, will contribute, in an essential manner, to a just appreciation of the condition of the separate states of which the confederation is composed.

At the termination of the struggle by which the British colonists in North America raised themselves to the rank of an independent nation, the government to which the interests of the new Republic were entrusted found itself placed in a situation of much embarrassment. After a contest of more than seven years' duration the commerce of the colonies was nearly annihilated, and a large debt had been contracted to meet the expenses of the war, while complicated accounts remained unadjusted between the general government and the separate states respecting the sums which each had received and expended. During the continuance of this contest the Colonies were united by no other tie than a sense of their common danger ; yet Congress, with no foundation for its authority except that derived from common consent, proclaimed the independence of the states, and carried on an expensive war to establish it. The articles of confederation, adopted in 1781, scarcely gave this body a more efficient power — it was, indeed, authorised by that instrument to make requisitions of money from the several states, but it was vested with no coercive means to enforce them. This limited and unsettled authority of the first Congress added to the difficulties of the government. The most likely source whence funds could be derived to defray the interest on the debt and to reduce its amount was from duties upon imports : but the states, by the articles of confederation, had reserved to themselves the sole right of framing their own commercial regulations, and, consequently, of levying imposts of this description ; and the burden to which they were severally subjected in making provision for the payment of their own debts, together with a mutual jealousy which already began to exist among them, caused them for a long time to resist the appeals which the government repeatedly made to them to provide from this source for the exigencies of the Treasury. It was not until the settlement of the constitution in 1789 that the general government was entrusted with more ample powers, by the eighth section of the first article of which it was authorised to impose taxes and duties, and to establish commercial regulations both with foreign nations and among the several states. Under this new form of government, and the able administration of General Washington, fresh energies seemed given to the country ; and the progress of its national and individual prosperity has since that

CHAP.
I.

Amount of
the debt,
April 1783.

Provisions
for the
mainten-
ance of
public
credit.

time surpassed, probably, what the world had ever before witnessed.

At the period first spoken of, at the close of the war in 1783, the debt of the United States amounted to upwards of forty-two millions of dollars; of this, about one fourth part had been borrowed, either in Holland under the guarantee of the French court, or directly from the Treasuries of France and Spain; and the remainder was due to individuals within the states. The interest on these loans amounted annually to $2,415,956 * ; in addition to the above sum the separate debts of the states amounted to upwards of $20,000,000.

At the time of the settlement of the constitution, arrears of interest had greatly swelled the claims of the public creditor ; but on the assembling of the first constitutional Congress an act was passed to make provision for the whole outstanding engagements of the government, and with a degree of integrity which is rare in the history of the financial embarrassments of states, the claims of the creditors at home were postponed till those of the foreign creditors were provided for. †

---

* The fractional parts of a dollar are omitted in the introductory chapters, but are retained afterwards, where detailed accounts are given. For the value of the dollar, see Appendix, letter A.

† From the difficulty which was experienced in providing the means of paying the interest on the foreign debt in the countries where the moneys were borrowed, a proposition was afterwards made to the creditors to commute the amounts of stock due to them into new stocks bearing respectively an additional interest of one half per cent. more than was originally agreed upon, but the principal and interest of which were to be pay-

OF PUBLIC CREDIT.

The arrangement of the domestic debt was attended with considerable difficulty. It was finally agreed to fund the arrear of interest at three per cent., and the principal at six per cent., suspending, however, for ten years, the payment of the interest on one third of the principal ; and, as a compensation for that suspension, a condition was attached to the debt which was supposed to enhance its value, viz. that the principal should only be redeemed at the rate of eight per cent. of the amount in each year.

At the same time the general government took upon itself $18,271,787 of the debts of the separate states*, and admitted its liability for a further sum of $4,221,100, arising from balances which were still found due to the creditor states on a final settlement of their accounts. These additional engagements were subjected to an arrange-

able only in the United States, and the principal to be redeemable at the pleasure of the government. This proposition was very generally acceded to, and the greater portion of the foreign debt was thus ultimately converted into domestic stocks bearing 4½ and 5½ per cent. interest.

It may be further observed, as a proof of the good faith of the government of the United States, that, during the war with this country in 1812, the interest on the portion of the debt inscribed in the names of British subjects was regularly paid to their agents in America; and if, owing to the interruption of direct commercial intercourse between the two countries, some delay was experienced in the receipt of the dividends in this country, from the agents having to seek for a circuitous route to transmit them, they were ultimately realised at a very favourable rate of exchange.

* See Appendix letter B.

ment similar to that which was adopted in the case of the claims of the home creditors.

Appropriations were made for the payment of the interest on these several debts, with priority according to the order in which they have been enumerated ; — viz.

1. On foreign loans.
2. On the domestic debt.
3. On the state debts which were assumed.
4. On the balances due to the creditor states.

A fund was also created for the redemption of the debt, which was placed under the management of the President of the Senate, the Chief Justice, and certain other public functionaries, who were constituted "The Commissioners of the Sinking Fund."

On the 19th of Nov. 1794, President Washington, in his address to Congress at the opening of the session, recommended the adoption of further means for the maintenance of the public credit and the ultimate redemption of the debt ; and an act was in consequence passed on the third of March, 1795, directing the creation of a fund, consisting of certain specified branches of the revenue, which should be invariably applied towards that object until the whole debt should be redeemed, and that this fund should be vested in the Commissioners of the Sinking Fund "as property in trust : " it was also enacted, that all priorities before established in regard to the different portions of the debt should cease, unless the creditors dissented ; so that the whole sum thus

appropriated towards the liquidation of the debt CHAP.
should constitute a common fund, chargeable with- I.
out distinction for the benefit of all the creditors
of the state.

The amount of debt which had been redeemed Amount of
by the Commissioners up to the 31st of De- the debt,
cember 1794, was $2,265,022 leaving a total Dec. 1794.
debt on that day, due by the United States, of
$76,096,468.*

Rapid advances had been made in lessening Progress of
this amount when the war with England, in its liquidation.
1812, caused a greatly increased expenditure.
The total debt at the beginning of that year
had been reduced to $45,154,189 inclusive of
$15,000,000 which had been borrowed to pay
the French government for the purchase of the
colony of Louisiana : but the means adopted for
reducing the original debt being persevered in,
and fresh provisions being made, as each successive loan was raised, to secure its final extinction, the financial credit of the country remained
unimpaired ; and so successful was the application
of its resources, that on the 30th September, 1820,
there remained only $20,570,627 of the funded
debt which was contracted before the year 1812.
Of that contracted subsequently to 1812 there then
remained unredeemed $70,654,933, making an ag-
gregate debt on the 30th of September, 1820, of
$91,225,560 ; but as the debt on the 30th of
September, 1815, was stated by the President in

* See Appendix, letter C.

CHAP.
I.

his message of November, 1820, to have amounted to $158,713,049 the sum repaid in this interval must have exceeded sixty-seven millions.* During this time the expenses of the government had been regularly defrayed in every branch of the civil, military, and naval establishments; the public edifices in Washington had been rebuilt after their destruction by the English in 1814, with considerable additions; extensive fortifications had been commenced and were in progress; permanent arsenals and magazines had been erected in various parts of the Union, and the Navy had been considerably augmented; and it must be acknowledged that the discharge of so large a portion of the public debt, and the completion of so many extensive and important undertakings in so short a time, exhibit, in a very strong point of view, the wealth and resources of the country.

Extinction of the debt of the federal government.

The further progress of the liquidation of the debt, may be traced in the various messages of the Presidents, and in the annual Treasury Reports; it is unnecessary, however, to follow up these details, and it will be sufficient to say, that, on the 1st of January, 1835, no portion either of the foreign or domestic engagements of the federal government

* In the President's message, the debt, on the 30th September, 1820, is stated to have been $91,993,883 : the amount given above is taken from the annual Treasury Report. The sum of $158,713,049 included various engagements of the government besides the funded and floating debt, which amounted only to $119,635,558 ; but the larger sum is assumed, because the items which swelled the amount had all been repaid in the interval alluded to.

remained unredeemed. President Jackson, in his messages of the two preceding years, had looked forward with much exultation to the final liquidation of the debt happening under his administration : during the last four years that the executive power had been confided to his charge, $58,000,000 had been applied towards the attainment of this object. " If Providence permits me to meet you in another session," he says, in his message of December, 1833, " I shall have the high gratification of announcing to you that the National Debt is extinguished. I cannot refrain from expressing the pleasure I feel at the near approach of that desirable event. The short period of time within which the public debt will have been discharged is strong evidence of the abundant resources of the country, and of the prudence and economy with which the government has heretofore been administered. We have waged two wars since we have become a nation with one of the most powerful kingdoms in the world ; both of them undertaken in defence of our dearest rights — both successfully prosecuted and honourably terminated ; and many of those who partook in the first struggle, as well as the second, will have lived to see the last item of the debt incurred in those necessary but expensive conflicts faithfully and honestly discharged ; and we shall have the proud satisfaction of bequeathing to the public servants who follow us in the administration of the government the rare blessing of a revenue sufficiently abundant, raised without injustice or oppression to our citizens, and unincumbered with

CHAP.
I.

Accumu-
lation and
distribution
of the
surplus
revenue.

any burdens but what they themselves shall think proper to impose upon it."

The surplus revenue beginning after this to accumulate rapidly, the most advantageous disposal of it became a question of considerable difficulty : the administration and its supporters were anxious to apply the money to military purposes, by extending the means of national defence ; but the opposition introduced a bill, which was finally passed on the 23d of June, 1836, enacting, that the money which should be in the Treasury on the 1st of January, 1837, should, after reserving the sum of $5,000,000, be distributed among the several states of the Union. The distribution was to take place according to the respective representation of the states in the Senate and House of Representatives, and was to be made in quarterly instalments ; but it was declared to be in the nature of a " deposit" only, to be resumed should the exigencies of the Treasury require it. The sum to be divided (which at the passing of the Act was stated by a Report from the Secretary of the Treasury as likely to amount to $22,000,000) eventually proved to be $37,468,859. *

Although the literal provisions of the Act of the 23d June expressly directed that the money should be " deposited" with the states, yet it was argued that the intention of those who passed it was to secure a permanent distribution of the surplus revenue ; and in accordance with this view, though

* See Appendix, letter D

in defiance of the obligations of the Deposit Act,
the amount received has in most of the states been
appropriated in a permanent manner; many of
them having expended it in works of internal improvement, or in paying debts previously incurred
for this purpose. In some instances it has been
lent upon mortgage to the citizens of the states;
and in one case, against every principle of justice,
since it had not been equally contributed, it was
divided numerically among all the inhabitants of
the state.

The last instalment, however, was not paid : a *Financial difficulties and sus-pension of the fourth instalment.*
series of events, which it will be necessary to detail,
so disordered the financial department of the general government before the distribution was completed that, after the first three payments had been
made to the different states, it became necessary to
have recourse to a new act of Congress, which
was passed on the 2d of October, to direct the
postponement of the transfer of the remaining
fourth till the 1st of January, 1839.* A subsequent act has since been passed to postpone the
payment indefinitely.

The events alluded to, which thus checked
the course of the nation in its onward career, have
had such a widely extended influence on its general prosperity, that before entering on the detail
proposed, a retrospect of the causes which led to
them will be attended with advantage.

---

* This law further provided that the amount deposited should
remain with the states until otherwise directed by Congress.

The first National Bank in the United States after the adoption of the constitution, was established in 1791, under the presidency of General Washington : the charter was granted for twenty years. Its establishment was strongly resisted at the time by the opponents of the government, and especially by Mr. Jefferson and Mr. Madison, who contended that Congress had no powers under the constitution to incorporate such institutions.

Before the expiration of the charter, the republican party, who thus opposed it, had come into power, Mr. Madison being President ; and a renewal of the charter was refused, but chiefly owing, it would appear, to the then existing state of political parties ; for Mr. Madison himself had waved the point of constitutional law, " as being precluded, in his opinion, by repeated recognitions, under varied circumstances, of the validity of such an institution in acts of the legislative, executive, and judicial branches of the government, accompanied by indications, in different modes, of a concurrence of the general will of the nation." * The Bank, in consequence, ceased to exist in 1811, when its period of twenty years was completed.

The war with England commenced in the following year, and occasioned great commercial dis-

---

* One of the objections made was, that seven tenths of the stock belonged to British subjects. The proposition for renewing the charter was lost only by the casting vote of the President of the Senate, and by a majority of a single vote in the House of Representatives.

tress, which it was soon seen was much aggravated CHAP. I. by the disorganised state of the currency, arising from the want of a controlling power to regulate the exchanges between the states. The government, who were conscious of this, in order to remedy these evils, nobly sacrificing the pride of consistency to the good of the country, resorted again to the expedient of a national institution ; and a new bank was established in 1816, during the second presidency of Mr. Madison, with a charter very similar to that of the one that preceded it. Bank of the U.S.
The charter of the new bank extended to 1836 ; and the institution appears to have fully answered the purposes for which it was established. Public and private credit were raised from a prostrate to a very elevated condition ; the finances of the nation were placed upon a solid foundation ; and a great reduction as well as a greater degree of steadiness was effected in the rate of the commercial exchanges of the country.* General Jackson, however, in the year 1829, being then in the second term of his presidency, expressed, in his annual message to Congress, a different opinion, and at the same time revived the question of the constitutional powers of Congress to grant incorporations. Opposition of the President to the renewal of the charter.
    The general feeling was certainly against him in both points. Mr. Gallatin, who had been Secre-

---

* These advantages had more especially been attained since the year 1819, previous to which time some imprudence was exhibited in the management of the bank.

CHAP.
I.

tary to the Treasury under Mr. Madison's administration, and is well qualified to take a comprehensive view of the whole subject, has, in his "Considerations on the Currency and Banking System
of the United States," ably proved the benefits of
a national bank ; and the arguments of Mr. Justice
Story, in his "Commentaries on the Constitution,"
present a powerful specimen of clear reasoning on
the point of law. The Senate and the House of
Representatives participated in the views which
were thus generally entertained, and by the reports of their respective committees expressed
their dissent from the opinions of the President ;
but this decided evidence of public opinion appears to have been without effect in influencing
the line of conduct which the President had determined to pursue.*

The subject was annually renewed by him in his
different messages ; — in that of December, 1832,
the solvency of the institution was also called in
question with the professed view of putting the
legislature on its guard with respect to the safety
of the public deposits ; but a Committee of Ways
and Means in the House of Representatives, after

* The Report of the House of Representatives (dated 13th
April, 1830) not only contains an excellent summary of the
arguments in regard both to the constitutional powers of Congress to incorporate banks, and to the expediency of re-
chartering the one in question, but enters into an interesting
detail of the origin and progress of the two banks, and of the
financial embarrassments which occurred in the interval when
no national establishment existed.

a full examination of the subject, reported to the house its entire conviction of the soundness and solvency of the institution, and that, in their opinion, the government deposits might be safely continued in it — and well they might; for it was shown that the claims against the bank, including the circulation, and the public and private deposits, amounted to $37,807,322, while its resources amounted to $80,865,465, leaving a clear surplus of $43,058,143.*

The subject of the renewal of the charter was at length, in the following year, formally brought before the legislature ; and on the 3d of July the Senate and House of Representatives, in accordance with their former views, passed an act to renew it. The President, equally firm in his opinion, refused to sanction the measure; and as, on being sent back to the two houses, it was not sustained by a majority of two thirds of each, as is required in this case by the constitution, the executive veto was decisive of the question.

In 1836, the charter consequently expired ; and although the corporation received a new charter from the legislature of Pennsylvania, and still retains the name of the Bank of the United States, it ceased from that time to be a national establishment.

From the time, however, that the President thus refused his assent to the bill for the renewal of the charter, till its final termination, three

* See Appendix, letter E.

years had to elapse; and during this interval the contest between the executive and the legislative bodies was carried on with increased acrimony. In September, 1833, the President, on his own responsibility, directed the removal of the public deposits from the Bank of the United States to certain state banks which he selected, in different parts of the Union. The Secretary to the Treasury, refusing to sign the order, was removed from office ; and a successor, partaking more of the President's views, was appointed, who, on the meeting of the legislature in December following, made a report to both houses, setting forth reasons in favour of the measure. The Senate rejected the reasons thus assigned as unsatisfactory, and passed a resolution on the 23d of March, condemning the conduct of the President as unconstitutional : this drew from the President a protest, which was communicated to the Senate, and was voted by that body to be a breach of its privileges, for which reason it refused to receive it or to enter it on its Journals. The House of Representatives, where the President's supporters were more numerous, without deciding positively on the sufficiency of the reasons offered by the Secretary, indirectly sanctioned the proceedings of the President ; and the Senate finally, though after a long course of violent opposition, became more pacified, and in January, 1837, expunged the obnoxious resolution of the 23d of March from its records.

Motives of the President. Such are the principal circumstances of this long-continued struggle. From amidst the excited feelings of parties it is not easy to arrive at the true motives of the President's conduct. His own reasons for withdrawing the deposits are shown at great length in a paper which he addressed, on the 18th of September, to his Cabinet ; in which, after frankly declaring his unalterable opposition to the Bank, as being both unconstitutional and inexpedient, he brings a variety of charges against it ; — asserting that it had employed means to retard the redemption of part of the public debt, in order to retain in its own possession the moneys which should have been applied to that redemption, and in other ways had been faithless as a public agent; but these charges are either denied, or it is argued that, if true, they afforded no legal ground for the President's interference. So determined an opposition to the establishment seems, on the whole, to lend some countenance to the general belief that he was influenced to a certain degree by political reasons arising out of the prominent part which the President of the Bank had taken in opposing his reelection to the head of the government, and his conviction that the influence of the Bank, widely disseminated by its numerous branches, was used in opposition to his administration. This belief seems corroborated by the further reasons assigned by President Jackson in the paper alluded to, in which he accuses the Bank of misapplying its funds in controlling the public press. " It is thus converted," he says, " into a vast electioneering engine, with means to embroil the country in deadly feuds, and, under cover of expenditures in themselves improper, to extend its corruption through all the ramifications of society." * — " Under these circumstances," he says in his message to Congress in December following, " it seemed to me that authority ought to be at once exerted, to deprive that great corporation of the support and countenance of the government in such a use of its funds and such an exertion of its power."

Disastrous conse- quences.

Whatever the real motives of the President may have been, the victory he thus obtained over the Bank, whether ultimately for good or for evil, has in its immediate consequences proved most disastrous. These and the measures adopted to arrest them will be presently considered ; in the mean time a short description of the territory of the United States will render it more easy to understand their influence on the trade and general prosperity of the country.

---

* A resolution of the Bank had placed its funds at the disposal of its president, to be employed in sustaining its political power, under the authority of which it appears that upwards of eighty thousand dollars had been spent in giving circulation to publications calculated to bring the country to a favourable decision upon its pretensions.

CHAP. II.

DESCRIPTION OF THE COUNTRY. — REMARKABLE FEATURES.
— THE MISSISSIPPI. — THE OHIO. — THE ALLEGHANY
MOUNTAINS. — NEW ENGLAND STATES. — TARIFF QUESTION.
— NOTE RESPECTING THE INDIAN TRIBES.

On looking at the map of the United States, the
attention is arrested by a great physical feature. —
The Mississippi, rising near Lake Superior, rolls its
waters in an almost undeviating southerly direction,
until, after a course of upwards of 3000 miles, it
empties itself into the Gulf of Mexico. This river
which thus runs through the whole length of the
United States, divides it into two parts:—the
eastern side of the valley through which it flows is
generally well cultivated, while the other side consists of an almost boundless tract of country of which
little is known except in the vicinity of the tributary streams ; of these, the two largest, the Missouri
and the Arkansas, taking their rise in the Rocky
Mountains, traverse these regions by a course, the
one of 2200, and the other of upwards of 3000
miles, before they reach the Mississippi, giving their
names to territories which have lately been admitted to the rank of states in the Union.

On the eastern bank of the Mississippi, at the
distance of about 1000 miles from the sea, the

The Ohio.

Ohio, another river of great magnitude, discharges itself into this vast recipient of the waters of central North America. This river, which rises near Lake Erie, and after a short course to the south follows a westerly direction, is more remarkable as a boundary line than the tributaries of the western bank of the Mississippi, from its constituting the great line of demarcation between the free states of the Union, and those which are still polluted with the stain of slavery.*

The difference of climate and produce on the north and on the south side of the Ohio is as marked as that of the moral condition of the respective cultivators of the soil. In the states south of the Ohio the cultivation of tobacco begins, although only partially in Kentucky and Tennessee. The soil, also, and climate best adapted for cotton is found to the south of the parallel of 37°†, while the cultivation of rice, requiring great heat and a marshy soil, is confined to this division of the United States.

Southern states.

Northern states.

In the states north of the Ohio, wheat is grown in abundance, and of a quality equal if not superior to any that is raised in Europe, while maize is still more generally cultivated, this prolific grain being adapted to a greater variety of soils.

* The Ohio, strictly speaking, only assumes that name at Pittsburg: the main stream above that city is called the Alleghany. From where the Ohio turns towards the south-west, the parallel of 39° 43′, which separates Pennsylvania from Virginia and Maryland, completes the line of separation between the free and the slave states.

† Both tobacco and cotton are grown in Illinois, but in no great quantities, and only for home consumption.

As the Ohio separates the northern from the southern states, so the range of the Appalachian or Alleghany mountains, extending from the vicinity of the St. Lawrence into Georgia, and running in a direction from north-east to south-west, presents a geographical limit scarcely less remarkable from the contrast which the regions on the one side offer to those on the other, both in regard to their physical character (more especially in the southern states) and to their political history. In the spacious valleys which lie concealed within the passes of these mountains, the soil is rich and productive, and to the east, from their base for a distance varying from 10 to 200 miles, the alluvium from the mountains constitutes a fertile tract well adapted for tillage ; but beyond this distance, in all the range from the Potomac round to the mouth of the Mississippi, there is a tract of sandy soil extending to the Atlantic Ocean, varying from 30 to 100 miles in breadth, which is very little raised above the level of the sea, and which is almost incapable of cultivation. The sea island cotton (the finest cotton imported into Great Britain) grows, however, on the small sandy islands contiguous to the coast of Georgia, and on the low grounds along the sea-shore. Extensive pine forests flourish in these unhealthy regions.

On the west side of the Alleghany mountains, a soil based on limestone well watered by magnificent rivers, and inexhaustibly productive, reaches to the Mississippi.

It is chiefly on the eastern side of the Alleghany

CHAP.
II.

Alleghany
mountains.

Eastern
states.

Western
states.

ridge that the original states of the Union are situated, and it is to the fertile regions on the western side, that the enterprising descendants of the original settlers have in later times emigrated, after having caused the greater part of the native Indians either to remove under treaties to the west of the Mississippi, or to exchange their right to the soil for annuities granted on their lives.* The government of the United States having by means of these treaties obtained a title to the disposal of the lands, have acquired in them a source of almost endless wealth. †

New England States.
The portion of the United States to the North of the Ohio has been characterised generally as fertile, but in the north-eastern extremity of this division there is a considerable tract differing from the rest in this respect, and which, on this account,

* See note at the end of the chapter.

† To facilitate the act of union, the claim of the original states to the lands which lie beyond the limits of the thirteen states first confederated, was ceded by them to the general government, though usually with some stipulation or reserve ; it was, however, understood that the proceeds of the sales of these lands were to be for the use of the general government, and subject to its control. Considerable embarrassment has lately resulted from a claim of the states which have since been established on these ceded lands to the right of applying the produce of the sales, made within their respective territories, to their own use. To obviate this, the President in his message of December, 1832, proposed that the public lands should no longer be made a source of revenue, but should be sold at such prices as would simply reimburse to the United States the cost arising out of the Indian compacts. As a source of national wealth, the value of the lands would be the same, or, indeed, greater, under this arrangement than before, by its affording to the purchasers the means of applying more capital to the cultivation of them.

as well as for its political and historical importance,
deserves a separate consideration. The River Hudson taking its rise near Lake Champlain, and running directly from north to south, separates this
tract from the rest of the states. The soil to the east
of this river is rocky, of little depth, and in many
places barren ; where cultivated, it is more adapted
for pasture or woodland than for tillage, as the severe
winters and ungenial springs often cause the corn
crops to fail. This description becomes more applicable to the country, in proportion as it recedes
from the Hudson; for in the vicinity of that river
the soil is richer, and Indian corn and rye form an
important part of its agricultural produce, while the
country is represented as offering to the traveller
a succession of hills with beautiful and constantly
varying prospects. The first description, however,
is true, as regards the general aspect of the country ;
but this tract, to which nature has been so little
bountiful, holds a conspicuous place in the history
of the United States, being not only the seat of
many of the original settlers, and called thence New
England, but the abode of those who first raised the
standard of insurrection against the mother-country.
Of the states which compose it, New Hampshire,
Massachusetts, Rhode Island, and Connecticut,
are original states of the Union ; Vermont was admitted a state in 1790; and Maine, which lies more
to the north-east than the others, and the boundary
of which, where it adjoins the British possessions
in Canada and New Brunswick, has been so long a
subject of dispute, was admitted only in 1820.

The enterprising character of the inhabitants of this district has enabled them, however, to overcome the disadvantages of a sterile soil. Possessing a long line of coast with many excellent harbours, they have established extensive fisheries; and availing themselves of the skill in navigation which a sea-faring life is calculated to produce, they have succeeded in establishing an important and profitable foreign trade. Their success, too, as manufacturers has been considerable, although this branch of industry has been fostered at the expense of all sound principles of political economy, by the imposition of oppressive duties on manufactured articles imported from abroad. Possessing, as the United States do, the raw material in great abundance, and with a capacity to increase the quantity almost indefinitely, their natural course of policy would be to turn this to account and become a great exporting country of raw produce, in exchange for manufactures raised at a less cost than they could produce them for at home, under the disadvantages of a thinly peopled country and high wages arising from the profitable employment for that population in agricultural pursuits. To have adopted an opposite course of policy seems unusually injudicious, and yet the establishment of manufactures appears to have been always a favourite object of American legislation, and to have arisen in a great measure out of their national jealousy of being dependent upon other powers. "It cannot be doubted," says President Monroe in his message of the 5th of December, 1821, "that the more complete our internal resources, and the less dependent we are on foreign powers for every national as well as domestic purpose, the greater and more stable will be the public felicity."*

As agricultural pursuits are, by comparison, less profitable in New England than in other parts of the Union, and as the skill of the people in mechanical arts must tend to lessen there the demand for labour, and, consequently, its price for manu-

* Mr. Jefferson's views were much opposed to these; but his preference for agricultural pursuits arose chiefly from his considering them more conducive to the happiness of the people and to the stability of the government.

"Those who labour in the earth," he says, in his usual glowing language, "are the chosen people of God, if ever he had a chosen people, whose breasts he has made his peculiar deposit for substantial and genuine virtue. It is the focus in which he keeps alive that sacred fire, which otherwise might escape from the face of the earth. Corruption of morals in the mass of cultivators is a phenomenon of which no age nor nation has furnished an example. It is the mark set on those, who, not looking up to Heaven, to their own soil and industry, as does the husbandman, for their subsistence, depend for it on the casualties and caprice of customers. Dependence begets subservience and venality, suffocates the germ of virtue, and prepares fit tools for the designs of ambition. This, the natural progress and consequence of the arts, has sometimes, perhaps, been retarded by accidental circumstances; but, generally speaking, the proportion which the aggregate of the other classes of citizens bears in any state to that of its husbandmen is the proportion of its unsound to its healthy parts, and is a good enough barometer whereby to measure its degree of corruption. While we have land to labour, then, let us never wish to see our citizens occupied at a work-bench or twirling a distaff."—*Notes on Virginia*, page 274.

facturing purposes, there is no doubt that this system, even when in full operation, proved less prejudicial to this part of the Union than to any other, and would be injurious only in a comparatively small degree to the northern states bordering on the Atlantic ; but the injurious effects in the purely agricultural states, and especially in the southern ones, were so strongly felt, that the state of South Carolina, incensed at last at the sacrifice of its interests to the prejudices of the northern states, refused to enforce the Customs' Acts, and threatened, if coercion was attempted, to secede from the Union. This decided conduct led to a modification of the system, a law having been passed to reduce the tariff duties progressively for ten years, that they might constitute at last a mere fiscal impost without partaking of the character of protective duties ; but this subject, though interesting, cannot here be further dwelt upon, being only so far connected with the present inquiry as it shows how little even this mistaken policy has been able to check the progress of the country in wealth and population.*

Note. — The public documents which relate to the treaties with the native Indians might create an impression that the emigration of the Indian tribes was voluntary ; but such a conclusion would be much at variance with the truth. To a strong at-

---

* It has been estimated, on apparently good grounds, that the *annual* loss to the country arising out of this desire to establish manufactures at home has not been less than $50,000,000. — *M'Culloch, Com. Dict.* page 848.

tachment to their native soil the Indians join a super-
stitious dread of alienating the lands which contain
the ashes of their fathers.   Far from being willing
exiles, those who have witnessed their departure
from their homes or who have met them in their
wanderings, describe their dejection as being very
great, and represent the scene altogether as truly
heart-rending.   M. de Tocqueville, who, in the
winter of 1831, saw a large body of Chactan-In-
dians arrive on the banks of the Mississippi, and
prepare to cross the river in search of a new
abode, says that the solemn scene will never be
effaced from his recollection : neither sobs nor
murmurs escaped from the assembled crowd ; a
mournful silence prevailed among them ; their mis-
fortunes were of long standing, and they felt them
to be without a remedy.   They had already entered the vessel which was to bear them away, but
their dogs remained still upon the bank, and when
at last these faithful animals perceived that they
were about to remove for ever, they raised the most
piercing yells, and instantly plunging altogether
into the icy torrent of the river, swam after the boat
which conveyed their masters from the shore.

The policy pursued by the governments of the
southern states in respect to the Indian tribes is as
destitute of good faith as it is of humanity.   The
lines marked out by treaties are of no avail *, for as

---

* The federal government, no doubt, shows itself more soli-
citous about the welfare of the Indian tribes than the governments of the separate states do, and acts with sincerer intentions,
but it has not sufficient power to put a stop to the oppressive
conduct of the separate states towards them.

the white population extends to the west, the poor Indians are driven farther off — with legal formalities, indeed, but without any regard to their rights of prior occupancy.

Sums of money, it is true, are paid to them to abandon their claim to the territories they give up ; but equally ignorant of the value of what they abandon and of what they receive in exchange, the sums paid to them have borne no proportion to the value of the land. In 1808, the Osages relinquished forty-eight millions of acres, for an annuity of a thousand dollars; and in 1818, the Quassaws yielded up twenty-nine millions of acres for a payment of four thousand dollars. These sums, indeed, ought not to be taken as a measure of the present liberality of the United States' government in their transactions with the aboriginal tribes, as between the 4th of March, 1829, and the 1st of December, 1836, 93,401,637 acres had been ceded, for which the United States stipulated to pay $26,982,068 besides an assignment of other lands ; and in several of the late treaties, the entire proceeds of the lands when sold have been assigned to the Indians. But even the sums, which they now receive for the extinction of their claims, are of little service to them. Deprived in their lands, of the source whence they could draw a precarious, indeed, but independent means of subsistence, they are left, when the money is expended, in a state bordering upon absolute destitution.* Their intercourse

* In some instances the money has been invested for their use by the government.

with civilised communities has no beneficial effect
in training them to habits of industry, or in fitting
them to cultivate the countries to which they are
thus half persuaded and half compelled to retire.
Not admitted to an equality with the European
settlers, they seem to learn only their vices; of
these none has proved so great a scourge to this
unhappy race as the intemperate use of ardent
spirits, the introduction of which has done more
harm to the Indians than any good they have
derived from their intercourse with the white
inhabitants of the Union. The people of the
United States seem to form too low an estimate
of the intellectual capacity of the Indian tribes,
and to act by them as if certain limits were fixed by
nature to its enlargement. The testimony of a
variety of writers may be adduced in opposition to
this opinion. By several of the early French mis-
sionaries the intellect of the Indians has been even
favourably contrasted with that of the peasantry of
France, and of the most enlightened countries of
Europe.* Viewing the conduct of the Americans
as well as their professed opinions, their object
seems to be the expulsion of the tribes from the
United States; or, judging from what is now going
on in Florida, when that is impracticable, to effect
their final extinction.

The work of extermination, indeed, has long
been going forward; no trace is to be found of
the original inhabitants of New England, nor of

* In Mr. Halkett's "Historical Notes respecting the Indians of
North America," a variety of interesting opinions on this subject
have been collected from sources entitled to the fullest credit.

the Lenapes who received William Penn on the banks of the Delaware, while M. de Tocqueville saw some of the last survivors of the Iroquois begging alms for their support.

The number of Indians who had emigrated from the eastern to the western side of the Mississippi is stated in an official document, dated on the 8th of March, 1836, to have then amounted to 31,357, while 72,181 still remained on the eastern bank.

The numbers by the annual census on the 1st of December, 1837, were 51,327 who had emigrated, and 49,365 who remained, which shows the rapid progress of their removal, as well as the rate at which the total number is diminishing. It is estimated that the indigenous tribes of the region between the Mississippi and the Rocky Mountains, comprise about 150,000; these added to the number who have already emigrated, will make upwards of 201,000 now to the west of the Mississippi and when all the tribes, "are removed *," there will be an aggregate Indian population in that country of more than 250,000. This does not

---

* This language is held in the official documents in the face of the treaties of 1790, and 1791, with the Creek and Cherokee tribes in the first of which, " the United States solemnly guarantee to the Creek nation, all their land within the limits of the United States;" and in the second they "solemnly guarantee to the Cherokee nation all their lands not hereby ceded."

In the contract of sale of the lands by the Quassaws, already referred to, that tribe reserved for itself a territory of a million of acres for a hunting ground. A solemn oath was taken that it should be respected; but this land has since been taken possession of by the states, and not a single Quassaw is now to be found to the east of the Mississippi.

include the Indians upon the peninsula of Michigan, and upon the shores of Lake Huron,
and Lake Superior, nor the various bands of the
great tribe of Chippewas, who occupy the regions
south of Lake Superior and at the sources of the
Mississippi. Much of the country inhabited by these
tribes is of such a character, that no reasonable time
can be assigned within which it is likely that they
will be required to emigrate ; but they will doubtless tend, at some future period, still further to increase the aggregate of the Indian population in
the west.

It is estimated that the tribes above stated, all
of which are either in contact with, or, as it is
termed, within " striking distance " of the western
and north-western frontier of the United States,
could furnish 60,000 warriors, if any circumstance
should occasion a war in which they could be
brought to unite ; and although from their habits
and constant hostilities among themselves, such a
coalition can scarcely be anticipated, yet the existence of such a large force on the frontier is evidently a source of considerable uneasiness to the
states, especially as in a moment of excitement it
is well known that the native Indians are either
ignorant of their comparative weakness, or appear
totally indifferent to it. This risk is, however, so
small, that although not entirely to be disregarded,
the above remarks on the present situation of the
Indian tribes may be viewed rather as recording
some interesting statistical facts than as being of
much weight in the question under examination.

CHAP. III.

EFFECTS OF THE PRESIDENT'S INTERFERENCE WITH THE BANK-
ING SYSTEM. — NATURE OF THE TRADE OF THE UNITED
STATES. — FACILITIES AFFORDED BY THE BANK OF THE
UNITED STATES INTERFERED WITH BY THE WITHDRAWAL
OF THE PUBLIC DEPOSITS. — SPECULATIVE SALES OF LAND
CHECKED BY THE SAME CAUSE. — DISTRIBUTION OF THE
SURPLUS REVENUE INJUDICIOUSLY EFFECTED. — SPECIE CIR-
CULAR. — EFFECTS OF THE TWO COMBINED. — MEASURES OF
THE PRESIDENT TO PROCURE GOLD. — DISASTROUS CONSE-
QUENCES. — FAILURES IN NEW ORLEANS AND NEW YORK. —
SUSPENSION BY THE BANKS OF SPECIE PAYMENTS. — IMPO-
LICY OF THE GOLD BILL. — PROOFS OF OVERTRADING. —
DECREASE IN SALES OF LAND. — OF IMPORTS. — OF EX-
PORTS. — OF BANKING TRANSACTIONS. — CAUSES OF RE-
NEWED PROSPERITY.

CHAP.
III.

Effects of
the Presi-
dent's mea-
sure.

WITH the light which the geographical sketch in the preceding chapter will throw upon the subject, we may now return with more advantage to a consideration of the measures adopted by the President in reference to the Charter of the Bank of the United States, and to the banking system generally, and to the effects which these produced on the industry and the prospects of the nation.

Nature of
the trade of
the United
States.

The soil constitutes the chief source of the wealth of the United States. Nearly nine tenths of the whole domestic exports are derived from its produce; and it is estimated that seven tenths of the population are employed in agricultural pursuits. Cotton, tobacco, flour, rice, and sugar, form the most important items in these exports; for which the United States receive in exchange either the manufactures of the country they are sent to, or such few products of the soil as their own climate will not allow them to raise.

The cultivation of these staple commodities is confined chiefly, as we have seen, to the southern states; and the growth of cotton is most extensive in those which border on the Mississippi and on the Gulf of Mexico. In these states, the growers of these different descriptions of produce having little realised capital, are obliged to have recourse to the capital or credit of their wealthier neighbours for the means of raising their valuable crops. The growers of rice and tobacco depend chiefly on the southern Atlantic cities, while the cotton planters usually obtain advances for the purchase of their slaves and the improvement of their plantations from the merchants or factors of New Orleans, or other ports on the Gulf of Mexico. They are supplied with clothing for their slaves, and other necessary articles of consumption, on credit, by the smaller country traders, who procure them on a still longer credit from the merchants of the Atlantic cities.

The cotton crop is usually ready in the month of October, and is sent down to the factors at the outports from that time till the beginning of summer. The factors ship it during these months

Facilities afforded by the Bank of the U. S.

to Europe, or to the northern states, and draw
bills for its value on the merchants to whose
care it is consigned. The Bank of the United
States, with its numerous branches, which per-
vaded all parts of the Union, was of much use
in assisting in these operations. These branches,
collecting revenue in the remotest parts, whether
arising from duties at the outports, or from sales
of land, were always ready to purchase the bills
thus drawn against shipments of cotton, as an easy
and safe means of remitting the sums they collected to the central establishment. As they paid
for these bills in the notes of the Bank, which enjoyed a universal credit, the factors on receiving
them were enabled, after repaying themselves their
advances, to settle with the planters for their
cotton ; the planters, in their turn, could pay the
country traders for the goods supplied to them on
credit, and the traders their debts to the merchants
at New-York or Philadelphia. By the time the
notes had performed these various functions, the
central Bank, to which the bills had been remitted, was placed, by their becoming due, in a
situation to meet the notes when they came to
be presented for payment : the circulation, thus
diminished for a time, could be renewed, when
the new crop coming on required a fresh issue
of notes to repeat the same functions, and to
traverse again the same route — at once aiding
commerce, and effecting in the best way the purposes of the Bank. In like manner, the Bank
and its branches could give drafts at any point of
the Union on any other where its offices existed,

at a per centage greatly less than it would cost to
transport specie.

The measure of the President which withdrew
the deposits from the Federal Bank, and dispersed
them among the different state banks of the Union,
put an end to this system of mutual accommodation. Local banks, whatever might be their wil-
lingness, could not give facilities in the same
manner and to the same extent. The Treasury,
moreover, no longer requiring the transmission of
the accruing revenue to head quarters, the sums
received remained fixed where the legitimate wants
of commerce did not require them ; and, by making
credit easily attainable, engendered a spirit of speculation in the districts where money was thus
rendered superabundant; while the belief, that these
balances were not likely to be required, removed,
at the same time, all feelings of restraint on the part
of the banks with regard to the extent of their
issues. This state of things, by greatly augment-
ing the profits of all banks which dealt in inland
exchanges (increasing, as it did, the general commercial dealings of the country), encouraged the
formation of new banks, which, by liberal issues of
their notes and grants of loans, gave a fresh impulse
to speculation.*

* The number of banks had before been greatly increased,
owing to the intimation by the President of his objection to a
renewal of the charter of the Federal Bank — all hoping to replace the branches that would cease to exist with the parent
establishment, or wishing, at least, to compete for the business
which would then be set free. — See Appendix, letter F.

Specula-
tive sales of
land
checked.

The effect was soon visible: in the states where the public lands are situated, sales hitherto had only been made as new settlers arrived, or as the means of the older settlers enabled them to add to their former possessions ; the occupation of the new lands, therefore, had, till this time, been going on slowly but steadily. Planters now increased the extent of their plantations, and the number of their slaves, by further purchases on credit, while new adventurers were daily coming forward : — the sales of land were thus suddenly and extensively increased; nor were the speculations confined to the purchase of new lands : every species of internal improvement was entered upon ; railroads and canals were projected in every direction, and town plots every where exposed for sale. This apparently prosperous state of things was at first a matter of exultation to the government. " Among the evidences of the increasing prosperity of the country," said the President, in his message of December, 1835, "not the least gratifying is that afforded by the receipts of the public lands." " This," he said, "attests the rapidity with which agriculture, the first and most important occupation of man, advances and contributes to the wealth and power of our extended territory." But these sales of the public lands, by adding to the amount of the public deposits, only added to the power of the banks to extend still farther their issues. The rapid growth of this spirit of speculation could not fail to strike the government, and was soon seen in its true light. From under five

millions of dollars in amount, in 1833, the sales of
land in 1834 produced more than six millions; in
1835 the sum had risen to nearly sixteen millions;
and in 1836 the sum paid by the purchasers of land
exceeded twenty-five millions of dollars.* By these
means, the public deposits, before the end of
October, 1836, amounted to $49,377,985, while
the deposit banks, with an aggregate capital of
$77,576,449 had lent on discounts or otherwise
$115,075,205. In exchange for these valuable
portions of public lands, the government, however, in this way got nothing but a credit on the
books of the Bank; and it soon became evident
that if this system, were permitted to go on, there
would be some risk of these bank credits becoming
altogether valueless; for the greater part of the loans
made by the banks being expended in the purchase
or in the improvement of lands, these deposits, if
not finally lost, could not be realised until real sales
had been made of the lands, over which the banks
retained a mortgage as security for their advances.

To check this evil two measures were resorted
to : one, to remedy the existing inconvenience, by
ordering the distribution among the states of these
public deposits or surplus revenue, which was effected by the enactment of June, 1836: the other,
to provide against a recurrence of the speculation
which caused the evil, which was done by a Treasury order, dated the 11th of July following, prohibiting the receipt at the Land Offices of any thing

Distribution of the surplus revenue

* See Appendix, letter G.

but specie in payment of future purchases. The
first measure, which, as we have seen, was forced
upon the government by its opponents spread
consternation, as soon as passed, among the banks
where the deposits were held, for although the
payments were to be spread over a whole year,
the withdrawal of upwards of thirty millions of
dollars, even in this manner, could not but be
productive of great embarrassment, when the sums
had been lent on securities not readily conver-
tible into money. But, if the measure was one
likely in itself to prove embarrassing, the mode of
carrying it into effect appears to have much aggravated the inconvenience of it. The great object
of the Treasury seems to have been to apportion
the amounts of surplus in the different states
beforehand, in the proportion in which the distribution would have afterwards to take place.
We have seen how, in the natural course of trade,
the planters, till the crops arrive at maturity, are
always indebted to the country traders, and these
to the merchants in the Atlantic cities, and that
from the time the crops reach the sea-ports a
stream of money flows constantly from the interior
towards those towns. The Treasury went on in its
equalising process, without any reference to the
business of the different sections of the Union, or to
the season of the year, and instead of aiding made
their transfers often work against the industry of
the country. The Deposit Act required, moreover,
that no more money should remain in any bank than
what was equal to three fourths of its capital ; and

Injudi-
ciously ef-
fected

a strict compliance with this regulation, owing to the constant incoming of the revenue, required almost weekly transfers and weekly selections of new banks. The transfers to execute these two subordinate purposes alone are stated by the Secretary of the Treasury to have amounted to no less a sum than $30,666,666. The second measure, known by the name of the Specie Circular, by which gold and silver were alone made receivable for public lands, has been still more severely criticised. It was followed, indeed, by the most calamitous effects : the first consequence was, that the banks nearest the Land Offices ceased making loans ; the next, that they strove to fortify themselves by accumulating specie, while some augmented largely the amounts of their already overgrown capital. It was at this moment that orders were issued from the Treasury to shift the public money from the places where it had been collected to other places, in anticipation of its distribution among the states. " The combination of the two measures," writes the President of the Bank, one of their most strenuous opposers, " produced a double result, — first, to require the banks generally to increase their specie ; and, next, to give them the means of doing it, by drafts on the deposit banks. The commercial community were thus taken by surprise. The interior banks making no loans, and converting their Atlantic funds into specie, the debtors in the interior could make no remittances to the merchants in the Atlantic cities, who are thus thrown for support on the banks of those cities, at a moment when they are unable to afford relief, on account of the very abstraction of their specie to the west. The creditor states not only receive no money, but their money is carried away to the debtor states, who in their turn cannot use it, either to pay old engagements or to contract new ones. By this unnatural process the specie of New York and the other commercial cities is piled up in the western states — not circulated, not used, but held as a defence against the Treasury; and, while the west cannot use it, the east is suffering for the want of it. The result is, that commercial intercourse between the west and the Atlantic is almost wholly suspended, and the few operations which are made are burdened with the most extravagant expense."

" In November, 1836, the interest of money has risen to twenty-four per cent.; merchants are struggling to preserve their credit by ruinous sacrifices; and it costs five or six times as much to transmit funds from the west and south-west as it did in November, 1835, or 34, or 32. Thus, while the exchanges with all the world are in our favour, while Europe is alarmed, and the Bank of England itself uneasy at the quantity of specie we possess, we are suffering, because, from mere mismanagement, the whole ballast of the currency is shifted from one side of the vessel to the other."

By an official report of the condition of the deposit banks in November, 1836, the amount of specie in twenty nine banks situated in the western states was under six millions of dollars; which, in proportion to their liabilities, was as one dollar only to about seven dollars and three quarters. This may hardly be thought to warrant the forcible expressions in the above extract ; but as the fact of this amount of specie remaining in the country, during such a state of things, is afterwards brought forward as a conclusive evidence that these commercial embarrassments were not the result of overtrading, it will be proper to see if it may not be accounted for on other grounds.

The very pressure for money alluded to, producing a fall in the price of all articles, whether of foreign merchandise or domestic produce, or securities, would alone account for an importation of specie, by causing it to be the most profitable means, either for the citizens of the United States to get their funds home from foreign countries, or for foreign capitalists to remit theirs to America for the purchase of cotton, or for investment in public securities. But another circumstance concurred to make the current of gold, for some time before this, set towards America. It had been a favourite scheme of General Jackson to make gold the standard of the currency of the United States ; and with this view a bill had been passed two years before, (on the 28th of June, 1834,) by which an ounce of gold, which by the mint regulations of 1791 was assumed to bear to silver the proportion of 15 to 1, was made the equivalent of about sixteen ounces of silver. Another law, which was passed on the same day, declared the British sovereign and certain other foreign coins

to be a legal tender.　The tendency of these measures being to give an advantage to foreign debtors
to pay in gold, large sums were transmitted to
America ; and, although prices could not fail to be
ultimately regulated by the new standard of value
impressed upon gold, it would be some time before
this took place ; and, until it did, these measures
must have had the effect of offering a premium on
the importation of the metal, thus enhanced in its
relative value to silver which had till then formed
the metallic basis of the currency.

It would not be easy to assign the exact period
when the effect of these bills ceased, but its influence was not, probably, over at this time.　Another
forced measure of the government, of more recent
occurrence, tended to bring gold into the country.
A sum of twenty-five millions of francs had been
awarded to America as an indemnity by France,
(under a treaty of the 11th of July, 1831,) the payment of which had been long delayed, but which
it was finally settled, about this time, should be
paid in certain instalments ; and orders were sent
from America to transmit the amount in gold.
Disastrous
conse-
quences.
Great Britain being the great emporium of gold in
Europe, the London market could not fail to be
sensibly affected by the heavy drains on it which
these measures produced ; the Bank of England at
the same time curtailed its discounts ; and this completed the measure of the disasters which were
impending over American commerce.　The export-
ers of produce to England had, in their distress,
drawn on their correspondents there for sums

greatly exceeding in amount the value of the property which they had consigned to them. Owing
to the pressure for money, produced by the de-
fensive measures of the Bank of England, the
American merchants in London and Liverpool refused any longer to accept the bills that continued
to be thus drawn upon them : the return of these
bills unaccepted to America was destructive of all
confidence and credit. General Jackson's term of
presidency expired on the 4th of March ; and so
little aware was he of the storm that was about to
burst over his country, that, in surrendering his
public trust, he, in his farewell address, congratulates
himself on having left the people prosperous and
happy. On the 7th of March, within three days, the
first mercantile failures took place at New Orleans,
after which they succeeded each other with fearful
rapidity. In two days houses in that city stopped
payment, owing, on an aggregate, more than twenty
seven millions of dollars. The following statement
from a deputation of the citizens of New York,
sent, in the beginning of May, to request the new
President to rescind the specie circular, and to
convene the Congress, will show the progress the
desolation by that time had made in that city : —
" Under a deep impression of the propriety of con-
fining our declarations within moderate limits, we
affirm that the value of our real estate has, within the
last six months, depreciated more than forty millions
of dollars ; that within the last two months there
have been more than 250 failures of houses engaged
in extensive business ; that within the same period

a decline of twenty millions of dollars has occurred in our local stocks, including those railroad and canal incorporations which, though chartered in other states, depend chiefly upon New York for their sale ; that the immense amount of merchandise in our warehouses has, within the same period, fallen in value at least 30 per cent. ; that within a few weeks not less than 20,000 individuals, depending upon their daily labour for their daily bread, have been discharged by their employers, because the means of retaining them were exhausted ; and that a complete blight has fallen upon a community heretofore so active, enterprising, and prosperous."

Suspension by the banks of specie payments.

The sequel is soon told. On the 10th all the banks in the city of New York, hopeless under such circumstances of being otherwise able to retain any gold in their coffers, by common consent, suspended payments in specie. As the news spread through the different states, the banks in almost every instance adopted the same course ; and in a short time scarcely one, throughout the whole Union, continued to pay the demands upon it in the established currency of the country.

Impolicy of the gold bill.

The greatest obloquy has been thrown upon General Jackson as being the sole cause of these disasters, but without sufficient discrimination. The policy of several of the measures to which we have alluded can scarcely, perhaps, be defended, and least of all the bill to alter the relative value of gold and silver. The proportion of 15 to 1, assumed in 1791, however near the truth it might have been at the time, had, indeed, considerably altered, owing to the quantity of silver produced in the mines having since increased, as compared with the quantity of gold; but the proportion of 16 to 1, assumed by the law of the 28th of June, 1834, was nearly as much above the real truth as the former proportion of 15 to 1 was below it. The disturbance caused by this undue estimate of the value of gold produced, as we have seen, a forced importation of it from Europe, which, meeting with a paper circulation already amply adequate to the wants of the community, naturally flowed back, in the common course of trade, to the countries it came from, entailing uselessly the expense of double commission, freight, and insurance; but the measure most condemned is the specie circular, which, together with the sub-treasury bill, required the collection of the revenue, whether arising from sales of land, or otherwise, to be made in specie. This bill was certain, however, to prove a means of putting an end to the extravagant speculations which had been entered into, and which the safety of the commercial interests of the country required to be effectually checked. The question ought to be, therefore, whether an equally safe remedy might not have been more gradually applied; but the discussion of this point, or that of the meed of praise or censure which should attach to the President for these transactions, would be of little service here. The President charges the country with overtrading as the cause of all the distress which ensued. Some who admit this, retort on the Pre-

CHAP.
III.

sident that his measures encouraged this over-trading : this, too, is beside the present question.*
Others, among whom the President of the Bank is the foremost, deny the existence of any over-trading. This is a proposition too essentially affecting the present inquiry to be allowed to pass without a stricter investigation.

Proofs of over-trading.

I have already alluded to the continuance of specie in the country, at the time of the commercial embarrassments, having been adduced as a proof that there had been no undue extent of trading ; but, if this circumstance has been satisfactorily shown to be attributable to other causes, the few following facts may be looked upon as no inconsiderable proofs of the truth of General Jackson's assertion.†

Decrease in sales of land.

The amounts of the sales of land had gradually but rapidly risen, as we have already stated, from under five millions of dollars, in 1833, to 25 millions in 1836. Had capital not been unduly diverted into this channel, there is no reason why this increased rate of sales should not have been at least maintained in a country possessing a rapidly increasing population ; yet, in the year 1837, the amount of sales fell again to under seven millions

* A powerful advocate of this opinion is the writer of a series of essays, entitled "The Causes of the present Crisis, shown by an Examiner," of which much use has been made in the foregoing account.

† The term overtrading is perhaps an incorrect one : an undue diversion of capital into one particular channel may, more strictly speaking, be assigned as the cause of the commercial embarrassment on this and on most other occasions.

of dollars, and in the first three quarters of 1838 to little more than two millions.

In 1833 the value of the total imports of the country amounted to 108 millions of dollars: in 1836 the amount had reached within a fraction of 190 millions. In a prosperous and sound state of things these amounts, too, should at least have been maintained; but for the year ending the 30th of September, 1838, the amount is stated in the last Treasury report to have receded to 112 millions: and, if the portion of these imports retained for home consumption be taken separately, the rapidity of the increase and decrease will be seen to be still greater in proportion. Nor was this diminution in the value of the imports ascribable solely to lower prices. If among the details of these imports the quantities of some of the more important items, as tending to the comforts and well-being of the people, be looked at, the falling off will appear still more remarkable. The number of packages sent from Liverpool to the northern Atlantic towns, from the month of April to September inclusive, in each of the years 1836–7, was as follows:—

Of cotton goods, in 1836, ... 20,140
          in 1837, ... 1,842
Of worsted stuff, in 1836, ... 6,687
          in 1837, ... 2,990
Of woollen goods, in 1836, ... 18,096
          in 1837, ... 4,400

These facts are strongly indicative of over specu- lation in 1836 and the years immediately preceding. The tables in the Appendix will more fully illustrate the subject; and it will be seen there, that the exports, which, till the year 1836, had likewise been progressively increasing in amount, also declined after that year, but in a much less proportion, which is still more remarkably the case if the exports of domestic produce only be looked at.*

Decrease in banking transactions.
The banks throughout the Union were naturally obliged, during this period of commercial distress, to lessen the extent of their transactions; but they attained, at the same time, a sounder condition.

In the course of 1837, and the early part of 1838, the total number of banks had, indeed, increased from 636 to 663, the increased capital being upwards of 27 millions of dollars; but the aggregate amount of loans and discounts, after those even of the new banks were included, had decreased upwards of 36 millions, while the circulation and claims on the banks by depositors had decreased more than 74 millions.†   That the transactions of the banks had not been still more contracted is owing, no doubt, to the suspension of specie payments having enabled them to extend a greater degree of accommodation to the planters in the south than they could otherwise have done.

This falling back, in a new and rising country, in the amount of the purchases of land, and of the general exports and imports, and in the extent of its banking transactions, will probably be looked upon

* See Appendix, letter H.   † See Appendix, I.

as conclusive evidence of former mis-trading; and CHAP. III. the fact is an essential one to establish, as satisfactorily accounting for the calamities that ensued — calamities that no acts of the executive, however impolitic, could well have produced, if they had had to act on a sound state of things; hence a recurrence of them is less likely to happen : and the facts above recorded are less detrimental, perhaps, to the financial credit of the country, seeing that in one case it would be at the mercy of a single individual, and that, in the other, the good sense of a whole nation must again be led astray before a recurrence of the same disasters can take place.

The fact of the exports of domestic produce having fallen off much less in proportion than the imports for home consumption is attributable to the assistance which it has been shown the suspension of specie payments allowed the banks to afford to the growers of the great staple productions of the country. Through the aid which the banks were still thus able to extend to the cotton planters, the quantity produced in 1837-8, as well as the quantity exported to Europe, exceeded that of all former years.

It is in the reduced consumption of the produce Causes of renewed of foreign industry, joined to the well maintained prosperity. efforts of their own, that we trace the means by which this country has thrown off the effects of the commercial embarrassment which has been described above. In August last, the northern banks, as they were the first to suspend specie payments, so they set the first example of resuming them; and

CHAP.
III.

before the end of the year, out of 829 banks and branches, upwards of 800 had either resumed, or had made arrangements to do so, early in January of the present year.

If, in this sketch of the financial history of the United States, the fact of the liquidation of its public debt has afforded a strong proof of the resources of the country, the rapid manner in which it has recovered from the commercial distress to which it was afterwards exposed will tend much to confirm it.

The luxuriant soil, the value of its products, and the industry of the people in turning these advantages to account, will, by the statements that have been made, be seen to have been the undoubted causes of the fortunate issue in both instances. Having thus exhibited the resources of the country in general, I shall proceed to examine how these are apportioned among the different states, so as to show the comparative means of each to meet its individual engagements.

CHAP. IV.

ADVANTAGES OF THE EASTERN OVER THE WESTERN STATES.
— PROSPEROUS CONDITION OF THE COLONIES BEFORE THEIR
INDEPENDENCE — TRACED TO THE CHARACTER OF THE
FIRST SETTLERS IN NEW ENGLAND. — ATTACHMENT OF THE
AMERICANS TO THEIR INSTITUTIONS. — ADVANTAGES OF
THE WESTERN STATES. — RICHNESS OF THE SOIL. — FA-
CILITIES FOR THE TRANSPORT OF PRODUCE. — RAPID PRO-
GRESS OF THE POPULATION. — COMPARISON BETWEEN THE
NORTHERN AND SOUTHERN STATES. — INTRODUCTION OF
SLAVES INTO THE LATTER. — OPINION OF M. DE TOCQUEVILLE
ON THE PROBABLE CONSEQUENCES. — MORAL INFLUENCE OF
SLAVERY. — GREAT VALUE OF THE PRODUCTIONS OF THE
SOUTHERN STATES. — MR. WHITNEY'S MACHINE FOR CLEANS-
ING COTTON. — APPLICATION OF PUBLIC FUNDS TO INCREASE
THE RESOURCES OF THE COUNTRY. — DIFFERENT MODES OF
THEIR APPLICATION.

IN comparing the states which lie to the east of the Alleghany mountains with those which lie between that range and the Mississippi, the most important difference, perhaps, in favour of the former arises out of the greater length of time which they have been established, and the greater stability which their institutions have in consequence acquired.

Although these colonies, before the declaration of their independence, were far from having reached

CHAP.
IV.

Advantages of the eastern states.

State of colonies before the

that point of wealth and prosperity which, as states of the Union, they have since attained, they had even at that time made a progress to which, in the opinion of no incompetent judge, Mr. Burke, nothing in the former history of mankind could be compared. " For my part," says that eminent statesman, " I never cast an eye on their flourishing commerce, and their cultivated and commodious life, but they seem to me rather ancient nations grown to perfection through a long series of fortunate events, and a train of successful industry, accumulating wealth in many centuries, than the colonies of yesterday; than a set of miserable outcasts, a few years ago, not so much sent as thrown out, on the bleak and barren shore of a desolate wilderness, three thousand miles from all civilised intercourse."

" After the war, and in the last years of it," he continues,. " the trade of America had increased far beyond the speculations of the most sanguine imaginations. It swelled out on every side. It filled all its proper channels to the brim. It overflowed with a rich redundance, and, breaking its banks on the right and on the left, it spread out upon some places where it was indeed improper, upon others where it was only irregular."

With this unquestionable testimony to the prosperous condition of the colonies at that period, we have now the advantage of being sufficiently removed from it to be able to judge of the results of the political changes which were then only in preparation, and, by the guide of principles founded

on better data, to trace them to their fundamental CHAP.
causes. These will be found in the earliest pages IV.
of their history.

If the first emigrants to the bleak and barren Character
shores of New England, driven as they were from of the first settlers in
the comforts of their homes, to incur the sufferings New England.
of exile, may in this respect be termed, in Mr.
Burke's language, " miserable outcasts," it must be
remembered that no motives of worldly advantage,
but the operation of a higher principle, had forced
them to abandon the place of their birth for a
country where they could follow their peculiar religious views without fear of disturbance ; that they
were not only men possessed of much intelligence,
but that all, without exception, had received a good
education, and that many of them were of no small
repute at home for their talents and acquirements.

The emigrants, whose numbers are variously
stated, at from 101 to 150, had intended to plant a
colony on the shores of the Hudson ; but they
were forced by adverse circumstances to land, in
the depth of winter, on that arid coast where the
town of Plymouth now stands. By the return of
spring more than one half of them had been cut
off by diseases or famine ; but " they were well
weaned," according to their own description, "from
the delicate milk of their mother country, and in-
ured to the difficulties of a strange land* : they
were knit together in a strict and sacred band, by
virtue of which they held themselves obliged to

* They had previously taken refuge in Holland.

take care of the good of each other, and of the
whole.   It was not with them, as with other men,
whom small things could discourage, or small dis-
contents cause to wish themselves at home again."

Although the laws which were promulgated
by these remarkable men, at this first era of the
American republic, are strongly imbued with those
notions of natural equality among men to which
their religious opinions had given rise, yet the
ideas which they formed of the duties of society
are more elevated and more comprehensive, perhaps, than those of any European legislators at the
time.   It is, however, the attention paid by them
to public education which more particularly stamps
their character with a high degree of civilisation.
In the year 1636, within sixteen years of the original settlement of the colony, 400*l.* was advanced
towards the establishment of a college; and Havard
University, an institution now of great celebrity,
was incorporated two years afterwards.

Though the settlers in the southern states were
derived from a different class in society, and had
different objects in view, which they struggled to
attain with a more turbulent and restless spirit,
yet their descendants were equally destined to participate in the blessings of a high degree of rational
freedom through the gradual spreading of the
principles adopted by the New England states,
which, passing successively to the more distant
ones, soon shed their influence over the whole
confederation.   The civilisation of New England
has, on this account, been compared by M. de

Tocqueville to a beacon lighted upon a hill, which, having first diffused its warmth on the neighbouring objects, tinges the distant horizon with its glow. The growth of the institutions of the northern and southern states, and the modifications of character arising out of the different origin of the settlers, and the prejudicial influence of slavery in the southern states, are ably shown by this reflecting and intelligent author.

The revolution, which subsequently separated the colonies from the mother country, may be traced to the influence of these early institutions in maturing the character of the colonists, and fitting them for governing themselves. The eminent men by whose ability and energy this revolution was achieved, added to these institutions others of which their country has equal reason to be proud; and, being coeval with the first establishment of the federal republic, even these have now been tried by the experience of more than half a century, which, if it be a short period in the history of nations, is sufficiently long to have shown their efficacy in times of foreign war and domestic troubles, and their tendency always to rise superior to the difficulties with which they have had to contend.

These institutions are highly prized by the people; and however much the characters of the inhabitants of the several states may differ one from the other — however much the enterprising merchant of New York may differ from the sober-minded and literary citizen of Boston, or both from

Attachment of the Americans to their institutions.

the aristocratic planter of Virginia — they all feel that they are what their fathers fought for, and what they have transmitted to them as an inheritance without a price. Such associations, by endearing the institutions of a country to a people, are likely with nations, as with individuals, to prove a stimulus to exertion, and an inducement, which will be ever strong in the minds of sensible men, to preserve and transmit unimpaired the fair fame they have derived from those who have preceded them.

Neither the local associations, nor those connected with their institutions which the older states possess, can be felt by the new settlers in the western states. The names even of these states are scarcely yet familiar to the ear, or, if they convey any impressions, they are such as are connected with the idea rather of wandering Indian tribes than of the abodes of a civilised people. The length of time, too, that the Atlantic states have now existed has been sufficient for the establishment of an extensive commerce, and for the growth of a considerable rural population. The states bordering on the Mississippi not only want these advantages, but also that accumulated wealth, the still more solid basis of commercial credit, which the eastern states enjoy.

Advantages of the western states.

On the other hand, it should be taken into consideration that, if the population of the western states is still small in number, it is made up almost exclusively of active and enterprising men, who have emigrated from the more crowded communities in the eastern and middle portions of the Union, and carried with them the steady cha-

racter of the American citizen.* Their connection,
too, with the federal government brings their lead-
ing men into constant communication with those of
the other states, whose experience they can apply
to the management of their own concerns; while in
the establishment of their institutions, and in their
modes of government, they have, from the first,
had models constantly before them, and prescribed
forms perfectly adapted to their wants.

The federal government, too, is enabled to exercise its beneficial influence in forming regulations
most conducive to the interests of these rising
states. Thus, in all the vacant lands which have
been surveyed and offered for sale, a reservation is
made of a certain proportion of every township, for
the endowment of schools and colleges.† Such a

* The numbers who leave Europe every year, driven either
by distress or by misconduct to America, appear to remain in
the large Atlantic cities, which contain at all times a large proportion of unruly and unprincipled characters. They have
hitherto, therefore, had no influence on the character of the rural
population of the western states. Their mode of life, indeed, is
so little adapted to rural pursuits, that the new states are likely,
on this account, to escape their contamination.

† In the new states, the part thus set aside constitutes one
thirty-sixth of the whole public lands within the state, and
must be applied for the benefit of the families living within the
surveyed township. Besides which, a *common* fund has, in
most instances, been created, to be applied, at the discretion of
the state, for the *general* purposes of education.

As an instance of the progress made in regard to education,
it may be mentioned that, in the state of Ohio, (by a report of
the 9th January, 1838,) it appears that at that time, out of a
population of 254,530 males and 238,307 females, between four

Richness
of the soil.

course of judicious policy can scarcely fail to produce a sensible change in the condition of these
new states.

The predominating advantage, however, which
the western states enjoy over the older ones is in
the inexhaustible richness of the soil. This, in
comparing the eastern with the western states,
ought more especially to be taken into consideration in reference to those southern states in which
tobacco is the staple produce. The cultivation of
this plant, which was introduced into Virginia by
the British settlers, in the year 1616, is known to
be extremely prejudicial in many respects. It is
productive of infinite wretchedness to those employed in it, who are said to be kept in a constant
state of exertion, beyond what the powers of nature
can well support, while little food of any kind is
raised by them; so that both the men and the animals on the farms are badly fed, and the earth is
rapidly impoverished.*

The nature of the cultivation of the western
states, especially of those to the north of the Ohio,
is the reverse of this in every particular. Far from
impairing the fertility of the soil, it every year adds
to the value of the ground, and increases both the
amount produced and its capability of future pro-

---

and twenty-one years of age, the total number in the schools
amounted, according to the most accurate evidence that could
be obtained, to 227,805.

    * The cultivation of rice, though it does not to the same ex-
tent exhaust the soil, appears to be attended with a still greater
degree of suffering to the labourers engaged in it.

duction. The crops, in the mean time, destined to
administer to the necessities, and not to the luxuries,
of man, feed the labourers plentifully; while the
richness of the soil requires from them only a
moderate degree of labour, except in the season of
harvest. Great numbers of cattle, too, suited either
for food or service, are raised at a small cost, and
thus plenty and happiness are diffused among the
people. Nor is much capital required for an enterprising settler. In many instances the first crop
of wheat will pay for the expense of purchasing the
land, for fencing and breaking up the prairie, for
seed, for getting in the crop, threshing, and carrying
it to market; and such is the inexhaustible quality
of the soil that, around the French towns in Illinois,
the same ground has been cultivated, and has produced corn in succession, for more than a century,
without any diminution of its fertility.*

* It may be doubted, however, if this extreme fertility of the
prairies, inducing as it does habits of indolence in the cultivator,
be an unmixed advantage. When the state of Connecticut, in
1786, surrendered its claims to a share of the public lands, a
district in Ohio, called thence the Connecticut Reserve, was retained contrary to the judgment of many of the ablest statesmen
of the day, it being so wet, when covered with forests, that it
was considered by them to be of little value. Being now well
cleared, this tract presents an extent of the finest arable and
meadow land; and in point of cultivation, and the general prosperity of the inhabitants, it equals, if it does not excel, any other
district in the western states. Thus it is observed that a soil
that demands labour in order that it may be made to yield, and
yields a large return when that is given, is often the soil that in
the end has the effect of making its owners the most independent.
— *North American Review*, No. C.

It has been remarked, too, that the abundance of land in

If we consider the extent of the tract thus favoured by nature, it is difficult to form too high an
estimate of its value. Reaching from the lakes on
the north, to the Ohio on the south, and from the
Alleghany mountains on the east, to the Mississippi on the west, this territory is nearly twice as
large as the kingdom of France, and contains
180,000,000 of acres of arable land, of which a
large proportion is of great fertility. It is nearly
encircled and much intersected by navigable waters,
while the Ohio and the Mississippi, with their
numerous tributary streams, afford an outlet for
its produce.

No rivers can be better calculated than these are
for facilitating the purposes of commerce. Rising
in mountains of little elevation, compared with the
length of their course, their descent is scarcely
greater than is absolutely necessary to carry off the
waters from the countries they traverse. At the
distance of 1364 miles from its source, the Mississippi attains an average depth of fifteen feet;
and ships of the burden of 300 tons can penetrate
to Cincinnati, in the heart of Ohio, more than
1500 miles from the sea; while steam navigation has
been carried to such perfection, that steam-boats
can perform this distance in ten or twelve days.*

America leads to an indifferent state of agriculture, from the
waste which it encourages. In Europe, the object is to make
the most of the lands, labour being abundant. In America, it is
to make the most of labour, land being abundant. — *Jefferson,
Notes on Virginia.*

* The steam-boat Mediator is stated to have performed the

Besides the outlet for their produce, which the Ohio and the Mississippi thus afford to cultivators, the state of Pennsylvania has established a communication between the former river and Philadelphia by a series of canals and railroads, and has thus opened to them the market of the Atlantic cities. The state of New York, by means of the Erie canal, has procured for them a similar advantage at a port more to the north, while a still more gigantic undertaking than either of these works is now in progress, to connect the Ohio at Louisville and Cincinnati with Charleston, which will bring the produce of these distant lands to the markets of the southern Atlantic states.

These advantages are such as to make it probable that the states of Ohio, Indiana, and Illinois, will, before long, hold as prominent a place in the Union, both for wealth and importance, as the eastern states now do ; the want of a sufficient population to give full effect to their institutions being the chief difficulty they now have to contend with, and becoming every year less.

In this respect, indeed, the progress of these states has been truly surprising. The first permanent settlement in Ohio was made at Marietta, on the 7th of April, 1788, by 47 persons from Massachusetts, Rhode Island, and Connecticut.* Such

Rapid progress of population.

---

passage, in July, 1836, from New Orleans to Louisville, in seven days and 15 hours. — *American Almanack,* 1837, p. 192.

* An article on the state of Ohio, in a late number of the *North American Review,* opens with the following anecdote:

was the nucleus around which this populous state has grown up. It was admitted to the Union in 1802, and up to 1816 it was the only organised government within the limits of the territory just described. In that year Indiana, having obtained the requisite number of 60,000 inhabitants, was added to the Union. Illinois and Michigan were then distant and feeble territories, with a few settlers thinly scattered over their surface; while Wisconsin, unknown even by name, was an undistinguished portion of the great north-western territory. " In the brief period of twenty-one years," says an official report, " such has been the influx of population into this great district, that Ohio, the eldest member in this brotherhood of nations, now numbers 1,400,000 inhabitants; Indiana upwards of 600,000 ; Illinois and Michigan,

---

— " A little after eleven o'clock, on the night following our elections in this place, (says a letter from Cincinnati, written in October, 1837,) I was called to the door by a very vigorous rapping. It was some one in great haste to know the result of the day's work, and who had mistaken our house for the one in which the votes were to be counted. After directing him aright, I threw the door open a little wider, that I might see what young patriot this was that so keenly desired to know the state of parties. The light of the hall lamp fell full on his face — it was Hezekiah Flint, one of the first band of white men that ever came to reside in Ohio."

Such an incident seems striking; and yet it is but 51 years since the above adventurers landed at Marietta: and many men of seventy, yet vigorous and stirring, must have been entering into busy life when the plain upon which Cincinnati is built was sold for less than fifty silver dollars.

both of which have organised their governments and come into the Union, 700,000* ; — while west of Lake Michigan, not only is Wisconsin rapidly rising, but, even beyond the Upper Mississippi, 30,000 citizens have already laid the foundations of another state." The population now embraced within the district in question falls little short of 3,000,000.

In comparing the northern with the southern states, the non-existence of slavery in the former is the circumstance chiefly to be considered as giving them an advantage over those where slave labour is had recourse to.

Comparison of the northern and southern states.

The introduction of negro cultivators in the southern states took place about the year 1618; and the men of this unhappy race being more capable of enduring fatigue, under a sultry climate, than Europeans, their number has been increased by constant importation. Their aid now seems generally to be thought essential to the existence of the countries where they are employed, as the greater part of the field labour in the southern states is performed exclusively by them.

Introduction of slavery into the southern states.

* This number seems to be over estimated : 500,000 would probably be nearer to the truth. For the gradual increase of the population in the United States, see Appendix, letter A.

† The Spanish government formerly caused a number of peasants to be sent from the Azores to a district of Louisiana, called Attakapas, by way of an experiment. These settlers still cultivate the soil without the assistance of slaves ; but their exertions are so languid as scarcely to supply their most necessary wants.

The experience of our West India colonies will in a few years show whether the same services may not be more advantageously obtained from the negroes as free labourers; and, if so, the stain upon the American Constitution, which tolerates the continuance of slavery, may be removed through the happy result of an experiment which has been so honourably made by the British nation. But, should this prove not to be the case, the slave states in America will probably continue to enforce compulsory labour from the negroes; nor is there reason to believe they will be exposed to any serious danger by doing so.

Opinion of M. de Tocqueville.
The high authority of M. de Tocqueville is opposed to this opinion. In whatever way he views the question he sees nothing but difficulties. That slavery will one day cease, either by the choice of the master or the will of the slave, is assumed by him to be beyond a doubt; but in either case he thinks that great calamities will ensue. Should the struggle take place while the northern and southern states are held together by their federal compact, and the former prove true to their engagements, it will end, he supposes, in the extirpation of the blacks; but, if the northern states should refuse to aid their brethren in the south, he thinks it likely that the white population in the southern states will share the fate of the Moors in Spain, and that the blacks will remain undisputed masters of a country which they alone seem capable of cultivating. The emancipation of the negroes

will only, in his opinion, hasten the catastrophe. Nothing but an intermixture of the races, which he holds to be impossible, could, he thinks, avoid the calamity. The deep attention which this author has bestowed on every subject connected with the moral and political condition of the United States renders any opinion which he advances worthy of a deliberate consideration ; but I cannot assent to his conclusions in this respect. In the West India Islands he conceives the ultimate extirpation of the white population to be still more certain ; but, if this even were the case, the situation of our West India colonies has little of resemblance to that of the southern states of North America. In the island of Jamaica, the proportion of the now emancipated negroes to the white population is about as nine to one, while in British Guiana there are more than twenty black men to one white. In the United States, South Carolina and Louisiana are the only states in which the black population has a numerical advantage, and in these the slaves exceed the free population by a very small fraction. The armed militia, which is organised in the slave-holding states, is amply sufficient, therefore, for the purposes of self-defence ; but the question cannot be regarded in a mere physical point of view : for the moral superiority which the white population possesses, arising out of its greater wealth and intelligence, must render its authority almost absolute as regards its power of resisting any acts of insubordination on the part of the slaves.

The misguided efforts of those, therefore, who would excite the negroes to a revolt, may lead, indeed, to their destruction, but can never effect a forced emancipation. The fact that the black population in the most southern states increases faster than the white, does not seem materially to affect the position, as this increase is less owing to the increasing number of births among the slave population than to the compulsory emigration of negroes from the more northern slave states: it is, therefore, so far voluntarily permitted by the states likely to suffer from it, and may at any time be checked when the excess becomes dangerous.

Moral influence of slavery.

The disadvantages of the system of slavery in the southern states may therefore, in a political point of view, be considered as confined to the influence which it produces on the habits and industry of the people, and on their moral conduct. The Ohio, we have seen, separates the free states from those where slave labour is resorted to; and the striking contrast between the banks on the two sides of the river is very remarkable, and strongly illustrative of this baneful influence. The different appearance of the two shores is thus described by M. de Tocqueville: — " Le voyageur qui placé au milieu de l'Ohio, se laisse entraîner par le courant jusqu' à l'embouchure du fleuve dans le Mississippi, navigue pour ainsi dire entre la liberté et la servitude, et il n'a qu' à jeter autour de lui ses regards pour juger en un instant laquelle est la plus favorable à l'humanité.

" Sur la rive gauche du fleuve la population est

clair-semée ; de temps en temps on aperçoit une
troupe d'esclaves parcourant d'un air insouciant des
champs à moitié déserts ; la forêt primitive reparait
sans cesse ; on dirait que la société est endormie :
l'homme semble oisif ; la nature seule offre l'image
de l'activité et de la vie.

"De la rive droite s'élève au contraire une rumeur
confuse qui proclame au loin la présence de l'in-
dustrie ; de riches moissons couvrent les champs :
d'élégantes demeures annoncent le goût et les
soins du laboureur ; de toutes parts l'aisance se
révèle, l'homme parait riche et content ; il tra-
vaille." The influence of slavery on the moral
condition of the people has also been exhibited
in a strong light by Mr. Jefferson, who could speak
of it from a still more intimate acquaintance with its
effects. "The whole commerce," he says, "between master and slave is a perpetual exercise of
the most boisterous passions, the most unremitting
despotism on the one part, and degrading submis-
sions on the other. Our children see this, and learn
to imitate it ; for man is an imitative animal. This
quality is the germ of all education in him. From
his cradle to his grave he is learning to do what
he sees others do. If a parent could find no
motive, either in his philanthropy or his self-love,
for restraining the intemperance of passion towards
his slave, it should always be a sufficient one that
his child is present. But generally it is not sufficient. The parent storms, the child looks on,
catches the lineaments of wrath, puts on the same
airs in the circle of smaller slaves, gives a loose to

his worst of passions, and thus nursed, educated, and daily exercised in tyranny, cannot but be stamped by it with odious peculiarities. The man must be a prodigy who can retain his manners and morals undepraved by such circumstances.

"With the morals of the people, their industry also is destroyed; for, in a warm climate, no man will labour for himself who can make another labour for him. This is so true that of the proprietors of slaves a very small proportion indeed are ever seen to labour."

"And can the liberties of a nation," he adds, "be thought secure when we have removed their only firm basis, a conviction in the minds of the people that these liberties are the gift of God? that they are not to be violated but with his wrath? Indeed I tremble for my country when I reflect that God is just; that his justice cannot sleep for ever; that considering numbers, nature and natural means only, a revolution of the wheel of fortune, an exchange of situation, is among possible events; that it may become probable by supernatural interference! The Almighty has no attribute which can take side with us in such a contest. But it is impossible to be temperate, and to pursue this subject through the various considerations of policy, of morals, of history natural and civil: we must be contented to hope they will force their way into every one's mind. I think a change already perceptible, since the origin of the present revolution. The spirit of the master is abating, that of the slave rising from the dust, his condition mollifying, the way, I hope, preparing, under the auspices of Heaven, for a total emancipation, and that this is disposed, in the order of events, to be with the consent of the masters, rather than by their extirpation." This state of things, however, unhappily continues. Modern writers describe oppression towards the slave as still producing, by a sort of retributive justice, the same state of moral degradation in the master: and the unenlightened policy of the state legislatures, which throws every impediment in the way of the intellectual improvement of the negroes, by attaching severe penalties to the teaching them to read and write, seems likely to perpetuate the evil. If better morals and more correct religious feelings can make their way through these obstacles among this unfortunate race, the progress, at least, must be slow and uncertain.

Against the disadvantages of a slave population is to be placed the great value of the produce raised by their labour: the most important by far of these productions, in the southern states, is cotton, of which the finest description grows, as we have seen, on the low grounds along the shores of Georgia. This plant was first cultivated for exportation about the year 1789, and what is technically called the " upland " cotton about the same time or a little earlier. It was found, however, so difficult to cleanse the cotton of the latter from the seed, that for some years it hardly repaid the expense of cultivation ; but by the invention, in 1793, of a machine to effect this purpose (the credit

Great value
of produce
in the
southern
states.

Mr. Whit-
ney's
machine.

CHAP.
IV.

of which is due to Mr. Whitney), an extraordinary change has taken place in the extent to which the cultivation of this plant has been carried.* In 1835, out of 361½ millions of lbs. of cotton wool imported into Great Britain, no less a quantity than 252 millions of lbs. was brought from the United States, and the quantity annually grown has of late years been considerably on the increase.†

Application of public funds.

While the industry and ingenuity of the people have been thus beneficially applied, according to the varying circumstances of the states, to the development of the resources of which nature has been to most of them so bountiful, the respective legislatures have not been backward in extending a fostering hand, and have given a fresh impulse to their exertions by the application of the funds of the state to objects of public utility.

Different modes of application.

When the states have not otherwise been possessed of funds available for this purpose, they have in many instances procured them by loans. The peculiar circumstances of each state has, in general, influenced the manner in which the sums in either case have been expended.

In the southern states the impulse which Mr.

* A description of this machine, and of the process of detaching the seeds from the fibres of the cotton, is given, in his usual graphic manner, by Capt. Hall. — *Travels in America*, vol. iii. p. 221.

† In 1835, the cotton crop of the United States was estimated at 480 millions of lbs.; the capital employed in the production, at 800 millions of dollars; and the number of hands employed, or of persons dependent on them, cost one million. For further statistical details see Appendix, letter L.

Whitney's machine has given to the culture of
cotton has caused it to outstrip the means of the producers to defray the expenses attendant on this increased cultivation; and the resources of the capitalists, especially in the newer states, being inadequate to meet the wants of the planters in this respect, the most profitable application of the sums raised by these states has been found in the formation and extension of banking companies, to supply that deficiency of capital through the means of a larger circulating medium.

The private resources of the citizens in the Atlantic states being, in general, adequate to the purposes of commerce, the public funds in these states have chiefly been employed in the construction of extensive works, which were either too costly to be undertaken by individuals, or where the prospect of a return was too remote to induce them to embark their capital in them.

In the newer states to the north of the Ohio, the formation of roads and canals, to facilitate the transport of their produce, offering also an advantageous outlay for capital, the public funds have been largely applied to works of internal improvement; but, although the nature of the cultivation is less costly in these than in the southern states, the means of the settlers to defray their agricultural expenses are, in general, inconsiderable, so that some portion has been applied also, in these newer states, to the institution of banks. These two modes of applying the funds of the states will require a separate consideration.

CHAP. V.

CHAP. V.

Funds chiefly obtained from loans.

THE consideration of the manner in which the funds of the different states have been applied to the development of their resources leads more immediately to the chief object which has been proposed in these remarks; for, as the greater part of the funds have been obtained by loans, it is with reference to this part of the subject that an inquiry becomes necessary into the means of the several states to fulfil their engagements.

Security derived from the nature of the expenditure.

Before entering, however, into the details which this investigation will require, it will be desirable, since the funds have, in almost every instance, been expended with a view to obtain either an immediate or prospective return in the way of interest, to consider, in a general point of view, how far this circumstance affords a security to the creditor of the borrowing state, independently of its general resources; for this profitable application of the amounts borrowed by the different states of North America should cause a great distinction to be made between their loans and those which constituted the debt of the federal government while that existed, or those that now form the national debts of European states; all of which have invariably been expended either to provide for the public defence, the protection of commerce, and the expenses of the civil administration, or in modes which leave no tangible traces behind them of the sums expended, and yield no pecuniary return to defray the interest upon the debts contracted. Although expenditures of the nature last referred to may be judicious in themselves, and may serve to secure to the states which engage in them substantial benefits which will repay them for the sacrifices they make in incurring them, the distinction laid down above ought not to be lost sight of, in estimating the respective security which loans contracted for such different purposes offer to the lender.

Although the expenditure of the sums obtained by loans in the several states, whether for purposes of internal improvement, or for the establishment of banking institutions, has been professedly for objects which will make a return equivalent to the outlay, yet the respective security which these two modes of expenditure offer to the lender, differs, also, in some essential particulars. I shall first consider the security which is derived from the application of the money to works of internal improvement, such as canals and railroads, and other works for facilitating commercial intercourse.

In such works a considerable time will, in general, elapse before any profitable returns are made ; and in a variety of cases many of them will doubtless fail altogether to produce a revenue sufficient to keep them in repair, and to pay the interest on the cost of their construction.   If this is foreseen in the case of any particular work, still it may not be a sound objection against engaging in it, as by its accomplishment the state may be adequately benefited, if it can attract, through its means, to itself a portion of trade which might otherwise be withdrawn, through other channels, to rival states; or such a work may, by its contributions to other main lines of improvement, compensate the state for the amount expended on its construction ; but the prospect that many, and the certainty that some, of the public works undertaken by the states will not produce a revenue adequate to their cost make it incumbent, where the results anticipated have not been verified by tried success, to examine whether the state possesses other means to redeem the sums borrowed, when the periods of payment arrive, and to preserve unimpaired the credit which it has pledged for the punctual payment, in the mean time, of the interest.   Indeed this is at all times desirable, as the rivalry of other lines of improvement, undertaken by individuals or even by adjoining states, each seeking to direct into its own channels as much traffic as possible, may interfere with the fairest prospects of works already in active and profitable operation.

In the case of many states, auxiliary funds are specially appropriated to this purpose — in others, the security of the loans are based solely on the general credit of the state. The appropriation of such funds is in all cases desirable, as, however great the resources of a state may be, its fiscal means are often extremely limited. This arises, not only from the most productive sources of revenue, such as the proceeds of the sales of public lands, imposts on commerce, and the revenue of the post-office, having been surrendered to the general government and belonging exclusively to it, but also from the anxiety always shown by the people of the United States to control their rulers by making them dependent on their will for the supplies, which they at all times very sparingly allot to them. This democratic feeling is carried so far, even in the wealthiest states, that the treasuries are constantly exposed to become bare ; and the accounts of almost all are complicated by the borrowing and repaying of temporary loans made by the monied institutions of the state to provide for unlooked for exigencies, or even for the ordinary demands of the public administration.*

* As these temporary loans and repayments all pass through the treasury accounts, the mere statement of the receipts and expenditures of the treasury gives a very imperfect notion of the resources of a state.

CHAP.
V.

Objects
proposed in
the im-
provements
in the
United
States.

First con-
ceived by
Mr. Morris.

Attempts
first made

In the public improvements which have been
undertaken by the different states, two objects
have been kept in view — one, to effect a safe
inland communication, by means of canals and
railroads, along the Atlantic shore, to serve as a
protection against foreign enemies, or the disasters of the sea, on a coast in many parts ill supplied with harbours * ; the other, by means of
similar undertakings, to connect the great lakes
and rivers in the north and west with the Atlantic.

Although the works to effect the former object
are extensive, they are not of the magnitude of
those which constitute the second description of
public improvements, which derive additional consequence from the great and increasing importance
of the regions, to the productions of which they
are probably destined to constitute the chief outlet.

The idea of uniting the western waters with the
Atlantic seems originally to have been suggested
by Mr. Gouverneur Morris, who, as early as 1777,
entertained a project of effecting a communication
between Lake Erie and the Hudson; but the state
of Pennsylvania appears to have been the first to
attempt to put such a plan into execution.

As early as 1790, the legislature of that state

* The coast of the northern states presents a variety of magnificent estuaries and spacious ports, which are constantly
accessible to vessels of the greatest burden ; but on the low
sandy coast which has been described as extending from the
Potomac round to the mouths of the Mississippi, the entrances
to the rivers are generally obstructed by bars, and the few
harbours which exist among the lagunes that are formed there
afford little shelter to vessels of considerable size.

appointed commissioners to explore several routes
between the Delaware and the lakes who reported
in favour of one through the valley of the Juniata,
by which it was shown that a communication
might be effected, if formed partly by canals and
partly by taking advantage of such rivers as were
navigable, or could be easily rendered so. The
state did not itself engage in the undertaking,
but two private companies were incorporated to
carry the plan into execution: one called the
Schuylkill and Susquehanna Company, in 1791;
the other, in the following year, by the name of
the Delaware and Schuylkill Company. But the
public mind was not then prepared for a work of
such magnitude; and, after four or five hundred
thousand dollars had been expended, the enterprise
was abandoned by both companies in 1795 and
1796. This plan was not again resumed in earnest
until 1825, when the extensive work already alluded
to was begun, by which the Ohio at Pittsburg is
connected by a series of canals and railroads with
the Delaware at Philadelphia. *

In the mean time, the state of New York had completed the canal which connects the Hudson with

* In this immense undertaking, the Alleghany ridge is crossed
at Blair's Gap, at the height of 2369 feet above the level of the
sea. The ascent and descent is effected by means of ten inclined planes, furnished with stationary engines (five on each
side of the summit level). The aggregate length of the bases of
these planes is 4.37 miles, the rise and fall in the whole distance is
2570 feet, of which 1398 are on the eastern, and 1172 on the
western side of the mountain; 563 feet are overcome by gradients,
and 2007 feet by the inclined planes.

Lake Erie. This celebrated work was commenced on the 4th of July, 1817, and completed in October, 1825. During the time it was in progress, a branch canal was commenced and finished to connect the waters of Lake Champlain with the main work. The Americans have contrasted this great undertaking with the canal of Languedoc, which, though only 148 miles in length, took Lewis XIV., with all his means, fourteen years to complete ; while the length of the Erie and Champlain canals together is 426 miles, and the time employed in their construction was little more than eight years. It is curious to trace the history of the Erie and Champlain canal, and to observe how unconscious the statesmen of the day appear to have been of the great benefits which the state was destined to derive from its completion. Documents exist to prove that, before it was begun, the legislature directed commissioners to solicit pecuniary donations in aid of the enterprise, not only from Connecticut and Vermont, but even from the states then in their infancy beyond the Alleghany mountains ; and so far was this timid and discreditable policy pursued, that the very preamble to the law of 1817, which finally directed the canal to be commenced, took care to express the humble hope that the states interested in the work would contribute their full proportion to the expense.

Nor were the doubts thus thrown upon the policy of the measure in its earliest stages the result of any hostile feeling, for they were partaken of by the warmest friends of their country. Even Mr. Jefferson pronounced the undertaking to be utterly visionary and chimerical, and at least a century in advance of the age ; nay, so little sanguine were the projectors themselves, that the comptroller of the state, on being called on to furnish an estimate of the revenues likely to be derived from the canal, stated, in 1821, four years after the work had been commenced, that for the ten years next succeeding its completion the tolls might amount annually to $150,000, while its original projector, Mr. Gouverneur Morris, a statesman whose comprehensive intellect and ardent temperament appear to have enabled him to look far beyond most of his contemporaries into the future, in endeavouring to impress upon the legislature the importance of the undertaking, asked whether it would be deemed extravagant to predict that the canal, within twenty years, would annually bring down 250,000 tons. In the ten years to which the comptroller looked forward, the amount of tolls actually received exceeded ten millions of dollars, and the amount of tonnage in 1836 which reached the Hudson was 696,347 tons, while the total tonnage of that year, ascending and descending, exceeded thirteen hundred thousand tons.

By the middle of that year the tolls, with the aid of the auxiliary funds, which were originally pledged for the payment of the money borrowed, had accumulated to an amount which enabled the state to discharge the whole of the debt contracted to

CHAP.
V.

pay the expense of the construction of the work; and the annual income which the canal now yields is sufficient not only to keep the work in a state of complete repair, but to defray the ordinary expenses of the government, and to leave a considerable surplus which has been appropriated to other works of national improvement.

Prospects of similar undertakings.

The state of New York is, however, the only one in which the public improvements have been long enough in operation to have thus afforded a complete proof of their success: and the Erie and Champlain canal is the only one of these of which this can as yet be said, the lateral canals, which have lately been finished, being still nearly unproductive. It must remain, therefore, a question of considerable doubt, whether an equally successful result will attend similar undertakings in other states. In order to form any well founded conjecture on the subject several circumstances must be taken into consideration: on the one hand the severity of the winters in the high latitude of New York places the canals of that state under a considerable disadvantage, when compared with those which have been made or are still in progress in lower latitudes and in milder climates. All traffic on the Erie canal is suspended during at least five months in the year; it being seldom navigable until the 20th of April, and rarely remaining open after the 20th of November, while the canals of Pennsylvania are generally navigable about the 10th of March, and usually remain so till the 25th of December. When the line of the Pennsylvania canal and railroad shall

have come, therefore, into full operation, which it
cannot yet be considered to have done, the mer- chants of Philadelphia will, by its means, be enabled to monopolise the western trade during portions of the spring and autumn, peculiarly valuable for commercial purposes. Even after the navigation is opened on the Erie canal, the intercourse be- tween New York and the western states is ob- structed for a considerable time by the ice which accumulates during the months of March and April in the harbour of Buffalo : this also will give a great advantage to the Pennsylvania line, as the navigation of the Ohio is open at Pittsburg during that important season of the year, so that the produce of the western states will find its way through the Pennsylvania canal to Philadelphia, and from thence to the adjoining districts, before vessels are able to navigate the eastern end of Lake Erie.* The Chesapeake and Ohio canal, which is to connect the Ohio at Pittsburg with the Potomac at Georgetown, will participate in this advantage.†

* The state of New York has chartered a company to con- struct a railroad, called the New York and Erie Railroad, to serve also as a winter communication between the city of New York and the harbours on Lake Erie, and to compete with the state of Pennsylvania for this lucrative portion of the trade.

† This canal, after leaving Pittsburg strikes to the south, and if executed according to the original plan, will traverse the Alleghany mountains by a tunnel four miles and eighty yards in length. Sections of the three great works referred to in this chapter, viz., the Erie, the Pennsylvania, and the Chesapeake and Ohio canals, are given on the map at the beginning of the volume.

On the other hand, it must be remembered, that the competition between these and other rival lines of communication will diminish the profits of all, unless the rapidly increasing resources of the western states shall keep pace with the increased means of transport. This is so uncertain an event, that, in any estimate that may be made of the future prospects of these and similar undertakings, it will scarcely be prudent, on the whole, to take the success of the Erie and Champlain canal as a criterion of the success of others ; but, even if it were so, it would lead to a very erroneous view of the extent of the resources which such works intrinsically possess, if the fact which has been stated, of the liquidation of the debt borrowed to construct the Erie and Champlain canal, be considered without reference to the share which the auxiliary funds, which were pledged at the first for its repayment, have had in producing this result.

Auxiliary
funds of
Erie canal.
It was not till the year 1826 that the tolls on the canal began to exceed the cost of maintenance : until that time, and partially for some years afterwards, it was from the auxiliary funds that the interest on the debt was defrayed, and it has been shown in the report of the comptroller of the state of New York, which was made to the legislature on the 3d of January of the present year, that had the works been limited till now to their own resources, and the interest been defrayed, as it then must have been by fresh loans, the debt, instead

of being cancelled, would now, at the end of twenty-one years, have exceeded by $57,674 the whole sum originally expended in the construction. The auxiliary funds must, according to this statement, have produced a sum greater than the whole amount of interest for twenty years on all the money borrowed. With a scrupulous regard for the maintenance of its credit, this state, at the commencement of the works, pledged also the tolls that should be received, for the payment of the debt, and it is from the two sources combined that the means of cancelling it have been obtained within nineteen years of its creation. This circumstance very forcibly proves how important it is that states, if they wish not only effectively to guard their credit and to give perfect stability to their engagements, but to attend to their truest interests, should never have recourse to loans in aid of such enterprises, without at the same time providing, either by auxiliary funds or by taxes, for the payment of the interest and for their final reimbursement. It is by this judicious policy alone that the Erie canal is at this moment the unburdened source of a large revenue to the state, enabling the legislature, without embarrassment, to act in the true spirit of its object, by reducing the tolls when the interests of trade require it, unfettered by any considerations of a mere fiscal nature. Without the adoption of such a system, 'a state will not only fail to derive this benefit, but must fail likewise to inspire capitalists with that full conviction of their security which will induce them to come forward on liberal terms to its assistance.

There seems little reason, however, to doubt that great advantages may be derived to the different states from their embarking in works of public improvement, should the tolls even fail eventually to produce an income equivalent to the interest on the cost of construction and to the cost of maintenance.

Benefit of public works.

However remarkable the success of the Erie and Champlain canal has been in a fiscal point of view, it would give a very imperfect idea of the benefit which the state of New York has derived from this work, were the revenue it produces alone made the criterion of the successful issue of the experiment. By diminishing the time and labour expended in the transport of produce, the sum annually saved to the citizens is very great, while the value of the agricultural productions of the interior, which would never have existed, or could not have been brought to market but by the aid of the canal, is so much added to the wealth of the community. The rapid growth, and in many cases the very existence, of the numerous towns which now line the borders of the Erie canal, may be traced to the traffic upon it, and exhibit in a strong light the advantage which the canal has afforded to the state. The effect which this traffic has had upon the population of Albany, Utica, Rochester, and Buffalo, will be perceived on comparing the number of the inhabitants in these towns in 1825, when the works were just completed, with the number at the last state census in 1835.

	Number of inhabitants in 1825.	Number of inhabitants in 1835.
Albany	15,974	28,109.
Utica	5,040	10,183.
Rochester *	5,271	14,404.
Buffalo	2,600	15,661.

The rapid increase of the population and wealth of the city of New York itself in the same period may also, in a great degree, be attributed to the facilities of communication which the Erie canal affords between that metropolis and the agricultural districts in the interior, though doubtless other circumstances have greatly contributed towards it.

The population of New York in 1825 was 166,086: in 1835 it had reached 270,089. The value of the real and personal property in the city, as assessed in the former year, was $101,160,046; in the latter year it was $218,723,703, and in 1836 had reached $309,500,920; while the aggregate value of the real and personal property in the state, the increase of which has been no less rapid, then amounted to $672,372,487.

If these results are even nearly arrived at by other states, in similar undertakings, the increased wealth which they thus derive from them will

* Rochester, in December, 1815, contained 331 inhabitants, and up to 1820 could count only 1502.

afford them increased means of fulfilling their engagements; and although, from the experience of
the state of New York, it has been shown that
auxiliary funds tend much to the security of the
public creditor, by rendering him independent of
all contingencies, it can scarcely be doubted that
the works, if judiciously planned and executed, will
either directly, or thus indirectly, contribute materially towards it, and in many cases render the
existence of such auxiliary funds a matter of less
importance.

Danger
from mag-
nitude of
under-
takings.
The greatest danger seems to be, that the newer
states may outstrip their means from the magnitude of the enterprises they have engaged in, and
be unable to complete them. Three great canals
(one of them as long nearly as the Erie canal), embracing in their aggregate length about 1000 miles,
are now in progress to connect the Ohio with
Lake Erie, while another deep and capacious channel excavated for nearly thirty miles through solid
rock, is to unite Lake Michigan with the navigable
waters of the Illinois; in addition to these, many
railroads are in course of construction; and the cost
of the works thus undertaken will exceed forty-
eight millions of dollars. The state of Indiana
alone has 6000 men engaged in its public improvements, while Illinois and Michigan are making corresponding efforts. The tendency of these works,
it will be seen, by a reference to the geographical
position of these states, is to co-operate with, rather
than to rival, the canals of New York, as the ob-

ject will be to send the produce of the countries they intersect to Lake Erie, that they may there enter the grand canal at Buffalo, and be conveyed to the Atlantic. This circumstance is much in their favour.

The state is sometimes the sole proprietor of such works, and derives the whole benefit arising from the tolls ; in other instances it is only a co-proprietor, in which case, an additional security is afforded to the public creditor, as it is usual for the state, before affording its aid to such undertakings, to secure itself by a mortgage on the whole work, while the sum advanced is usually limited to one half, and often to a smaller proportion of the amount to be expended. In some instances, the works are carried on solely at the expense and for the benefit of incorporated companies, who are authorised to borrow funds in their own names, by issuing bonds under the guarantee of the state. In this case, so long as the interest is regularly paid by the company, the state, in a fiscal point of view, remains wholly unaffected by the aid it affords in affixing its guarantee : at the same time, the contingency, that it may hereafter be called on to pay the interest, or ultimately to redeem the capital of the bonds thus issued, ought not to be overlooked — it is, indeed, the guarantee of the state that gives the loans obtained under it, the currency and credit which they enjoy in foreign countries, where it would be difficult to acquire such information respecting the resources

The state not always the sole proprietor.

of the different companies, and the merits of the several undertakings, as would warrant capitalists to lend their funds without this additional security. In treating of the debts of the different states, engagements of this nature will therefore be considered as forming, as much as any other, a part of their liabilities.

CHAP. VI.

THE case where the credit or the funds of the states have been applied to the creation or extension of banking institutions is next to be considered.

Although the primary object contemplated by the states, in promoting the welfare of such institutions, has been to afford the means of a judicious increase of the circulating medium, and thereby to give impulse and vigour to agricultural labour, activity to commercial enterprise, and an increased value to the lands of the state; yet, in a variety of cases, the state, by retaining a greater or less share in the bank, has also had in view the

CHAP. VI.

Application of funds to establish banks.

CHAP.
VI.

Security
which this
affords.

Auxiliary
funds not
required.

creation of a revenue by participating in the profits of the establishment.

In considering this application of the funds, when the sums have been obtained by loans, a material difference in the degree of security which the lender derives from the nature of the undertaking, compared with what he derives from an application of the funds to works of internal improvement, arises out of the earlier returns which banking institutions make for the capital invested.

We have seen that the length of time during which railroads and canals must necessarily remain unproductive renders the pledge of auxiliary funds desirable, to prevent the accumulation of an arrear of interest while the works are in progress ; but as the capital of a bank, if it is well conducted, will begin to make a return from the first, a collateral security of this nature is not required. The provisions of the charter of the bank, and the degree of prudence and integrity shown in the management of its affairs, are what the lender should rather look to in this case, as affording a security arising out of the application of the funds, apart from that which he derives from the general resources of the state. These points can only be thoroughly investigated by a reference to each separate case, and they will in this way, as far as it is practicable, be presently considered : the different degrees of connection that exist in different cases, between the bank and the state, are no less deserving of attention, and will be first taken into consideration.

There are several instances to be found of banks which are the exclusive property of the states in which they are situated; and some few where the capital has been altogether raised by a creation of state debt. This arrangement affords less security to the public creditor than when the state is a co-partner; as in the latter case, the bonds which are issued in payment of the share which the state holds in the bank, and which constitute the state debt, are made payable to the order of the bank, and are indorsed by it, and have by this means the additional guarantee of the capital subscribed by the remaining proprietors.*

CHAP.
VI.

Banks
owned
solely by
the state.

This identity between the government and the bank is objectionable on other grounds; for although the act of the legislature, which incorporates the bank usually places the president and directors under restrictions as to the proportion to be observed between its issues and other liabilities, and the amount of its capital; yet, in places where wealth is likely to have a preponderating influence, those at the head of the banking establishments will

* The capital of the bank of the state of Alabama, which is solely owned by the state, besides the borrowed capital arising out of the state loan, consists of certain trust funds set aside for the purposes of education, called the " University fund," and of the " three per cent. fund," arising out of three per cent. on the amount of the sales of public lands which is given to the state for internal improvements; but these funds afford no additional security to the holder of the state bonds, as the agreement which pledges the general revenue of the state for the payment of the principal and interest specially exempts these items from the pledge.

CHAP.
VI.

probably be chosen to the legislative and executive offices of the state, in which case the control exercised by them in their latter capacity can be little depended upon in checking their own acts as directors of the bank; and should the necessities of a government become at any time urgent, it would be under a strong temptation to draw on the bank, till the bank became as necessitous as itself: much room is also left under this system for the exercise of a dangerous monopoly. Although liable to these objections in theory, it must be stated, however, that no serious charge of an indiscreet exercise of their power has been brought against the directors of banks so constituted.

Banks where the state is co-proprietor.

The cases in which the state is co-proprietor in a bank are very numerous, and while this system, as we have seen, affords a greater degree of security to the holder of the state's engagements, the benefits which the state derives from it are very considerable.

Bank of Louisiana.

The Bank of Louisiana was one of the earliest institutions of this nature, and its charter seems to have served as a model for similar establishments in other states; for this reason, and on account of its having now been sufficiently long in operation to have presented several interesting results, some details may be entered into, as illustrative of the general proceedings of banks founded on this principle. This bank was established by an act, which was finally approved of by the legislature on the 10th of April 1824, and soon afterwards

commenced business: the charter extends to
1870. The capital consisted of $4,000,000, of
which one half was subscribed by the state, and
paid for by an issue of bonds bearing interest at
5 per cent.; the remaining half was subscribed by
individuals, and was to be paid for in specie, although the enforcement of this provision was afterwards relaxed: the credit of the state being then
untried, the bonds were only received at the rate
of $83\frac{1}{3}$ per cent of their nominal amount, so that
bonds for $2,400,000 were given as the state's
subscription, which were to be redeemed in equal
portions at the end of ten, fifteen, twenty, and
twenty-five years from the date of the act; the
bonds were not to be sold by the bank otherwise
than for specie, and not below the rate at which
they received them: the bank was allowed to
appoint the place where the half-yearly interest
was to be paid; but any additional charge, loss
on exchange, or other expenses which might be
consequent upon the payment at any other place
than New Orleans, were to be defrayed by the
bank.*

The faith of the state was pledged for the payment of the principal and interest of the bonds,
but so long as the share of the state in the profits
of the bank was more than sufficient to pay the

* The state bonds were sold at a profit of £322,000; but,
by an engagement to pay the interest in London at the rate of
4s. 6d. per dollar, the bank loses the premium on the current
rate of exchange, between England and America which will ab-
sorb nearly one half of this profit before the bonds are all repaid.

interest, the payment was to be made by the
bank, and the surplus was to be retained under
the joint administration of the treasurer of the
state and the officers of the bank, to constitute a
sinking fund for the redemption of the principal ;
and it was enacted that, until the full liquidation
of the first series of $600,000, no part of the
surplus profits on the state's share should be
otherwise appropriated than to the payment of the
principal of these bonds : but it was stipulated
that, after the redemption of this first series, one
fourth part of the half-yearly dividends upon the
stock held by the state might be applied towards
the current expense of the government ; no greater
portion of the dividends, however, was to be so applied until a further sum of $600,000 had been
redeemed, when one half of the dividends might be
applied to the use of the state ; after which no
greater amount was to be applied by the state to its
own use until the whole of the bonds were paid off.

Many judicious regulations were laid down by
the charter for the management of the bank, with
a view both to the accommodation of the public
and the security of the institution : one half of
the capital was to be appropriated solely for the
purpose of being lent upon notes or bonds secured
by mortgages or immoveable property ; but no
mortgages were allowed to be taken upon land not
in a state of cultivation, and not more than one
half of the nett value of the real property to be
mortgaged, after deducting all previous mortgages
or incumbrances, was, in any case, to be advanced.

The rate of interest to be charged by the bank
was limited to 9 per cent. per annum upon loans and on discount of bills, and to 6 per cent. when the period did not exceed four months.

The success of this bank has now been fairly tried: a half-yearly dividend of four per cent. has been regularly paid to the shareholder; and at the expiration of the first ten years, the sinking fund had accumulated to a sum sufficient to effect the liquidation of the first fourth part of the loan; the second series, which becomes due in the course of this year, has in like manner been provided for, and notice has been given that it will be paid on an appointed day: for the last five years, therefore, the state has had the power of applying one fourth part of the dividends falling to its share to the general purposes of the government; and henceforward, till the remaining portion of the bonds are redeemed, it will have the disposal of one half, or 4 per cent. per annum, on its share of the capital. If the same prosperous course is continued, the state, at the expiration of ten years more, will have become possessed of one half of the capital of the bank, and will be in the enjoyment of the full dividend upon that share, without a single dollar having been advanced by the treasury.

Besides the instances in which the state is either the sole owner or the co-proprietor of the institutions which have arisen out of the application of the public funds to banking purposes, there are other cases in which the states assist by their credit, without deriving any direct advantage beyond reserving a power under the act which incorporates the bank, of taxing the dividends, or requiring a payment for the privileges granted in the charter, although sometimes the state stipulates for an eventual share of the profits in consideration of its guarantee. The mode of putting the banks thus constituted into operation is not necessarily in all cases the same; but, in general, the property of the individuals who embark in the undertaking is mortgaged in the first instance to the bank, which pledges the mortgages so obtained to the state; and the state, on the actual deposit of the title deeds, issues its bonds to the bank for a stipulated proportion of the amount, by the sale of which the capital is either wholly or in part raised. The state stipulates, in almost all cases, for the right of examining into the condition and management of the bank; and as the value of the property mortgaged is ascertained by the appraisement upon oath of commissioners appointed by the legislature, whose appraisement is often again subjected to revision, the system seems to offer a considerable security to the holder of the state's bonds — and one which is constantly increasing, for in a country progressively improving, the property thus pledged must every year acquire a greater value : in some instances, the state further requires that the whole profits of the establishment should be set aside until the bonds issued by the state are redeemed. There are several banks founded on this principle in the southern states.

These banks are denominated Property Banks. The present position of the Union Bank of Louisiana may serve to illustrate the practical working of this system. The Union Bank was incorporated in April 1832, and commenced business on the 23d of October: $7,000,000 of state bonds, bearing an interest of 5 per cent., and redeemable in equal series at fixed periods, were issued by the legislature in its favour, mortgages to the amount of $8,000,000 on real property being pledged with the state, and an agreement being entered into, that no profits should be divided among the shareholders till the first series of the bonds should be redeemed, and afterwards only in proportion as the successive portions of them should be cancelled. During the seven years which have since elapsed the interest on the bonds has been punctually provided for, the surplus profits have accumulated to nearly two millions of dollars, and the security held by the state, including these profits, is now valued at more than sixteen millions. *

CHAP.
VI.

Union
Bank of
Louisiana.

* A premium of $394,000 was obtained by the sale of the bonds, which is included in the above sum of two millions. If this and some bad debts are deducted, the accumulations since 1832 will amount to about a million and a half, although the bank has only lately completed its capital. If the surplus of the security, after providing for the redemption of the bonds, is available in these cases as a security for the general liabilities of the bank (as it apparently must be), it will add much to the stability of institutions established on this principle. It is true, indeed, that the value of their notes could not be maintained solely on such a basis, even if the whole of the securities were exclusively pledged for their redemption; for

It will be seen that the banks thus variously constituted afford, in the principles on which they
are formed, different degrees of security to the
holder of the state's engagements. The property
banks are, perhaps, on the whole, those which afford
the best security, while they appear, at the same
time, to be more conducive than any others to the
interest of the places where they have been established. When the capital of a bank is raised by
subscription, and the profits are divided half yearly
among the stockholders, a large portion is usually
held by the wealthy citizens of the eastern states, or
by capitalists in Europe, who draw from the state
not only a fair return as interest on their capital,
but a share, also, of the profits derived by the bank
from deposits, and from the use of a paper currency. In the case of the property banks, the
capital being borrowed from foreign capitalists, and
not owned by them, they receive a limited interest
only, the banking profits remaining in the state,
and becoming the property of the stockholders
when the bonds are redeemed.

Necessity
of the
banks.

A considerable advantage attending loans based
on banking institutions is, that these establishments

---

when a bank at any time fails to redeem its notes in specie,
after being required to do so, the value of the notes must become
depreciated, however ample the resources of the fund may be,
if the needy circumstances of the holders will not permit them
to wait for the tardy redemption which a legal process must
require. At the same time, a fruitful source of panic is avoided,
when it is known that there is in existence a capital pledged
to the state, and held by it in trust for the creditors.

from being connected with the operations of trade, and depending on a punctual discharge of their engagements for that public confidence upon which their prosperity essentially depends, are not likely to put it lightly at hazard by deviations from that regular conduct which can alone insure a continuance of it.

The late recourse to a general suspension of cash payments, which has been already alluded to, bears so directly on this remark, that the circumstance deserves a careful consideration. During the period of commercial difficulties in 1814, the same policy was had recourse to by all the banks south of New England; and the readiness with which the expedient was in both cases resorted to does not evince the existence of that high degree of commercial integrity that ought to characterise the transactions of a people anxious to maintain an unsullied credit. The lax sentiments on the subject, which were expressed on the last occasion, seem to have been partaken by all classes of the community. In the case of most of the banks, a forfeiture of the charter, or some other severe penalty, is attached to the non-fulfilment of specie payments ; but the legislatures of the different states showed, in general, little disposition to put these penalties in force, and readily passed acts in the hour of need to suspend the operation of the penal clauses. The subject, indeed, is so lightly viewed, that in the charter of some of the banks, the power of suspending cash payments for

CHAP. VI.

maintaining their credit.

Suspension of specie payments.

a limited period is, with a rare degree of foresight, expressly provided for.*

The excuse urged for the late general suspension

---

* When the project of a national Bank was under discussion, in 1814, during Mr. Madison's administration, the expediency of a similar clause was strongly contended for, which, joined to the plan of the advocates of this scheme to sustain the public credit by founding the capital of the Bank on a pledge of state stock, led to some severe strictures on the part of Mr. Webster. " What sort of an institution is this?" he asked: "it looks less like a bank than a department of government. It will be properly the paper money department. Its capital is government debts; the amount of its issues will depend on government necessities; government, in effect, absolves itself from its own debts to the bank, and, by way of compensation, absolves the bank from its own contracts with others. This, indeed, is a wonderful scheme of finance. The government is to grow rich, because it is to borrow without obligation of repaying; and is to borrow of a bank which issues paper without liability to redeem it. If this bank, like other institutions which dull and plodding common sense has created, were to pay its debts, it must have some limits to its issues of paper; therefore there would be a point, beyond which it could not make loans to government. This would fall short of the wishes of the contrivers of this system. They provide for an unlimited issue of paper in entire exemption from payment. They found the bank, in the first place, on the discredit of government, and then hope to enrich government out of the insolvency of their bank. With them, poverty itself is the main source of supply, and bankruptcy a mine of inexhaustible treasure. They rely not in the ability of the bank, but in its beggary; not in gold and silver collected in its vaults to pay its debts and fulfil its promises, but in its locks and bars, provided by statute, to fasten its doors against the solicitations and clamours of importunate creditors. Such an institution, they flatter themselves, will not only be able to sustain itself, but buoy up the sinking credit of the government."

of cash payments is founded on the necessity of the case, and in a consideration of the results to which an opposite course of conduct would have led. This, after all, resolves itself into the shallow plea of expediency. Setting aside, however, the consideration of the injustice done to all those who have settlements to make with foreign creditors — a difficulty attending a suspension of specie payments which can never be got over — the effect has certainly been, not only to protect the banks themselves from severe losses, but, by enabling them to afford that aid to commerce which has been referred to in a preceding chapter, to ward off many of the evil consequences which would otherwise have followed such ill judged speculations as had been entered into. The investigations which took place by the committees of the legislatures in the different states have thrown much light on this subject; and whether the reports may or may not be thought to justify the course that has been adopted, they exhibit the condition of the banks at the time of the suspension, in a way which proves them to have been entitled, at least, to the credit of possessing ample effects, and points out the necessity of distinguishing between their incapacity to pay their engagements in specie, and their insolvency.

It appears, indeed, that, under all the circumstances of the case, to have attempted to continue specie payments would have led to the most disastrous consequences, both to the banks and the community : the banks would have been com-

pelled to press their debtors to the utmost extent,
and to have incurred heavy and vain sacrifices to
procure specie, the whole of which would have
been immediately withdrawn again from their
vaults, to meet the heavy demands for foreign
payments.*

By suspending specie payments, the banks were
able to unite the double object of showing leniency
towards their debtors, and of obtaining more ample
security for the sums that were due to them. This
was usually effected by their allowing protested
or doubtful bills to be exchanged for promissory
notes, payable by instalments, at more distant dates,
and covered by a collateral security; but as the
dates of these promissory notes have extended, in
many instances, beyond the periods when the banks
have been enabled to resume their payments, the
banks which have had recourse to this means of
recovering the sums that were due to them, have,
in many cases, been inconvenienced by the loss of
an efficient control over their funds, and have been
obliged themselves to have recourse, in their turn,
to an issue of post notes to supply the capital
that has thus been rendered for a time unavailable.
The precarious nature of the cotton crop, by ex-
posing the banks which make advances on it to great

---

* Part of the difficulty of the banks in the cotton-growing
districts seems to have arisen from the large amount of notes
made payable at New Orleans or other distant points; which
circumstance has induced some of these banks to change the
character of their circulation, and to make their notes payable
only at the place of issue.

vicissitudes, renders a judicious distribution of their CHAP. VI. funds of such importance, that their return to a sounder condition ought to be narrowly watched. Till they arrive at it, no reliance can be placed upon their power of continuing to pay in specie, nor upon the return of the country to a healthy state. Many of the banks still further added to their issues at the time referred to by purchasing bills secured on the shipment of cotton, which was consigned to agents of their own appointment at Liverpool. This had equally the effect of relieving the commercial distress, while it enabled the banks to procure funds in Europe which could be converted into specie. This course is still persevered in by many of the banks; but as it puts their funds more out of their control than when simple advances are made on the cotton to the growers of that article, it seems quite inconsistent with the principles of sound banking. The practice, indeed, of making advances on the security of the ensuing crops, though productive of great profits to the banks, is one which should itself be used with caution, as a failure in the crop, by depriving individuals of the means of fulfilling their engagements, must always lead to commercial embarrassments and to drains upon the resources of the bank.

The circumstance, even, of an insufficient supply of water in the rivers to enable the drawers of bills of exchange to ship their cotton to the factors at the outports in time to meet their bills, has been stated as materially adding to the distresses of the winter of 1836, although the crop of that

Danger to which banks are exposed.

year was unusually large, and the prospects in the autumn most promising. While unlooked for events of this nature, which are beyond human control, and others to which the cotton crop, from its magnitude, is exposed, cause banking institutions to be attended with danger, they render them essentially necessary to the welfare of the states which produce that staple commodity; and if the country be sometimes paralysed by the injudicious conduct of these establishments, the benefits which they confer on it appear, on the whole, to counterbalance the evils.

The states pay their dividends in specie.

In reference, however, to the financial difficulties of the year 1837, and the consequent suspension of cash payments at that time throughout the Union, it ought to be observed as creditable to the respective states, and as auguring well for their credit in times of future difficulty, that, during this period of suspension of cash payments, their several engagements to the public creditor were in almost every case discharged in specie, or if that could not be obtained, in its equivalent. The state of New York paid the interest on its debt in specie; and a portion of the principal becoming due in 1837, the creditors (as specie to a sufficient amount could not be procured) were paid at the rate of 109 dollars in paper, for each 100 dollars they were entitled to. The state of Indiana paid its interest in specie, which it purchased at a premium of 11 per cent. The state of Ohio and others, which have made the interest on their loans payable in the city of New York, from the paper of the banks of that city being at the time 9 per cent. below the value of specie, paid 109 dollars for every 100 that was due. The states of Maryland and Pennsylvania were among the exceptions to this honourable line of conduct; but the former state subsequently passed a law requiring all future interest on its loans to be paid in specie; and Pennsylvania has just done her creditors the tardy justice of passing a similar enactment, and is about to make compensation to them for the dividends which were paid in depreciated paper.

From what has been said, it will be seen that, in judging of the degree of security which the application of the funds of the state, whether to purposes of internal improvement or to the establishment of banks, affords to the lender, the probability of the permanent prosperity of the undertakings ought not, in either case, to be lost sight of; and as this must be always a subject of considerable doubt, it is of no less importance to keep in view the wealth and general resources of the borrowing state. In the following chapter an attempt will be made to bring such facts before the reader as will enable him to form a judgment on these points.

In some states, loans have been raised for miscellaneous objects, some of which yield no profitable returns: these will be simply enumerated in their proper places, as the amounts are too small to have a material influence on the general question.

CHAP. VII.

PLAN PROPOSED TO BE FOLLOWED IN INVESTIGATING THE
CONDITION OF THE DIFFERENT STATES. — STATISTICAL DE-
TAILS RESPECTING THE STATE OF MASSACHUSETTS — OF
NEW YORK — PENNSYLVANIA — MARYLAND — VIRGINIA —
SOUTH CAROLINA — GEORGIA — KENTUCKY — TENNESSEE —
OHIO — LOUISIANA — INDIANA — MISSISSIPPI — ILLINOIS
— MAINE — ALABAMA — MISSOURI — MICHIGAN —
ARKANSAS — THE TERRITORY OF FLORIDA.

CHAP.
VII.

Plan pro-
posed to be
followed.

IN investigating the resources of the different states, I shall limit the inquiry to the condition of such only as have had recourse to loans, and still have a public debt. Although the order in which they are considered is immaterial, yet, for the sake of arrangement, the condition of the original states will be first inquired into in the order in which they are geographically situated, beginning at the north with Massachusetts. The condition of the newer states will then be considered in the order in which they have been admitted into the Union. Although Florida ranks only at present as a terri-tory *, yet as it is likely in the course of the next

* While the number of the inhabitants of a territory falls short of 5000 it is under the rule of a governor and judges. When the population reaches 5000 it is placed under a higher form of territorial government, having its own legislature, and a delegate to watch its interests in congress, but without having a vote in the proceedings. This is the present condition of

year to become a state, and as it has already con- tracted a debt on its own responsibility, its condition and prospects will be included in this examination.

When the objects sought to be attained by the different states in the application of their several loans can be ascertained, the manner in which the sums have been expended will form the first subject of investigation ; and if it has been for purposes of internal improvement, the present productiveness and future prospects of the undertakings will be considered. When particular taxes have been appropriated, or other auxiliary funds pledged, as a security for the loans, the particulars, as far as I have been able to ascertain them, will next be stated: and lastly, the general resources of the state, and more particularly its financial position, will be inquired into.

When the loans have been applied to public works

When the proceeds of the state loans have been applied to the formation or the extension of banks, the condition of the different establishments will be exhibited, in some of the most important particulars, at the latest times at which I have been able to procure returns. The situation of the banks immediately before the suspension of cash payments, and at an early subsequent date, will also, where it is possible, be shown. By comparing the condition of the several banks at these different periods, a

When applied to establishing banks.

Florida. When the territory contains 60,000 free inhabitants, it is allowed to form a constitution for itself, and is received into the Union as an independent state.

judgment may, in some degree, be formed of the
prudence with which their business has been conducted; but the details which the returns of the
banks afford convey in general very inadequate information in this respect.

Experience proves that loans made for long periods, however perfectly they may be secured, can
never safely sustain a large circulation, and that
banking operations, to be usefully or even safely
conducted, ought to be grounded on a rapid return of the moneys that are lent. Without attention to this salutary rule, a bank will soon find
itself obliged to restrict its business to its own
capital, or to run risks incompatible with its safety;
but in the periodical statements rendered by the
banks, the amount of the capital employed in the
discount of bills is not always distinguished from
that lent upon mortgage or other securities, and
the average period for which the loans are made,
or which the bills discounted have to run, is still
more rarely stated; no data, therefore, to judge of
the good or bad management of the banks are
afforded in these most essential particulars.

An objectionable feature in the management of
some of the banks, which is made apparent in their
returns, is the extent to which they often allow
themselves to become indebted to other banks.
When these other banks are in the same state or
town, this relative position of debtor and creditor
is usually only temporary, as, in some places,
the banks make weekly, and in others daily exchanges of each other's notes, which generally

constitute the sole claim which they have one upon the other; but when large sums are due to banks in other states, much alarm and derangement is often created by a sudden call for repayment.

It would be tedious in the case of each separate bank to point out this and similar deviations from the rules of sound banking, it will be sufficient therefore to call the attention of the reader generally to the subject, in order that each may form an opinion for himself from the data that will be laid before him. In the remarks which I shall have occasion to make on the manner in which these different establishments bear upon the credit of the respective states, I shall rather attempt to give an historical account of the rise and progress of the different institutions, and of the connection which exists between each, and the state which has established it.

In the case of loans raised for banking purposes, auxiliary funds, as I have before had occasion to remark, being less required, none have been set apart by the states in their loans for this object.*

A sinking fund arising out of the profits of the business has usually, however, been created; and where this is the case, the nature and extent of the fund will be taken into consideration. The interest on bonds granted to banking establishments appears to be invariably paid by the respective banks in whose favour they have been issued, without pass-

* The stock owned by the states in other banks has sometimes been pledged for the interest and payment of bonds granted to more recently established ones.

ing through the accounts of the treasury. This, however, by no means does away with the necessity of examining into the financial condition of the states whose bonds are so circumstanced, which will equally, therefore, form a part of the proposed inquiry, although in regard to the southern and western states, where the banks are chiefly situated, very little information in this respect has been obtained.

When statistical information respecting points in which all the states are interested can be arranged in a tabular form, it will be reserved for the appendix, and presented in that form, as exhibiting in a clearer manner the comparative situation of the different states under these particular points of resemblance.

MASSACHUSETTS.

Amount of
debt and
liabilities.
The debt and existing liabilities of this state consist of

Moneys borrowed to meet the ordinary demands on the treasury - -	$277,864 34*
Due on state warrants and other engagements	15,333 58
Bonds issued, or authorised to be issued, on account of works of internal improvement -	4,650,000 00

Making together $4,943,197 92

* The two last figures, separated by a space from those preceding them, represent *cents*, or the hundredth parts of a dollar. This is the mode of notation commonly made use of in the United States, and which will be adopted in this chapter, and in the appendix.

The debt contracted for purposes of internal improvement consists of bonds issued or to be issued.

CHAP.
VII.

Loans for
public im-
prove-
ments.

For the state's subscription to the stock of the Western railroad corporation - - $ 300,000 00	
For the state's first loan in aid of ditto ▪ 2,100,000 00	
For the state's loans to the following railroads, viz. to the Eastern railroad - - 500,000 00	
To the Norwich and Worcester railroad - 400,000 00	
To the Andover and Haverhill railroad ▪ 100,000 00	
To the Nashua and Lowell railroad - - 50,000 00	
For the state's second loan in aid of the Western railroad - - - - 1,200,000 00	
$ 4,650,000 00	

The bonds of this state are in all cases made payable to bearer, so that no form is necessary in transferring them from one holder to another. Those issued as a loan to the Western railroad company are expressed in British sterling money, and are made payable in London.* The others are payable at the treasury at Boston in current money.

The bonds issued as the state's subscription to the stock of the Western railroad are redeemable

* The bonds of this state are extremely simple in their form. Those for the Western railroad are in the following terms : — " Be it known that there is due from the commonwealth of Massachusetts to the holder of this certificate five hundred pounds sterling, to be paid at the banking-house of Messrs. Baring, Brothers, and Co. in London, on the first day of October, 1868, with interest at five per cent. payable at the same place semi-annually, on presentation of the interest warrant. In testimony whereof," &c.

CHAP.
VII.

on the 15th July, 1857. Of those issued as a loan to that corporation, part are redeemable in 1858, and part in 1868.

The bonds issued to the other railroad companies fall due on different days in the year 1857.

Rate of
interest,
and where
and when
payable.

The bonds for internal improvement all bear interest at the rate of five per cent. The interest is payable at the places where the respective bonds are redeemable, and is in all cases paid, in the first instance, by the treasury, but the different railroad corporations reimburse the sums paid on their account; so that the interest on the portion of the bonds for the state's subscription to the stock of the Western railroad is the only actual charge on the resources of the state. The days on which the interest is payable varies in the different loans.

Works on
which the
money
raised has
been ex-
pended.

The first of these loans for railroads was authorised in 1837; in the course of which year bonds were issued to the extent of five hundred and fifty thousand dollars: but though the state of Massachusetts was thus late in adopting any general system of internal improvement, the individual enterprise of the inhabitants had long been directed to this object, and several works have been executed by private companies, unaided by the funds of the commonwealth *; two of these, the Boston and Worcester railroad, and the Boston

---

* The first canal of any extent constructed in the United States was in this state, viz. the Middlesex canal, which was commenced in 1789 and completed in 1808. It was in Massachusetts also that the first railroad was begun; viz. the Quincy railroad, which was completed in 1827.

and Lowell railroad, have been for some years in active operation.

The Western railroad, the chief work in which the state is interested, is a continuation of the first of these lines: it commences at Worcester, and is to extend from that town to Springfield on the Connecticut river, and thence to the boundary line of the state of New York — a distance altogether of 117 miles: it will there unite with the lines of railroad now in progress in that state, so as to form an uninterrupted communication between Boston and Albany, the seat of government in New York. The line from Worcester to Springfield, a distance of 54¼ miles, will, it is supposed, be opened in the course of this year.

A charter was granted to a company to execute this work, and a capital was raised of nine hundred thousand dollars, of which one third was subscribed by the state, and two thirds by individuals: it was estimated that the work would cost three millions of dollars, and the state issued bonds in favour of the company for the two million one hundred thousand dollars necessary to make up this sum.

By a report made by the company on the 1st of January last, it appears that the part to the east of the Connecticut river will, by the time it is completed, cost $1,864,729 12, and that to complete the part of the road which lies to the west of that river a further sum of $2,326,442 61 will be required, making the total cost of the road $4,191,171 73. This sum being nearly one million two hundred thousand dollars more than the resources of the company, application was made to the state for a further grant, and the amount required has accordingly been voted by the legislature. As no part of this railroad is yet open, there are no data to judge of the returns that may be expected from it.

Eastern railroad.

The Eastern railroad is to extend from Boston by Salem to Newburyport, and may ultimately be carried to Portsmouth in New Hampshire : it was opened from Boston to Salem on the 28th of August last. The estimated cost of the whole line from Boston to Portsmouth, a distance of fifty-three miles, is one million six hundred thousand dollars; but it will only be carried by the Massachusett's company to the boundary line of their own state. $831,903 30 had been expended up to the 31st of December last, of which $470,575 00 had been received from the shareholders as instalments on their shares, and the remainder procured by a sale of the state's bonds.

The amount of traffic upon the part of the railroad that has already been completed has greatly exceeded the estimate of its projectors. If it should be maintained during the year at the rate shown by the returns from the time it was opened to the end of December last, the net revenue on this portion alone will amount to $88,400 57 ; and if from this be deducted 7 per cent. (viz. 5 per cent. interest on two hundred and ninety thousand dollars of state stock, and 2 per cent. on that amount as a sinking fund), the balance of $68,100 57 will yield

a return of above 14¾ per cent. on the amount
advanced by the shareholders; but even should the above rate be maintained on the portion of the work already finished, as this extends only from Boston to Salem, forming a communication between the latter flourishing town and the seat of government, and passing through one of the most densely peopled districts of the United States, so limited an experience can scarcely be made a criterion of the prospects of the remaining portion of the line. The density of the population, however, through which the whole line passes, affords it a fair prospect of success : it must be considered too, that the returns have hitherto been derived only from passengers.

The Norwich and Worcester railroad is another extension of the Boston and Worcester line. It is nearly finished; but no part of it is yet opened. The length of this work is fifty-eight miles : the greater part of it lies within the state of Connecticut, the legislature of which has chartered a company to execute the portion which falls within its territory.* The capital embarked in this work amounts to one million and a half of dollars.

Norwich and Worcester railroad.

The Andover and Haverhill railroad is now in operation : in the last year, after paying interest on the portion of state stock that had been as-

Andover and Haverhill railroad.

* This company has had banking privileges given to it. It is not an unusual condition in the charter of a banking company in the United States, that it should execute part of a canal or railroad, or subscribe for a part of the stock.

CHAP.
VII.

Nashua and Lowell railroad.

Advantages of these works to the state, and prospects of success.

signed to it, a dividend of three per cent. on the capital was paid to the shareholders.

The Nashua and Lowell railroad is an extension of the private undertaking between Boston and Lowell, and is to connect the latter town with Nashua in New Hampshire, from whence it is meant to extend it to Concord, the capital of the state; but the state of Massachusetts is interested to so small an extent in this work, that no further details respecting it need be entered into.

The whole of the works to which the commonwealth has thus contributed the aid of its funds are executed in the most substantial manner, and are well adapted to promote the welfare of the state, by connecting the distant parts of it, as well as the capitals of the adjoining states, with Boston and the manufacturing districts in the neighbourhood; Worcester and Lowell respectively being the places where the chief woollen and cotton manufactories are established.* By means of the

---

* The town of Lowell presents a striking instance of the rapidity with which population and wealth occasionally spring up in America. In the year 1820 the site of the city formed part of the township of Chelmsford, and contained about a hundred inhabitants; in 1822 the first cotton mill was erected, and by 1830 the population of this thriving town had advanced to 6500; in 1833, the number of inhabitants was estimated at 15,000: and there were then no·fewer than twenty-two cotton mills in operation, affording employment to 5730 people; these numbers will appear surprising, if it be considered that in Manchester the number of cotton mills in 1832 was only sixty-eight, and the number of people employed in them 20,585; the population of Lowell, however, according to the state census

Western railroad, the state of Massachusetts will likewise be brought at Albany into connection with the Erie canal, and will be enabled to participate directly in the commerce of the western states. Massachusetts will thus obtain a portion of the valuable agricultural produce of those states and find there an extensive market for the surplus produce of its own industry and its extensive foreign trade, without having recourse to the circuitous channels of New Orleans, Baltimore, Philadelphia, and New York, through which ports the western states are at present almost wholly supplied with New England manufactures. The expense attendant on this circuitous transmission so enhances at present the price to the consumers in the west. that the produce of the fisheries and of the other branches of industry in New England will, it is supposed, be nearly doubled by the opening of this new avenue to the western states.

Such an increased demand for the fabrics of Massachusetts will be of great service to the state ; for it will be remembered that New England is

---

on the 1st May, 1837, had only reached 18,010. If the falling off in the *rate* of increase be looked at in connection with the date of the coming into operation of the tariff bill, (the 3d of March, 1833,) it may be thought to afford a confirmation of the opinion advanced in a former chapter, that it was chiefly the protection of the former high duties that fostered manufactures in this and the other towns in New England A naturally favourable position, affording a great supply of water-power for machinery, has no doubt had a great influence on the prosperity of Lowell, but could scarcely alone have effected it

CHAP.
VII.

more extensively engaged in manufactures than any other district in the United States, and the state of Massachusetts is decidedly superior in this respect to any other in the Union. From an official account which has been lately published, founded on the returns of the assessors of the different towns, it appears that in the year ending the 1st of April, 1837, though an unprosperous year, from the commercial difficulties which preceded it, a capital of $54,851,643 00 was invested either in manufactures or in fisheries; the number of hands employed in these branches of industry was 117,352, and the value of the articles manufactured or produced was $91,765,215 00; and as this statement embraces none of the products of agriculture or of commerce, with the exception of wool and of the fisheries, it is far from presenting a complete view of the active industry of the state.

The traffic which so extensive a trade is calculated to bring to the railroads of this state, renders it likely that the tolls, when they come into full operation, will defray the expense of the repairs and interest, and leave a surplus to be applied towards the liquidation of the debt.

Sinking fund.

A general sinking fund, established to aid this object, has been placed under the control of the treasurer of the commonwealth, and to this all sums received as premium on the sale of the state's bonds are appropriated. Some particular loans appear also to have special sinking funds attached to them. Thus, in the case of the

bonds issued to the Eastern railroad company, two
per cent. on the amount of the capital, exclusive of
five per cent. for interest, is set apart to be applied
to the redemption of the bonds before any profits
are divided among the shareholders ; and, by the
act authorising the issue of bonds as the state's
subscription to the Western railroad company,
one half of the amount which may in future be
received for the sale of the lands of the commonwealth is to constitute a sinking fund for their
redemption * ; but the published statement rendered by the treasurer on the subject of the finances
of the state affords an imperfect view only of the
various provisions which have been made for the
liquidation of the debt.

The amount of the debt of the state of Massachu- Unsatisfac-
setts is so inconsiderable, that the want of means to tory condition of
investigate this point is, in its case, of little import- the treasury.
ance ; but the instance of this state very fully ex-
emplifies the general advantage of a sinking fund,
as, although Massachusetts ranks among the wealthiest of the states in the Union, and although the
public expenditure is framed there with the strictest
attention to economy, and the government is car-

* The state of Massachusetts, in ceding her land to the
general government, in April 1785, retained a claim to all lands
east of the Hudson ; and on the separation of Maine in 1820,
stipulated that one half of the proceeds of the land unsettled
at the time should be paid over, as sales were effected, by that
state. This condition gives Massachusetts a large pecuniary
interest in the settlement of the question of the boundary between
the British provinces in North America and the United States.

ried on in the most frugal manner, the receipts into the treasury for the last four years have proved inadequate to the demands upon it.

The receipts and expenditure during these years have been as follows : —

	Receipts.	Expenditure.
31st Dec. 1835	$446,378 64	$495,438 37
1836	402,697 13	435,456 10
1837	460,543 34	512,745 52
1838	419 323 03	491,675 74

Though the expenditure in the last year falls short of that of the preceding one, yet from the receipts having fallen off in a still greater proportion it will be seen that the deficiency was greater in that year than on any previous occasion. As the treasurer has authority to borrow money in anticipation of the revenue, there has been no difficulty in meeting the public engagements; but the necessary result of this continued excess of the expenditure over the ordinary receipts has been the accumulation of a floating debt, which on the 1st of January of the present year amounted, with the outstanding demands on the treasury, to $293,197 92; as there was, however, an available balance in the treasury on that day of $125,206 93, the real deficiency may be stated at $167,990 99. As it appears by the statement rendered by the governor, at the opening of the present session of the legislature, that the utmost that can be depended upon from the receipts of 1839 is that they will meet the expenditure of the year, there is no immediate prospect, unless other means are

resorted to, of the money so borrowed being
speedily reimbursed.*

This unsatisfactory condition of the treasury
appears to have resulted from various alterations
which have been made within the last few years
in the fiscal arrangements of the state.

By an act of the 31st March 1834, one half
of the amount received for the sale of the lands
of the commonwealth was transferred from the
general revenue, and placed to the credit of the
Massachusetts school fund, as was likewise the
interest on a sum which the state had received
for certain claims on the United States for militia
services. By an act of the 15th April 1837, already referred to, the remaining half of the proceeds
of the sales of lands was transferred to the sinking
fund. But a still more important change in the
circumstances of the treasury arose out of an alter-
ation in the mode of defraying the expenses of the
two houses of the legislature.

The amount of compensation to the members,
though paid by the treasurer in the first instance,
used formerly to be repaid by the several towns and
cities of the state, the charge resting on them by
the original terms of the constitution. The alter-
ation alluded to consisted in the transfer of this
charge to the treasury, and in the abandonment of
an annual state tax, which had been levied from the

* The portion of the surplus revenue allotted to Massachusetts was deposited by the state with the several cities and
towns in the commonwealth, and not applied to the use of the
treasury.

first settlement of the country to defray this expense. The chief and almost the only sources of revenue which the treasury possessed, after these changes had taken place, consisted in taxes levied on the capital of banking establishments, and on sales by auction. As the produce of these had however been sufficient, up to the time when the changes were effected, not only to defray the ordinary expenses of the commonwealth, but to allow of liberal appropriations to objects of national importance; and as the revenue derived to the treasury from these sources was progressively increasing, it was not considered necessary to provide for the additional expenditure which the payment of the legislature occasioned.

A variety of circumstances have since, however, tended to increase the amount of the compensation to the houses of legislature beyond what was then contemplated. The rate of the compensation has been increased, while the size of the house of representatives has been augmented, and the length of its sessions has been protracted. By the combined operation of these causes, the pay of the legislature, which in 1825 had amounted only to $36,603 00, was swelled in 1837 to $163,794 50; and although during the last year, owing to a recent amendment in the constitution, this charge had been considerably diminished, it remained greater than in any previous year, excepting in 1836 and 1837.* Taxes on the active

---

* The number of the representatives in the legislature of Massachusetts is twice as great as that of any other state in the

capital of the community might be easily levied to meet the deficiency in the revenue, yet being prejudicial in their effects, the legislature is more likely to turn its attention with a jealous vigilance to a diminution of its expenses, than to such sources of revenue.* A committee has in consequence been appointed to consider the possibility of reducing the state expenditure; and in a report dated on the 12th of February last, it was suggested, among other means, that the towns and cities should be again compelled to pay their own representatives, and that all state provision for paupers, which forms a large item in the expenses of the state, should be abolished.

The following table will serve to show the gradual increase that has taken place in the expenditure of this state : —

1825	$198,621 23	1830	$330,440 28	1835	$495,438 37
1826	252,297 16	1831	381,481 68	1836	435,456 10
1827	293,633 71	1832	304,613 69	1837	512,745 52
1828	307,769 03	1833	367,353 92	1838	491,675 74
1829	293,942 45	1834	362,380 41		

Union. While each city and town paid its own representative, the expense deterred many from exercising their right of choosing one; but when the expense came to be defrayed by the treasury, the full number being returned, it was felt to be inconveniently great: by the amendment in question, it would be reduced from 634 to 417.

* The great resources of the state arise from its commerce, but the constitution of the United States precludes recourse to this branch of industry for taxation, all taxes derived from commerce being applicable to the purposes of the federal government.

The progress of the bank and auction tax, since 1835, has been as follows : —

Bank Tax.		Auction Tax.	
1835	$304,211 11	$45,090	19
1836	317,546 98	57,845	62
1837	379,175 12	56,942	90
1838	354,562 00	41,292	14

The following statement will show the particulars of the receipts and expenditure for the last year, although it will appear from what has been said above, that they can scarcely be taken as a criterion of the future financial prospects of the treasury.

Receipts : —

On account of the bank tax	- -	$354,562 00
On account of the auction tax	- -	41,292 14
Interest on deposits in city bank	-	4,398 29
On account of miscellanies	- -	5,385 71
One half of the amount of notes given for land in Maine	- - -	13,684 89
		$419,323 03

Payments : —

Officers' salaries and incidental charges for the support of government	- -	$ 73,956 26
Pay of council	- - -	3,635 50
Pay of the senate $ 9,335 50; of the house of representatives 100,476	- -	109,811 50

On rolls of account, viz : —

For paupers	- - $46,268	45
For assessors, sheriffs, &c.	3,729	54
For printing newspapers, &c.	5,348	61
For miscellanies, including military expenses	- 8,964	34
		64,310 94

County treasurers, balances of their accounts - - - -	68,680	75
State printers - - -	19,225	67
Military appropriations and pensions -	8,432	70
Militia services - - -	30,545	00
Agricultural societies, bounties on silk, &c.	7,055	52
Appropriations to the lunatic hospital and charitable institutions - - -	31,707	55
Miscellaneous objects - - -	47,782	75
Interest on money borrowed - -	10,289	60
For prosecuting claim on the United States	1,242	00
Interest on western railroad scrip -	15,000	00
	$491,675	74

If the amount paid to the two houses of the legislature, and the provision for state paupers, had been deducted from the expenditure, as here shown, the bank and auction tax, at the reduced amount even of last year, would have been ample to meet the remainder.

The resources of this state are so great, that it is more the spirit of the people than the circumstances of the commonwealth that render even these retrenchments necessary. There appears to be more realised wealth in Massachusetts, compared with the population, than in any other state of the Union*, while the inhabitants are in possession of

Realised wealth of the state, and extensive trade.

* The population of Massachusetts, according to the census of 1830, was 610,014, and the property of the state in that year was assessed at $208,360,407 54. The population of the state of New York, according to the same census, was 1,918,608, and the real and personal property was assessed at $319,118,296 00, being scarcely one half of its relative proportion. The state of New York has increased more rapidly

CHAP.
VII.

a most thriving trade. The shipping belonging to this state amounts to 470,388 tons, exceeding that of any other state, and constituting about one fourth of the whole shipping of the United States; 1731 vessels, with a tonnage of 295,031 tons, entered, and 1681 vessels of 274,705 tons cleared, at the different ports in 1836. The value of the imports for that year was $25,681,462 00, and of exports $10,380,346 00; but these numbers were unusually large, the value of imports into Massachusetts in the preceding year having been $19,800,873 00, and the amount in the year following, $19,984,668 00. These statements of the exports and imports refer only to the foreign trade, the value of the exports and imports coastwise not being ascertained. Of the exports about one half is of domestic produce. Under these cir-

---

since in population than Massachusetts, and the rate of increase in property may also have been greater; but this difference is not nearly made up. At the same time, unless the manner in which the valuations are taken is known, and it varies much in different states, no certain conclusion can be drawn from such data. The expense of supporting the poor is greater in Massachusetts in proportion to the number of inhabitants than it is in New York; but to judge by the returns of the savings' banks, the prosperity of the lower orders in the former state must be considerable. In Massachusetts, according to the returns of the last year, there were thirty banks in the state; the number of depositors was 33,063, and the sum deposited on their accounts £4,869,392 59. The number of depositors in the bank of Boston exceeded fourteen thousand, and the sum deposited was more than two millions.

cumstances this state, though debarred from direct taxation on these particular branches of industry, could clearly provide for a much larger expenditure, or could support a larger debt, should circumstances require it.

NEW YORK.

I HAVE already had occasion to mention that the portion of the debt of this state which was created to defray the expense of the construction of the Erie and Champlain canal has been completely discharged; and although the whole of the creditors have not yet received payment of their claims, this is effectively the case, for the outstanding amount has been paid over to a board of commissioners who hold it on trust until, by the terms of the loan, the creditors can be compelled to receive payment of the sums due to them, and to surrender their certificates.*   The outstanding balance may, on this account, be disregarded in considering the liabilities of the state.

Extinction of Erie and Champlain canal debt.

---

* The total amount borrowed was $7,672,782 24, of which $5,412,947 59 has been paid, and certificates of stock cancelled to that extent; the remaining portion, $2,259,834 65 (of which $548,520 53 bears interest at 6 per cent., and $1,711,314 12 at 5 per cent.) is not redeemable till 1845.

The commissioners have repeatedly given notice to the remaining creditors, both by public advertisements and by written circulars, whenever their residence could be discovered, that they have received the money and are prepared to pay it; and, in order to avoid the responsibility of keeping so large an amount invested for their behalf, have offered the creditors premiums of 6, 9, 18, and even 24 per cent. if they would come forward and receive payment.

CHAP.
VII.

Present
debt
and liabili-
ties.

Since the year 1825 the state has created fresh debts in completing the following lateral canals, viz : —

For the Oswego canal - - -	$ 421,304 00
For the Cayuga and Seneca canal - -	237,000 00
For the Chemung canal - - -	316,000 00
For the Crooked Lake canal - -	120,000 00
For the Chenango canal - - -	2,362,535 66
	3,456,839 66

It has also commenced the construction of the Black River canal and the Genesee Valley canal, and has created debts on these accounts; viz.

For the Black River canal - -	591,446 10
For the Genesee Valley canal - -	2,000,000 00
And has borrowed towards defraying the expense of enlarging the Erie canal -	1,000,000 00

Making the total outstanding debt for lateral canals and for the enlarging of the main line - - - -	$ 7,048,285 76

The state owes besides,

To the bank safety fund - - -	586,532 43
To the canal fund (without interest) -	800,000 00
And the Astor stock, created in 1832 to extinguish a claim of Mr. Astor to certain lands sold by the state, the title to which had proved defective, amounting to - - - - -	561,500 00

Making the total debt of the state	$ 8,996,318 19

The last three items form what is called the
"General Fund Debt," as distinguished from that portion of the debt which has been raised for the purpose of constructing canals, which is called the " Canal Debt."

The canals specified above have been constructed entirely by the state. Several others have been constructed by private companies. The most extensive of these is the Delaware and Hudson canal, which was undertaken chiefly to supply the city of New York with coal from the Pennsylvania coal fields. To assist in this important object, the state lent its credit to the company, and under two acts, of the 10th March, 1827, and the 2d May, 1829, issued certificates of state stock to the extent of eight hundred thousand dollars.

In like manner, although the state has hitherto declined to construct railroads on its own account, preferring to leave such undertakings to incorporated companies, it has lent its credit to the New York and Erie railroad company, by a law passed on the 23d April, 1836, and directed the issue of state stock to the amount of three millions of dollars: making the engagements entered into on behalf of these two corporations $3,800,000.

It has since issued certificates of stock to the following companies; viz. —

To the Canajoharie and Catskill railroad company - - - -	$100,000 00
To the Auburn and Syracuse railroad company	200,000 00

To the Ithaca and Owego railroad company $ 287,700 00
And it had previously lent its credit to the
    Nevisink navigation company, to the extent
    of   -   -   -   -   10,000 00

                 Making in all   4,397,700 00
       Add amount of debt as above   8,996,318 19

    Total amount of debt and liabilities $ 13,394,018 19

The amounts here mentioned as liabilities do not
appear in any way in the treasury accounts ; but
as the state may hereafter be called upon to pay
the interest, or ultimately the capital, of the stock
thus issued, the existence of such liabilities ought
not to be overlooked, and on this account they
are here specified among the engagements of the
state.

Form of
security
and mode
of transfer.

The difference in the nature of the state's engagements, in regard to its canal and railroad stocks,
has led to the adoption of two distinct modes of
issuing and transferring the certificates which are
the evidence of the owner's title to them.

The canal stock is registered in the name of the
proprietor, and is transferable, either in whole or in
fractional amounts, at the treasury or at the Manhattan bank in the city of New York, which has
been selected by the legislature for that purpose.
A transfer can only be effected by the owner ap-
pearing, either in person or by attorney, when the
original certificate is given up and cancelled, and a
new one issued in the name of the person to whom
the stock is transferred.

The certificates of the railroad stocks, which are made out in even sums, not exceeding a thousand dollars, are issued by the comptroller of the state, and are made payable to the order of the companies to which they are respectively issued. The transfer of the stock is effected in this case, not at the treasury or at its deputed bank, but at particular banks which have been designated by the several companies themselves. The proprietor is equally obliged, as in the case of the transfer of canal stock, to attend in person, or by his attorney, to sign an acknowledgment of the transfer; but the original certificate, instead of being cancelled, is delivered to the new proprietor, a memorandum of the transfer to his name being indorsed on the back of it.

The stock issued to the Delaware and Hudson canal company is transferable at the office of the company, under the same rules and forms as have been instituted in respect to the transfer of the canal stocks of the state.

The principal of the canal stock is payable at the treasury, and is redeemable at the pleasure of the state at any time after the following periods; viz. —.

CHAP.
VII.

Where and when redeemable.

After the 1st July, 1845	-	-	- $2,362,535 66
1st July, 1846	-	-	- 571,304 00
1st July, 1849	-	-	- 87,000 00
1st Aug. 1850	-	-	- 1,027,446 10
31st Dec. 1855	-	-	- 1,000,000 00
31st Dec. 1860	-	-	- 2,000,000 00
			$7,048,285 76

CHAP.
VII.

The principal of the stock issued by the comptroller to the different incorporated companies is
payable at the respective transfer offices, and is
redeemable at any time after the following periods;
viz. —

That issued to the Delaware and Hudson canal
company, under the act 10th March, 1827 — after
the 31st December, 1847.

That under the act of the 2d May, 1829 —
after the 31st December, 1849.

That to the Canajoharie and Catskill railroad
company — after the 1st July, 1858.

That to the Auburn and Syracuse railroad company — after the 1st September, 1858.

That to the Ithaca and Owego company — after
the 1st January, 1864.

That to the New York and Erie company —
20 years after the date of issue.*

Rate of in-
terest, and
when and
where pay-
able.

The interest on the canal stock is payable at the
treasury, and that on the different railroad stocks,
and on the stock issued to the Delaware and Hud-

---

* The stock allotted to the New York and Erie railroad company is to be issued in instalments as certain portions of the
work are completed. It does not appear whether the several
issues are to be redeemable at the end of twenty years from the
date of the first issue, or from the date when each separate
issue is made. It does not either any where appear when the
sum issued to the Nevisink navigation company is subject to
redemption. The above account of the periods of the redemption of the other stocks may not be invariably accurate as the
facts are collected from a variety of sources — no statement on
the subject being given in the treasury report.

son canal company, at the respective places where the capital is redeemable. Of the canal stock, $548,520 53 (part of the uncancelled Erie canal debt for which funds have been provided) bears interest at the rate of 6 per cent. : the remainder of the state canal stock bears interest at 5 per cent.

The following stocks also bear interest at 5 per cent. ; viz. —

The portion of the stock issued to the Delaware and Hudson canal company, under the act of 10th November, 1827.

The stock issued to the Nevisink navigation company.

That issued to the Canajoharie and Catskill, and to the Auburn and Syracuse railroad companies.

The following bear interest at $4\frac{1}{2}$ per cent. : —

The remainder of the stock issued to the Delaware and Hudson canal company.

The stock issued to the New York and Erie railroad company, and that issued to the Ithaca and Owego company.

The interest is in all cases payable quarterly, on the first days of January, April, July, and October.

The interest on the general fund debt is paid at the treasury. The Astor stock bears interest at 5 per cent. The debt to the bank safety fund appears to have been originally at $4\frac{1}{2}$ per cent., but is now at 5 per cent. The debt to the canal fund, under

Works on
which the
loans have
been ex-
pended.

an arrangement which will be afterwards explained, bears no interest.

The following table shows the length in miles of the different canals already completed by the state, as well as the cost of construction : —

	Length.	Cost.
Erie Canal - -	- 372	$7,143,789 86
Champlain -	- 79	1,257,604 26
Oswego - -	- 38	565,437 35
Cayuga and Seneca -	- 23	236,804 74
Chemung - -	- 39	331,693 57
Crooked Lake -	- 8	156,776 90
Chenango - -	- 97	2,270,605 22
	656	$11,962,711 90

Main de-
sign.

The whole of these may be looked upon as constituting one work ; the main object being to connect the valley of the Hudson with that of Lake Champlain, on the north, and the great central basin of the Canadian lakes on the west — while the various lateral canals are destined to bring into the main trunk the produce of the neighbouring countries, and to transport, at a cheap rate, the manufactures and produce of foreign countries into the inmost recesses of the state.

Erie canal.

The Erie canal constitutes the great trunk. This work, which is admirably executed in all its details, extends from the Hudson at Albany up the valleys of the Mohawk and Seneca, and thence across the country to the Tonnewanta ; by that river to the Niagara, and along the latter and Lake Erie to Buffalo.

The Champlain canal extends from the Erie canal up the valley of the Hudson, leaving the latter at Fort Edward, and passing down the valley of Wood Creek to Lake Champlain, at Whitehall.

Champlain canal.

The Chenango canal, the longest of the lateral canals that have been completed, extends from the Erie canal, at Utica, up the valleys of the Saquoit and Oriskany creek, and down that of the Chenango to the main branch of the Susquehanna, at Binghampton.

Chenango canal.

The Oswego canal passes down the valley of the river of that name, extending from Syracuse, on the grand trunk, to Oswego, on Lake Ontario — one half of which distance is slack water navigation, with a tow-path on the bank of the river.

Oswego canal.

The Cayuga and Seneca canal extends from Lake Seneca, at Geneva, to the Erie canal, at Montezuma, passing down the valleys of the Cayuga and Seneca outlets. A lateral branch of two miles joins the main trunk with Lake Cayuga. One half of this also is slack water navigation.

Cayuga and Seneca canal.

Crooked Lake canal connects that lake with Lake Seneca. These two works thus throw open three fine lakes to an easy access from the sea; and the Chemung canal, from the head of Lake Seneca to Elmira, on the river Tioga or Chemung, connects the whole with the Susquehanna. The original projectors of the Erie canal contemplated its connection, not only with Lake Erie, but also with the river Ohio, by means of a south-west branch, uniting with the river Alleghany at Olean: of the two lateral canals now in progress

Crooked Lake canal.

Chemung canal.

CHAP.
VII.

Genesee
Valley
canal.

Black Ri-
ver canal.

Works
aided by
the credit
of the state.

Delaware
and Hud-
son canal.

(which were commenced only in 1837) the Genesee Valley canal is intended to carry this plan into
effect. The canal, as laid down, is to extend
from Rochester up the valley of the Genesee, and
thence by that of Oil Creek to the Alleghany at
Olean, a total distance of 107 miles.

The other or northern branch of the canals now
in progress, called the Black River canal, will
extend from the main trunk at Rome to the foot
of the high falls of the Black River, near Leyden,
below which the river is navigable (or can be
made so at a trifling expense), to its outlet in Lake
Ontario.

Before entering upon an examination of the
financial condition of the above works, which are
those which have been exclusively executed by
the state, it will be convenient to consider the
nature of the works undertaken by the several
companies to which this state has extended the aid
of its credit, in order that the different improvements in which the state has either a direct or
contingent interest, may be brought under view
in one place.

The financial condition of the companies will,
at the same time, be considered, as, their accounts
being unconnected with the state treasury, no
more fitting opportunity of considering them will
be afterwards presented.

The Delaware and Hudson canal company was
incorporated on the 23d April, 1823, for the purpose already referred to, of constructing a canal
and railroad from the river Hudson to the coal-

mines at Carbondale in Pennsylvania. The canal CHAP. extends from the Hudson, at Kingston, a point 90 VII. miles above New York, to Port Jervis, on the Delaware, after which it unites with the Pennsylvania section of the work. The capital of the company is one million five hundred thousand dollars, of which the company is authorised to employ one third in banking operations in the city of New York.

The traffic on the canal is considerable, but the amount of tolls seems small when compared with the outlay. The total sum received from the completion of the work, in 1830 to 1836 inclusive, amounted to $226,773 79, averaging little more than thirty-two thousand dollars in each year. The increase, however, had been nearly progressive. In the last three years of the time referred to, the tolls were respectively as follows : —

In the year 1834 - - - $36,946 07
1835 - - - 41,976 82
1836 - - - 45,154 73

At the end of the latter year, the property of the company, exclusive of coal-mines, but including the value of the canal, the canal boats, barges, &c. was estimated at $2,786,025 00.* This statement of the condition of the company affords considerable evidence of its general prosperity ; and the state, having a mortgage on the whole property, must be very amply secured for the guarantee it has afforded.

* The cost of the part of the canal which is comprised within the state of New York was $1,574,068 00.

The object of the New York and Erie railroad was to establish a communication which would be open earlier in the spring, and could be continued later in the autumn, than that afforded by the Erie canal. The line is confined by the charter to the southern counties of the state, which border on the adjoining states of New Jersey and Pennsylvania. This work, one of the greatest of the kind that has been projected, has been commenced at Tappan, on the west side of the Hudson, near the southern extremity of the state, and will terminate at Dunkirk or Portland, on Lake Erie; the distance between the two points in either case being about 481 miles. If extended from Tappan, down the eastern bank of the Hudson, to the city of New York, the total length will be 505 miles.

It was originally estimated that this work, from which most important benefits to the state are anticipated, would cost $5,474,000 00. It appears now, that six millions of dollars, a tolerably close approximation, will defray the entire expense. One half of this sum, or three millions of dollars, has been raised by shares, and constitutes the capital of the company. The remaining three millions will be obtained, as required, through means of the pledge which the state has made to that extent of its credit.*

In addition to the resources above mentioned,

---

* Certificates of the last million may not be issued by the state till a double track of rails has been completed for the whole distance.

valuable donations of lands in the most important
village or town sites have been made to the company by individuals owning property on the line of the road.

Although not far advanced, the nature of the work, and the ample funds of the company, appear to afford to the state, in this instance also, an ample security for the pledge it has made of the public credit.

The Auburn and Syracuse railroad forms a connecting link in a more extensive chain of works. The Ithaca and Owego railroad is to connect Lake Cayuga with the Susquehanna ; but these, and the remaining works to which the state has lent its credit, are not of sufficient importance to require a more detailed description.

In the charters by which these and all other railroads in the state have been incorporated, the state has reserved to itself the right of ultimately appropriating the works to itself, on making such financial arrangements with the proprietors as circumstances may render equitable.*

Reverting to the works undertaken solely by

---

* The total length of railroads undertaken by incorporated companies, either finished, commenced, or authorised, and the capitals of the companies respectively, are as follow : —

		Miles.	Capitals.	
Incorporated railroads	finished	218	$ 5,065,000	00
Ditto	commenced	938	16,000,000	00
Ditto	authorised	1704	31,064,000	00
		2860	$ 52,129,000	00

of the Erie
and Cham-
plain
canals.

the state, the condition of the Erie and Champlain canals and their finished branches will be first
considered.

The first tolls were received on the Erie canal
on the 1st of July, 1820. The rapid and nearly
constantly progressive increase on this and the
other canals, as they were completed, may be seen
in the following table. It ought to be observed that,
previously to 1833, the rates had been reduced
nearly 20 per cent., and again in 1835, about
15 per cent.

Year ending 30th Sept.	1820	$	5,437	34
	1821		14,388	47
	1822		64,072	40
	1823		152,958	33
	1824		340,761	07
	1825		566,112	97
	1826		762,003	60
	1827		859,058	48
	1828		838,444	65
	1829		813,137	45
	1830		1,056,922	12
	1831		1,223,801	98
	1832		1,229,483	47
	1833		1,463,715	22
	1834		1,339,799	56
	1835		1,548,972	39
	1836		1,614,680	38
	1837		1,326,780	90
	1838		1,481,602	41

Of the late-
ral canals.

The lateral canals have, however, contributed
very little towards these results; for, of the amount
received in 1838, $1,423,337 65 was derived from
the Erie and Champlain canals, and $58,264 76

only from the lateral canals — at present, there- CHAP.
fore, the latter are a great charge on the state ; the VII.
expense of repairs and of the collection of tolls in
1838, and of interest on the debt contracted for
their construction, having amounted to $287,425 35,
leaving a deficiency of $229,160 59.

The following statement shows the deficiency
on each canal : —

On the Oswego	-	-$ 54,460 70
On the Cayuga and Seneca	-	15,517 62
On the Chemung	-	- 29,833 11
On the Crooked Lake	-	10,037 55
On the Chenango	-	- 119,311 61
		$229,160 59

The aggregate deficiency on each since their
completion, and the total amount of those deficiencies, are as under.

On the Oswego canal	for 9 years	$226,316 19
On the Cayuga and Seneca	9	110,346 80
On the Chemung	6	190,513 99
On the Crooked Lake	5	52,228 54
On the Chenango	2	238,792 13
	Total,	$818,197 65

No judgment can yet be formed of the prospects of the two lateral canals which are still in
progress ; the cost of them will, it is estimated,
exceed five millions of dollars. The account of
the funds and the expenditure of these is at
present kept distinct from that of the other canals.
It appears, by the statements rendered, that
$2,230,829 72 of the amount raised for their con-

struction, remain unexpended, and are deposited in different banks in the city of New York. As the interest on the loans has hitherto been paid out of the principal of the sums raised, these canals have not as yet proved any charge on the treasury.*

Sinking fund.

When the canals were commenced in 1817, a special fund was created for the security of the public creditors who should advance money for their construction ; and, up to the year 1825, the power of borrowing, which was vested in the canal commissioners, was by law strictly limited to amounts for the payment of the interest of which the income of the fund at the time of borrowing " should be deemed ample and sufficient." The fund consisted of certain duties on salt and on sales by auction, which had formerly belonged to the general fund, of the tolls to be received from the

---

* The amount received for the loan on account of the Black River canal, including the premium, was   - $613,076 29
While there has been expended on account of
  this canal, including interest on the loan   -   122,793 52

                                   Leaving unexpended   490,282 77
The amount received for the
  loan, on account of the
  Genesee Valley canal, in-
  cluding the premium, was $2,002,106 55
While there has been ex-
  pended, including interest
  on the loan   -   -   -   261,559 60

                                   Leaving unexpended   1,740,546 95

                                   Total unexpended $2,230,829 72

canals when constructed, and of some other items of inconsiderable amount.

In 1825 the lateral canals were commenced ; but the policy by which the state up to that time had been governed, in respect to the borrowing of money, was abandoned, and the loans for the construction of these canals were authorised, without any specific funds being set apart for the payment of the interest ; the interest being simply made a charge upon the treasury. In 1835, when the amount necessary for the liquidation of the Erie and Champlain canal debt had been collected and invested, the object of the legislature being virtually fulfilled, the salt and auction duties were re-transferred from the canal fund to the general fund ; but the canal fund continued to exist; and, though reduced to the property in the canals themselves and the tolls derived from them, it had, from the prosperity of the works, become a fund of considerable magnitude ; the nett revenue from the tolls (after deducting all expenses of collection and of maintenance and repairs) having about that time reached the sum of $1,107,871 30.*

The fund being thus set free, the legislature determined to enlarge and otherwise improve the main canal ; and, by an act of the 11th May, 1835, the whole income, with the reservation of three hundred thousand dollars, which was to be applied annually to the ordinary use of the government, was appropriated to this purpose. By a

---

* The above amount was received in 1836: the receipts have not been maintained since at the same rate.

subsequent act (passed 26th May, 1836), the annual sum to be appropriated to the general use of the treasury was increased to four hundred thousand dollars, and made subject to the payment of the deficiencies in the income of the lateral canals — which at present amount, as we have seen, to more than one half of the sum.

Enlarge-
ment of
Erie canal.
The improvements to which it is thus contemplated to apply the income of the canal fund are of the most extensive kind. It is not only proposed to enlarge the canal, so as to make its capacity three times as great as it is at present, but to change the direction of its present line for several miles of the route. The greatly enlarged dimensions of the canal will, it is calculated, owing to the greater size of the boats by which it will be navigated, reduce the cost of transportation at least one half, and add greatly to the traffic upon it. *

It was at first estimated that the cost of these improvements would amount to twelve millions of dollars, but the sum required will probably fall little short of fifteen millions. So many years must elapse before the revenue of the canal fund alone can produce this sum, that the committee of ways and means, in the course of the last session, suggested that the state should be authorised to borrow money to complete the proposed alterations within as short

* The canal at present is forty feet wide at the surface of the water, twenty-eight feet at the bottom, and four feet deep. It is proposed to make it seventy feet wide at the surface with a slope of two feet to one at the side, and seven feet deep : there are also to be double locks of enlarged dimensions throughout the whole line.

a time as possible, so as to secure the full benefit of the diminished cost of transportation at a correspondingly early period. Such a course would, in some respects, be highly advantageous ; for to effect any saving in the cost of transportation, by making use of a larger class of vessels, the enlargement must be completed throughout the whole line, or the expense and delay of repeated shipments would be incurred ; and, if the completion of the works should be delayed for eighteen or twenty years, the loss of interest on the sums annually expended would be very considerable. The only loan, however, yet made, is for the sum of one million of dollars mentioned among the details of the canal debt of the state. The comptroller, in his report, made on the 3d of January of the present year, strongly opposed the recommendation of the committee and condemned the principle of making further loans for this object, maintaining that the surplus income only of the fund should be applied to it ; but the policy of this state fluctuates so much, owing to the predominance of one or the other of the contending parties, at the constantly occurring election of the governors, that it is not easy to foresee how long this course, certainly the more prudent one for the state to adopt, may be persevered in.*

* In New York, and in several other states, the governor holds office for two years. In some states the term of office is only for one year — in others three — but in no case does it exceed four years.

The sum expended by the canal commissioners, in the last year, on account of the enlargement of the canal, amounted to $1,161,001 80, while they received for the loan, including the premium, $1,005,050 00; making an excess of expenditure, above the loan, of $155,951 80, which will cause so much less to be expended in the present year.

Income of the Erie and Champlain canal fund.
The total income from the Erie and Champlain canal fund, from all sources, including the interest on $2,259,834 65, (the sum set apart for the liquidation of the remaining debt of the Erie and Champlain canals,) amounted, in 1838, to

$1,553,136 84

Of this amount there was expended,

For the repairs of the canals	$449,058 64
For interest on the debt -	129,374 05
Sundry payments - -	26,892 65
	605,325 34

Making the revenue derived from this fund $947,811 50

If from this amount the above sum of $155,951 80 be deducted, as likewise four hundred thousand dollars for the ordinary use of the treasury, there will still remain $391,859 70 to be expended in the next year on the enlargement of the canal.

Condition of the treasury.
The financial condition of the treasury is the next subject for consideration.

Receipts and expenditure in 1838.
It appears by the report of the comptroller, dated on the 3d of January of the present year, that the balance on the treasury, on the 1st of Oc-

tober, 1837 (when the last fiscal year commenced), CHAP.
amounted to   VII.

	$1,526,032 40
That the receipts during the year ending 1st	
Oct. 1838 amounted to - - -	4,371,923 68
Making together	$5,897,956 08
And that the payments out of the treasury in	
the same period amounted to - -	5,786,981 51
Leaving the balance, on the 1st Oct. 1838	$110,974 57

This statement, taken by itself, does not, however, afford a correct view of the financial position
of the treasury. The receipts and payments here
referred to comprise, not merely the revenue of
the state, and its expenditure for the purposes of
the government, but a variety of sums which have
been received into the treasury for a time, and
subsequently paid out, as well as moneys obtained
on loans, and sums paid out on account of many
separate funds, such as the common school fund,
the literature fund, the bank fund, &c. When
the different claims between the treasury and
these several funds are adjusted, there appears,
instead of a balance of $110,974 57, to be a
deficiency of $70,762 81 ; the total sum due from
the general fund to these particular funds being
$203,741 37.

If these extraneous items be deducted from the
gross amounts of the receipts and payments at the
treasury, the amount of revenue applicable to the

ordinary expenses of the government, and the amount of those expenses, will become apparent.

The total amount of receipts being, as above		$4,371,923 68
There are to be deducted		
The amount of loans and of moneys temporarily received into the treasury -	$2,138,459 50	
Receipts on account of the canal fund - -	1,435,908 85	
Receipts on account of the common school and literature funds - -	199,308 25	
Receipts on account of the bank and United States deposit funds - -	319,611 87	
		4,093,288 47
Leaving for revenue for state purposes, on the general fund account - -		$278,635 21
The total amount of payments being -		$5,786,981 51
There are to be deducted, on the other hand,		
Moneys paid out of the treasury which had been temporarily paid in - -	$156,197 08	
Payments on account of the canal fund - - -	1,435,858 85	
Payments on account of the common school and literature funds - -	186,876 57	
Payments on account of the bank and United States deposit funds - -	3,163,718 51	
Balance of outstanding warrants - - -	40 95	
		4,942,691 96
Leaving the expenditure for state purposes		$844,289 55

The revenue was made up of the following items : —

Auction duties	-	-	-	-	$142,102 35
Salt duties	-	-	-	-	108,929 55
Miscellaneous	-	-	-	-	27,603 31
					$278,635 21

The expenditure consisted of

Salaries of officers of government and office expenses - - - - -	$66,115 71
Compensation to members of the legislature and incidental expenses - - -	82,852 32
Court of errors and contingent expenses -	19,302 90
Annuities to Indian tribes - - -	18,018 38
State prisons and apprehension of prisoners -	7,727 26
Brigade inspectors - - -	4,062 00
Commissary department - - -	11,979 78
Blind and deaf and dumb institutions - -	21,387 09
Printing - - - -	29,663 83
Interest on state debt - - -	51,090 91
Interest on temporary loans - - -	60,878 20
Miscellaneous expenses - - -	13,531 13
Special appropriations and temporary expenses	228,519 45
Deficiencies in the lateral canals - -	229,160 59
	$844,289 55

The expenses comprised in the above summary, under the head of " special appropriations," &c., consisted, in great part, of sums granted towards defraying the cost of a new state hall and a house for the governor ; of liberal grants to hospitals and charitable institutions ; of sums paid for the purchase of Indian lands, and expenses incurred in calling the militia of the state into service for the

CHAP.
VII.

Deficiency
in the ge-
neral fund
revenue

defence of the frontier. It included also a sum advanced for canal purposes, which, from not being included in the canal deficiencies, would appear to have been for some incidental expense not likely to occur again.*

Many of these items are evidently not of annual occurrence; but as, without further information, a distinct line cannot be drawn between such as are so, and such as are properly incidental, I have included the whole in the annual expenditure. By this means, however, there appears to be a larger deficiency in the revenue of the general fund than possibly exists in reality; for the difference between the revenue and the expenditure in the last year amounts, thus, to no less than $565,654 34; while the deficiency in 1839, according to the estimate furnished by the comptroller, will not exceed $271,800 00; but, as in the estimates of the receipts of the current year there is included a sum of eighty thousand dollars which it is supposed will be received from sales of land for arrears of taxes in five preceding years, the amount ought rather to be stated at $351,800 00. In the year 1835 the deficit amounted to $98,589 95, and

* The principal appropriations alluded to were for the following objects, viz. : —

The new state hall - - - $23,300 00
The governor's house - - - 18,000 00
The New York hospital - - - - 22,500 00
The lunatic asylum - - - - 28,500 00
Foreign poor - - - - 10,000 00
Expense of militia - - - - 20,000 00
Commissioners of canal fund for interest on
advance to the Chenango canal - - 16,731 36

in 1836 to $180,403 85.* From this it would appear that the annual deficiency is on the increase. In the last year, part of the deficit may be traced to a considerable falling off in the auction duties : the sum received in 1838 being $72,356 27 less than was received from the same source in the year before, and $105,000 00 less than was received on the average of the three years immediately preceding.†

The sum of four hundred thousand dollars, appropriated annually out of the revenue of the canal fund to the use of the state, is not included in the statement just given of the revenue of the general fund. This arises from a legal technicality in the act by which the appropriation is made ; as, to avoid the appearance of diverting this amount from the canal fund, it is stipulated that the payments made under it shall constitute a debt from the general fund to the canal fund ; and it is the two years' payment since the passing of the act that constitutes the debt of $800,000 00, without interest, which is specified among the items of the general fund debt. If this annual sum had been considered as forming part of the revenue of the general fund, the deficiency in the last year would have been reduced to $165,654 34 ; and, if special appropriations to this amount be deducted, as not properly included

Compensated by the surplus in the canal fund revenue.

* I have been unable to ascertain the deficiency in 1837.

† It seems doubtful whether this falling off in the auction duties was caused by the late general derangement in commercial affairs, or by a change which has taken place in the mode of appointing auctioneers.

CHAP.
VII.

in the annual charge, the revenue may be looked on as having been fully adequate to the charge upon it. In like manner, the contemplated deficiency of $271,800 00 in the ensuing year would, by the addition of $400,000 00 to the receipts, be converted into a surplus of $128,200 00; while it is estimated that the surplus of the canal fund, applicable to the extension of the Erie canal, will amount, in 1839, to $620,000 00.

Origin and progress of the different funds.

Allusion has been repeatedly made to the general fund, in contradistinction to the common school fund, the literature fund, and other funds which exist in the state, of which the incomes are applicable to special purposes, while that of the general fund is strictly applicable to the ordinary expenses of the government. It will afford a striking proof of the rapid growth of the wealth of the state, and throw, at the same time, considerable light upon its financial condition, if the state of these funds, at an earlier period than we have yet considered, and their subsequent progress be referred to.

In 1817, the year in which the canals were begun, the state possessed property in bank stocks, mortgages, and other securities, to the amount of

$2,973,617 70

Producing an annual income of about   -   - $180,000 00
The state derived a revenue from auction
   duties of   -   -   -   -   191,123 38
And from salt duties imposed in that year and
   producing in 1818   -   -   -   48,784 27

Making a revenue from these sources of $419,907 65

Two special funds, the common school fund CHAP.
and the literature fund, established to aid in a ge- VII.
neral system of education, were then in existence.
The principal of the two together amounted, on the
1st of January, 1817, to $1,008,938 36. To dis-
tinguish these from the first mentioned fund, the
latter was styled the general fund. When the
canals were commenced, in 1817, another special
fund, as we have already seen, called the canal
fund, was created, to which the salt and auction
duties were transferred ; thus reducing the income
of the state, derived from the general fund, to
$180,000 00. A property tax, which had been
levied to defray the expenses of the war, and had
been afterwards continued at a reduced rate, was
sufficient, however, with the above-mentioned sum
of $180,000 00, to provide for the payment of the
ordinary expenses of the government. This tax,
though applicable to the ordinary expenses, does
not appear to have formed part of the revenue of
the general fund.

In 1826, when the rapid increase in the canal
tolls began to take place, the state tax was dis-
continued, upon the ground that the principal of
the stock held by the state in banks, mortgages,
&c., constituting the capital of the general fund,
would be sufficient to carry on the government
until the debt, for which the salt and auction duties
were pledged, should be extinguished; when these
revenues would be liberated and placed at the service of the state. Between that time and the year
1836, the whole of the capital of the general fund
was accordingly expended, principally in defraying

the expenses of the government, although the large sum of $233,616 19 was taken from it, and added to the common school and literature funds, and a portion exceeding five hundred thousand dollars expended on the state hall and on the public prisons. The state has, however, borrowed, on the other hand, $586,532 43, which constitutes the debt of that amount due by the general fund to the bank safety fund.

The common school fund and literature fund now amount together to $2,197,800 38. The portion of the surplus revenue of the United States appropriated to this state, which constitutes the " United States Deposit Fund," has likewise been applied to purposes of education : the income derived from these three funds in the last year amounted to $394,736 97.

It appears, therefore, that, in the twenty-one years that have elapsed since 1817, while the common school and literature funds have more than doubled in amount, and large sums have been expended in the construction of public buildings, the productive property of the state has increased from $2,973,607 70 yielding an annual income of about $180,000 00, to a capital (now invested in canals) producing a net income, viewed under the most unfavourable light, of $718,650 91.*

County and town levies. Though no state tax has been levied since 1826, yet county and town taxes are annually assessed on all real and personal property for the

---

* This sum is the difference between the revenue of the canal fund and the deficiency in the lateral canals.

support of paupers, of an internal police, in further
aid of schools, and for the construction and repair
of highways. The aggregate amount of the county
tax in the last year was $862,115 39, and of the
town tax, exclusive of that levied on the city of
New York, $753,389 21. If to this be added
$1,244,972 15, the amount levied on that city,
the aggregate amount of the tax for the town and
county expenses will be $2,860,476 75.

An assessment is annually made to determine
the amount of this tax, and the returns of the
several districts afford another unerring proof of
the great increase that has taken place in the value
of property throughout the state since the completion of the canals.

The total value of the real estate on which
the above tax was levied in the last year was
$502,864,006 00, and the total value of the per-
sonal estate $124,680,778 00, making the aggre-
gate value of the real and personal estate
$627,544,784 00.

The following tables, drawn up from the returns
of former years, will clearly demonstrate that the
canals have been the efficient cause of the increase,
for it will be seen that there had, in the ten years
immediately preceding their construction, been an
absolute falling off in the amount of the assessment
of real and personal property in the state ; and that,
in the city of New York, the amount during the
same period had been nearly stationary, while, in
the ten years immediately following their construction, the increase is equally remarkable in both.

Official valuation of the real and personal estate of the State of New York, from 1815 to 1825 inclusive.

Year.	Real Property.	Personal Property.	Total.
1815	$239,667,218	$41,587,905	$281,255,123
1816	250,182,474	40,680,034	290,862,508
1817	265,710,214	38,457,247	304,167,461
1818	271,721,102	37,611,638	309,332,740
1819	243,942,231	37,054,513	280,996,744
1820	222,148,986	33,403,379	255,552,365
1821	207,446,531	33,199,982	240,646,513
1822	198,439,210	32,864,290	231,303,500
1823	215,238,913	46,903,723	252,142,636
1824	211,577,310	57,908,315	269,485,625
1825	199,533,471	63,893,875	263,427,346

The like from 1825 to 1835 inclusive.

Year.	Real Property.	Personal Property.	Total.
1825	$199,533,471	$63,893,875	$263,427,346
1826	214,802,204	64,590,093	279,392,297
1827	238,430,138	65,823,585	304,253,723
1828	275,861,471	68,785,292	344,646,763
1829	238,747,841	70,794,638	309,542,479
1830	250,975,885	68,142,411	319,118,296
1831	271,053,169	70,801,274	341,854,443
1832	294,596,149	75,956,259	370,552,408
1833	Returns incomplete.	—	—
1834	347,608,841	118,849,137	466,457,978
1835	403,517,585	125,058,794	528,576,379

Decrease in the valuation of the real and personal property of the state, in the ten years
next preceding 1825   -   -   - $17,827,777
Increase in the ten years next subsequent   - $265,149,033

Official valuation of the real and personal property of the City of New York, from 1815 to 1825 inclusive.

Year.	Real Property.	Personal Property.	Total.
1815	$57,000,000	$24,636,042	$81,636,042
1816	57,308,200	24,766,000	82,074,200
1817	57,799,435	20,996,200	78,895,735
1818	59,827,285	20,426,806	80,254,091
1819	60,500,295	18,612,766	79,113,061
1820	52,084,328	17,446,425	69,530,753
1821	50,619,720	17,665,350	68,285,070
1822	53,330,574	17,958,570	71,289,144
1823	50,184,229	20,756,591	70,940,820
1824	52,019,730	31,055,946	83,075,676
1825	58,425,895	42,734,151	101,160,046

The like from 1825 to 1835 inclusive.

Year.	Real Property.	Personal Property.	Total.
1825	$58,425,895	$42,734,151	$101,160,046
1826	64,912,850	42,534,931	107,447,781
1827	72,617,770	39,594,156	112,211,926
1828	77,139,880	36,879,653	114,019,533
1829	76,834,880	35,691,136	112,526,016
1830	87,603,580	37,684,938	125,288,518
1831	97,221,870	42,058,344	139,280,214
1832	104,042,405	42,260,213	146,302,618
1833	114,124,566	52,366,976	166,491,542
1834	123,249,280	63,299,231	186,548,511
1835	143,732,425	74,991,278	218,723,703

Increase in the valuation of the real and personal estate of the city in the ten years preceding 1825 - - - - $1,439,634

Increase from 1825 to 1835 inclusive - - $135,648,027

CHAP.
VII.

Extent of
the trade
of the city
of New
York.

The admirable situation of the city of New
York has undoubtedly contributed much to its
prosperity, and will probably enable it to retain
the foremost place which it now holds among
the cities on the Atlantic coast. The harbour,
for such the bay may be considered to be, is one
of the most capacious in the world, and sheltered
on every side. The navigation is rarely impeded
by ice, as the strength of the tide and the
vicinity of the ocean keep it generally open, even
when the Chesapeake and Delaware bays are
frozen over. Ships of the largest burden can at
all times enter and lie close to the quays, while
the river Hudson, at the confluence of which with
the East river the town is situated, is navigable
to a considerable distance up the interior. These
natural advantages have been greatly improved by
means of the canals, which bring into the Hudson
the produce of the western states, and make New
York the emporium to which the produce of
European nations is sent to be dispersed to almost
every point of the Union. More than one half of
the total value of the imports into the United
States is imported into New York. Its proportion
of exports is less considerable, but it amounts to
between one third and one fourth part of the total
exports from the states generally. The number
of vessels that load and unload at New York is
very considerable; and the tonnage belonging to
the port is greater than that of Liverpool or any
other city in the world, with the single exception
of London. With such advantages, this state can

yield to none in the security which its resources
afford to the holders of its engagements.

PENNSYLVANIA.

THE public debt and the engagements of this
state, according to the last annual report on the
finances of the commonwealth, consisted, at the
close of the fiscal year, on the 31st of October,
1838, of

Loans not pertaining to canals and railroads - - - -	$1,680,000 00
Loan for the Eastern penitentiary, per act 21st March, 1834 - -	120,000 00
Loan for the Union canal company, per act 1st March, 1833 -	200,000 00
Temporary loan, per act 16th June, 1836 - - - -	200,000 00
Ditto, per act 14th April, 1838 -	800,000 00

Appropriations to miscellaneous objects; viz.—

For Turnpike and state roads - -	$69,302 72	
Bridges - -	82,512 50	
Colleges, academies, &c.	525,000 00	
Common schools -	616,511 61	
Penitentiaries -	21,314 98	
Miscellaneous, viz. Geological survey, &c. }	231,088 05	
		1,545,729 86
Appropriations for internal improvements - - - -		532,057 01

Debts pertaining to public improvements by canals and railroads - 22,229,003 32
Debt due to the United States on
 account of surplus revenue - 2,867,514 78
            Total, $30,174,304 97

The faith of the state is also pledged for
$300,000 00 to the Pottsville and Danville Rail-
road Company, and for the payment of the interest
on $200,000 00 of the stock of the Bald Eagle
and Spring Creek Navigation Company.

The temporary loans contracted in June, 1836,
and in April, 1838, amounting to one million of
dollars, and a portion of the canal debt, making in
all $1,694,000 00 have, however, either become
payable since the date of the report, or will be
due in the course of the present fiscal year. The
repayment of these sums will lessen to that extent
the liabilities of the state ; but, on the other hand,
two loans amounting to $2,480,000 00 have since
been contracted (under an act of the 26th of
January, 1839), and another of $1,150,000 has
been authorised by the legislature, (by act 27th
June, 1839,) which will add so much to the
amount. Deducting and adding these sums respectively, the debt will be increased on balance to
$32,110,304 97.

As, however, the excess of the sums thus raised,
over the amount of the loans falling due will, together with the ordinary revenue of the state, provide for the portion of the appropriations likely to

be immediately called for*, and as the revenue of the state hereafter will, it is supposed, be sufficient to meet the remaining appropriations as the several sums may be required—the whole of the liabilities under the head of appropriations ought, in considering the future prospects of the state, to be deducted from this amount.

The portion of the surplus revenue received by the state ought not either, under the prevailing notions entertained upon the subject by the other states of the Union, to be considered in the light of a debt; if this amount be likewise deducted, the sum forming the permanent debt of the state will be $27,165,003 32.

Form of security and mode of transfer.

The stock of this state is invariably registered in the name of the proprietor, and can be transferred only by him in person or by his attorney. The transfers are effected at the bank of Pennsylvania. The principal of the state debt, when due, is payable at the treasury, and is redeemable at the following periods.

When and where redeemable.

$ 150,000 00	on the 1st Jan. 1840.
930,000 00	1st June, 1841.
300,000 00	1st Dec. 1846.
1,000,000 00	1st Dec. 1850.
2,000,000 00	1st Dec. 1853.
800,000 00	1st Jan. 1854.
2,200,000 00	1st Dec. 1854.
2,783,161 88	1st July, 1856.
4,000,000 00	4th March, 1858.
3,070,661 44	1st July, 1858.

* Of the appropriations to miscellaneous objects $767,659 68 only is likely to be required in the year 1839.

1,200,000 00	1st July, 1859.
2,648,680 00	1st July, 1860.
2,265,400 00	1st July, 1862.
1,280,000 00	1st July, 1864.
959,600 00	1st July, 1865.
1,150,000 00	loan authorised 27th June 1839, to be redeemable within twenty-five years.
428,500 00	time not specified.

$27,166,003 32 *

Rate of interest, and when and where payable.

The interest is payable at the bank of Pennsylvania, at the rate of 5 per cent. per annum, and is paid half yearly, on the 1st of February and the 1st of November.

Works on which the loans have been expended.

The great work undertaken by this state is the Pennsylvania canal and railroad, which forms a complete line of communication between Philadelphia and Pittsburg on the Ohio, and by means of its numerous branches is calculated to benefit almost every section of the state.

Pennsylvania canal and railroad.

The Columbia railroad, which forms the first portion of the main work, commences at Philadelphia, and extends to Columbia on the Susquehanna. A canal has thence been carried up the east bank of the river to the mouth of the Juniata, and up the valley of the latter river to Hollidaysburg, at the eastern base of the Alleghany mountains. The Alleghany portage railroad, which has been already described, then begins, and forms a communication across the mountains with Johns-

---

* There is a discrepancy of $1000 in the two results; but there is no means of determining in which the error lies.

town at the western base; a second canal, following the course of the rivers which run into the Ohio, connects Johnstown with Pittsburg.

The project of uniting the western waters with the Atlantic, as we have already seen, was early formed by this state, but was abandoned for a time, after various unsuccessful attempts had been made to carry it into effect. It was not till after the exertions of the neighbouring state of New York had been crowned with success by the completion of the Erie canal and the attainment of a large revenue from it, that the attention of Pennsylvania was again roused to the subject, and the extensive work, which has just been described, determined on. A law authorising its construction at the expense of the state was passed on the 25th of February, 1826; the work was commenced at Harrisburg on the 4th of July; and the greater part was completed in about six years. The whole line between Philadelphia and Pittsburg was opened in 1834.

The lateral canals were commenced about the same time. The Delaware division of the Pennsylvania canal was the first of these that was completed. This, which may rather be considered as a separate canal than as a branch of the main line, commences at Bristol, on the Delaware river, eighteen miles above Philadelphia, and is carried up the east bank of the river to Easton. This important canal is the channel by which the coal from the productive mines in this state reaches Philadelphia.

Lateral canals.

A series of canals carried up the valleys of the Susquehanna and its two branches forms the most extensive of the actual tributaries of the main line. The Susquehanna division leaves the grand trunk at the junction of the Juniata and the Susquehanna rivers, and proceeds along the west bank of the latter to Northumberland, where the two branches of the Susquehanna unite their waters ; the part of the northern branch division, which is already completed, extends from that point to Lackawannock. This branch will be further extended up the valley of the river till it joins the boundary line of New York. The west branch extends from Northumberland to Dunnstown. It also is now being extended in two directions to the Bald Eagle and the Tangascootac creeks.

Extension of main line.
It was part of the original plan of the projectors of these works to extend the main line to Lake Erie, and this extension is now also being carried on. Advantage will be taken of the Ohio from Pittsburg to the mouth of the Big Beaver river ; — a canal has there been commenced, which has been completed to Newcastle, and thence by French creek nearly as far as Conneaut Lake ; it will be eventually carried to the town of Erie, situated on the lake of that name. The whole distance from Philadelphia to Erie by this route will be 524 miles, of which 118 miles will be effected by railroads, 28 by the Ohio river, and 378 by canals.

Gettysburg extension.
The extension of the Columbia railroad to Gettysburg, near the Maryland line, forms the last of

the series of works in which the state is at present engaged.

These works, it will be seen, constitute a very comprehensive plan of internal improvement, but it does not appear to have been conceived or executed with the ability which has been so remarkably evinced by the projectors of the works of a similar nature in the state of New York. The direction of the main line does not seem to have been sufficiently well considered in the first instance, so that more advantageous lines have since been laid down, and in some instances executed, by chartered companies, which must have the effect of abstracting much business from the state line. Another great fault seems to have consisted in the false economy of hastening on the works which prevented a sufficiently substantial execution of them in the first instance, and has entailed an unnecessary cost on the state by causing much to be done over again. The scantiness of the sums granted at any one time for repairs has led to the commission of a similar error, by causing the repairs to be inadequately effected.

The following table shows the length in miles of the different portions of the main work, and the expense of construction : —

	Length.	Cost.
Columbia railroad, from Philadelphia to Columbia - -	82	$3,330,127 55
Pennsylvania canal, eastern and Juniata divisions, from Columbia to Hollidaysburg - -	172 43	4,594,146 03

Alleghany portage railroad, from Hollidaysburg to Johnstown -	36	$1,634,357 69¾
Pennsylvania canal, western division, from Johnstown to Pittsburg - - -	105	2,823,192 71
	395 43	$12,381,823 98¾

Length and cost of lateral canals.

The following will show the same particulars of the branch canals which are already completed.

	Miles.	Cost.
Delaware division, from Bristol to Easton - - -	59 75	$1,238,027 69
Susquehanna division, from Duncan's Island to Northumberland	39	1,039,256 77½
North branch, from Northumberland to Lackawannock -	73 25	1,398,412 77
West branch, from Northumberland to Dunnstown - -	72	1,580,351 84
Beaver division, from Beaver to Newcastle - - -	24 75	481,282 98
French Creek division, from Franklin to French Creek feeder - - -	22 25	442,558 34
French Creek feeder, from Bemis's Dam to Conneaut Lake	23	292,103 72
	314	$6,471,994 11½

The above only shows, however, the amount actually expended in the first instance. The large sums which have since been expended for reconstruction and repairs not being included,

If to the above the Bald Eagle and Lewisburg cross cuts and the different feeders be added, it will make the aggregate of state canals and railways in operation above 720 miles.   There are besides, in course of construction,

	Length in Miles.	Estimated Cost.	Expense already incurred up to 31st Oct. 1836.
The North branch extension	90	$ 2,923,294 99	$ 3,086 11
The Erie extension - -	112	*	9,018 95
The Tangascootak extension	7½	225,960 77½	108,240 77½
The Gettysburg extension (railway) - - -	41¾†	1,631,806 00	2,253 57½
			$ 122,599 41

The following table will show the increase of the traffic on the state canals and railroads, and the amounts received in tolls since they were first opened for public use.

Years ending	Amount of Tolls received.
31st October 1830.	$ 27,012 90
1831.	38,241 20
1832.	50,909 57
1833.	151,419 69
1834.	309,789 15
1835.	684,357 77
1836.	835,931 83
1837.	975,350 49
1838.	959,336 32

These tolls, which are still little more than adequate to the payment of the interest on the cost

* The cost of the Erie extension is variously estimated, according to the different lines that have been proposed.

† If to these there be further added 382½ miles of canal, and 564½ of railroad, either in operation or in course of construction, which have been undertaken by incorporated companies, there will result an aggregate of upwards of 1918 miles of canal and railroads within the state of Pennsylvania.

of construction and the repairs and superintendence of the main line, fall considerably short of the
amount required to defray the charges on the
whole of the improvements, the regular expenses
on which in 1838 were, independently of repairs,
as follows : —

Interest - - $1,111,500 16		
Toll collectors, lock keep-		
ers, &c. - -	68,500 00	
Expense of motive power	240,682 97	
		$1,420,683 13
While the repairs amounted to		512,290 00
Making a total expenditure of		$1,932,973 13

The branch canals, on which so large an expenditure has been incurred, and which remain
thus comparatively unproductive, must continue
in a grea degree to be a charge upon the main
line until the whole works are completed, and
hence the policy which the governor has lately
strongly urged on the legislature, that the funds of
the commonwealth should be applied exclusively
to the completion of the main line to Erie, and of
the most important parts of the works already commenced, rather than that fresh sum should be devoted to undertakings, however promising, in other
sections of the state. *

* A project is in contemplation, and partly commenced, to
construct a canal from Newcastle on the Beaver division, to
Akron on the Ohio and Erie canal. This would be a highly
important work, and is strongly advocated both by the states of
Pennsylvania and Ohio. To the former indeed, it would, if

By this means the system of internal improve- CHAP. ment, which has hitherto been a heavy charge upon VII. the treasury, may possibly, as in the case of the canals of New York, become its main reliance. It had been estimated, and was confidently expected, that the tolls, which in the last year amounted to $958,336 32 would have reached twelve hundred thousand dollars, and the failure is attributed principally to a disastrous breach in the canal having suspended the navigation on a considerable portion of the work for upwards of five months, during which time a great part of the trade was diverted to other routes in other states. From the present appearance of the trade, if no accidental causes intervene, it is estimated that the tolls in the present year will reach to fifteen, or not improbably, to sixteen hundred thousand dollars.

Though this estimate, like many former ones, may prove to have been made on too sanguine a view, yet the success of the three great private canal companies of the state, the Schuylkill *, the

---

executed, be of paramount importance; for a large portion of the produce of Ohio, now carried through the Erie canal to New York, would, if this communication were in existence, be carried in preference by the Pennsylvania line to the Philadelphia market, and increase, probably to nearly a corresponding amount, the quantity of foreign merchandise that would be received back through it in return. This preference of the Pennsylvania line would be founded on many considerations — principally on the distance by it being nearly 200 miles shorter than by the Erie canal, while the dangerous navigation of Lake Erie would, by the Pennsylvania route, be altogether avoided.

* The Schuylkill navigation company has a capital of

CHAP.
VII.

Union, and the Lehigh, may certainly justify very great expectations for the future success of the state works; and the nature of a considerable part of the traffic likely to arise on them affords a prospect of a more steady continuance of that prosperity than even the Erie canal can count upon : for coal and iron, and other heavy articles of indispensable use, which are the produce of Pennsylvania, must find their way to her markets through all changes of circumstances, while a carrying trade, which forms the chief traffic on the Erie canal, must always feel the disastrous effects of commercial distresses such as the United States have recently experienced.

As an indication of what may be expected from the coal trade, when further developed than it is at present, it may be remarked that the Delaware division, which is supported almost exclusively by the tolls on coal, not only maintains all costs of repairs, but pays the full interest on the cost of its construction.

$1,665,600 00, and has borrowed $1,538,626 93 as a permanent loan. The tolls, which had come in slowly till 1825, amounted in that year to $15,775 74.

In 1826 to	$43,108 87	In 1832 to	$264,829 70
1827	58,149 74	1833	325,486 63
1828	87,171 56	1834	299,841 05
1829	120,039 00	1835	433,643 64
1830	148,165 95	1836	522,633 26
1831	134,006 92	1837	604,189 00

In 1836 the current expenses, including repairs, amounted to $102,718 06, and the interest on loans to $77,215 14. The shares of $50 each were as high, in April, 1833, as $129 per share, and have since been sold at between three and four times the original cost.

The state, besides appropriating the tolls on the public works to the payment of the interest on the loans raised to construct them, has set apart other branches of revenue for this purpose, and for reimbursing the principal. These consisted up to the year 1836 of a tax of $2\frac{1}{2}$ per cent on collateral inheritances, of a tax on personal property, of the auction duties, of the county rates and levies, of escheats, and of dividends on various amounts of turnpike, bridge, and navigation stock held by the state. The premiums obtained on loans, and the premiums received on the granting or renewal of bank charters, seem also to have been occasionally appropriated to this purpose.

In the act for reincorporating the bank of the United States, as a bank of the state of Pennsylvania, which was passed in 1836, the tax on personal property, and the county rates and levies, which produced altogether about three hundred thousand dollars per annum, were repealed; but it was provided at the same time that the bank, in consideration of its charter, besides paying a premium of two millions and a half of dollars, should make an annual payment of one hundred thousand dollars for twenty years*; no mention, however, is

---

* In the excellent arrangement made for the state in the act referred to, it is further stipulated that the bank when called upon shall subscribe to certain specified improvements to the extent of $675,000 00; that it should lend the state, if required to do so, six millions at 4 per cent interest (or take a 5 per cent. stock at 110), and at all times make temporary loans when called upon, not exceeding one million of dollars at a time, at the same rate of interest.

made in the act of these sums being substituted for the repealed taxes, so that they seem to be thus withdrawn from the sinking fund, but the state of this fund does not appear to be very clearly defined. It is stipulated that, when the revenues arising from the specified sources are not sufficient for the payment of the interest on the loans, the deficiency is to be taken from the treasury. As this seems generally to be the case, the state of the treasury becomes a matter of considerable importance.

Financial condition of the treasury.
This, unless the prospective returns of the canals be looked to, does not appear to be very favourable; but the statements rendered, even by the state authorities, are so contradictory, that it is not easy to arrive at a satisfactory conclusion.* A further difficulty in obtaining at once a clear view of the resources of the state is presented by the circumstance that a large portion of the receipts in each year, in the accounts rendered, is derived from loans and from incidental sources which

---

* The discrepancies referred to arise rather out of the different views taken of the financial position of the state by the governor whose term of office has just begun, and those taken by Governor Ritner whom he succeeded, than out of any difference in their statement of the facts of the case. The strong manner in which the present governor shows his opposition to the acts of his predecessor seems very prejudicial to the interests of the state: he opposed, for example, the renewal of the bank charter, and denied its validity; and, acting on this opinion, instead of having recourse to the bank for the loans raised this year — which he might have obtained under the terms of its charter at 4 per cent. — he preferred borrowing at a higher rate of interest, rather than do what might be construed into any recognition of its authority.

cannot be relied upon as permanent revenue; while the expenditure includes the outlay for the construction of the public works in progress.

The following table will show the amount of the receipts and expenditures, including such items, from the year 1828, together with the amount of outstanding debt at each period, from which an average result may, to a certain extent, be derived : —

(margin note: Receipts and expenditure since 1828.)

Years ending	Receipts.	Expenditure.	Amount of Debt.
Nov. 30. 1828	$ 3,129,470 09	$ 3,107,552 50	$ 5,350,192 04
1829	3,610,338 02	3,624,777 51	8,327,849 31
1830	6,331,449 31	6,357,394 50	12,310,020 48
Oct. 31. 1831	3,033,978 57	3,058,926 54	14,217,856 01
1832	4,594,889 22	4,602,204 88	17,405,628 64
1833	4,047,050 62	3,796,794 48	20,298,431 88
1834	4,876,748 05	5,190,079 15	23,448,747 05
1835	3,273,533 21	3,131,860 31	24,955,435 56
1836	3,804,642 54	3,675,638 11	24,970,762 16
1837	6,067,276 47	4,173,940 26	28,058,139 52
1838	2,769,087 29	4,889,863 73	30,174,304 97

The amount of receipts in 1837 is rendered unusually large from its including the three instalments of the surplus revenue; taking, therefore, the amounts of the eight years from 1829 to 1836 inclusive, as a fair data to form an estimate upon, the aggregate receipts will be seen to amount to

$ 33,570,629 54

The debt amounted on the 31st of
  October, 1836, to   -   -   - $ 24,970,762 16
But in this were included appropriations to miscellaneous objects
  amounting to   -   -   -   641,758 84
  _____
Making the amount of debt on loans $ 24,329,003 32
On Nov. 30. 1828 it
  amounted to   -   - $ 5,350,192 04

Deduct   appropria-
tions   -   - $ 210,192 04
Making the amount
of debt on loans -   5,140,000 00
                                          5,140,000 00

The increase of actual debt, therefore,
in these eight years, was   -   -   19,189,003 32   19,189,003 32

Leaving the receipts, exclusive of loans $ 14,381,626 22

The expenditure in the same years amounted in the
aggregate to   -   -   -   -   - $ 36,542,227 98
The expenditure on public works to 31st October,
1836, amounted
On the main line to   -   -   -$ 12,381,823 98¾
On the branch canals to   -   -   6,471,994 11½
On the canals and railroad under
construction to   -   -   -   122,599 41

Making the total expenditure on
public works to 31st October,
1836   -   -   -   -   18,976,417 51¼
While prior to 30th November,
1828, it amounted to   -   -   4,771,967 24

Making the expenditure on public
works during the same eight years   14,204,450 27¼   14,204,450 27¼

Making the expenditure exclusive of public works 22,337,777 70¾
The public property, however, on
31st October, 1836, in bank stock,
turnpike, bridge, and canal stock
amounted to -   -   - $ 5,115,798 50
While the same on 30th November,
1828, amounted to   -   -   4,590,748 31

Deduct therefore the amount of
additional investments   -   -   525,050 19   525,050 19

And the total expenditure applied to the purposes of
the government and the repair of the works will be $ 21,812,727 51¾

An amount which exceeds that of the receipts into
the treasury, during the same period of eight

years, by $7,431,101 29¾, or at the rate of nearly $960,000 00 per annum.

CHAP.
VII.

Receipts
and ex-
penditure
in 1838.

The present financial position of the state, without reference to the future prospects of the canal tolls, is not more satisfactory.

The whole amount received during the year ending 31st
October, 1838, amounted to - - - $ 2,769,087 29

Of this amount the following items may be looked on as incidental : —

Loans	-	-	-	-$ 775,000 00	
Premiums from banks		-	-	- 127,053 53	
Interest on deposits		-	-	- 137,668 86	
					1,039,722 39

Leaving for ordinary revenue $ 1,729,364 90

The total expenditure during the same period amounted
to - - - - - -$ 4,889,863 73
Of which the extraordinary expenditure for internal improvements, turnpike, and state roads, amounted to 2,011,456 24

Leaving for ordinary expenditure - - - 2,878,407 49
Deduct ordinary income - - - - - 1,729,364 90

Excess of ordinary expenditure over ordinary income $ 1,149,042 59

The realised property of the state consisted, on the 31st October last, of

Bank stock	-	-	-	-$ 2,108,700 00
Turnpike and bridge stock		-	-	- 2,726,396 58
Canal and navigation stock		-	-	528,000 00
Railroad stock	-	-	-	- 179,564 59
Public works, canals, railroads, &c.			-	25,109,644 92
Moneys due on lands, about		-	-	1,000,000 00
				$31,652,306 09

The income derived from these funds, which constituted the principal source of the ordinary receipts, consisted, in the last year, of

Dividends on bank stock -	-	$158,230 00
on turnpike, bridge, navigation, and railroad stock	- -	43,389 08
Tolls on public works —		
From Canals - - $415,631 00		
Railroads - - 305,827 70		
Motive power - 237,877 62		
		959,336 32

The revenue derived from other sources consisted of

Tax on bank dividends	- $113,826 89	
Premium from bank -	- 100,000 00	
Auction duties and commission	88,791 95	
Land and land office fees	- 61,765 57	
Retailers' licenses -	- 76,525 61	
Tavern licenses -	- 50,311 32	
Collateral inheritance tax	- 22,295 70	
Tax on writs, &c. -	- 21,972 01	
Miscellaneous -	- 32,920 45	
		568,409 50
Total of ordinary income		$1,729,364 90

The following items constituted the ordinary expenditure : —

Canal expenditure -	- -	$1,932,973 13
Expense of government -	- -	299,154 01
Education, viz.		
Common schools - - $363,372 92		
Colleges and academies - 51,455 18		
		414,828 10

Militia expenses	-	-	-	30,664	24
Pensions and gratuities	-	-		47,091	53
Interest on loans not pertaining to canals				99,000	00
Penitentiaries, prisons, and miscellaneous				54,696	48

Total of ordinary expenditure $2,878,407 49

There appears thus to be a permanent deficiency in the revenue; to meet which, instead of having recourse to new loans, so as to constantly increase the permanent debt of the state, it is proposed by the present governor to have recourse to a system of taxation; and the treasurer, in his last report, alludes to the large amount of property in stocks and money existing in the state, as sources from whence a considerable revenue may be derived.

If, as it appears from his statement, many years may elapse before the canal revenues meet the interest on the loans and the expenditure connected with them, such a course seems necessary to maintain the credit of the state on a solid basis; but Governor Ritner, in his message to the House of Representatives, on the 6th of December, 1837, presents things under a much more favourable aspect.

Equally averse with the present governor to any permanent increase to the state debt, he urges, from the cheering prospects of the work, the possibility of dispensing with that alternative, and directs attention to the near approach of the time when the canals are not only to pay their own expenses, but to yield a large revenue to the state.

The canal commissioners, in their last report,

CHAP.
VII.

dated on the 21st December, 1838, hold out an equally cheering prospect ; but their expectations of the amount of the profits, likely to be derived from the tolls when the whole works are complete, exceed all reasonable bounds. * The facts, however, already stated, and, above all, the experience of the Schuylkill canal and other private undertakings, afford sufficient ground to believe that the works may ultimately cease to be a charge upon the treasury ; but, should this never prove to be the case, the great wealth of the state appears to offer a sufficient guarantee that its public credit may be maintained at an easy cost to the inhabitants.

Commerce
and ship-
ping.

Coal trade.

The city of Philadelphia, second only to New York in size, stands next to it and Boston in the extent of its foreign commerce and shipping ; but it is for the abundance of its coal and iron ore that this state is chiefly eminent ; nor is the near vicinity in which these two main elements of its wealth are found to each other a less remarkable feature in its rich mineral formation : they frequently form strata of the same hill. The quantity of coal in the state is almost without bounds. On the eastern side of the Alleghany ridge, where the coal-fields

* According to their computation the tolls will not fall short of $7,430,600 00. The cost of superintendence and repairs will then, it is estimated, amount to a million of dollars; and the interest at 5 per cent. on 45 millions (to which sum it is considered that the state debt may by that time have amounted) will constitute a further sum of $2\frac{1}{4}$ millions to be deducted, leaving a net annual revenue of $4,180,600 00 applicable to the reduction of the debts, or to the purposes of government.

are at present chiefly worked, the coal is principally of the anthracite or non-bituminous kind: the three fields or deposits which contain it embrace an area of nine hundred and seventy-five square miles; but the bituminous coal-fields, which lie beyond the Alleghany mountains, are those the future productiveness of which seems to surpass all calculation. The area they cover is not less than twenty-one thousand square miles, and the quality of the coal appears to be of the best description.

The city of Pittsburg, placed at the junction of the two rivers which afterwards assume the name of the Ohio, is situated in the midst of this vast region of coal, and owes, doubtless, to this circumstance much of the celebrity which it has acquired as the manufacturing emporium of the west, and as one of the chief manufacturing towns in the United States. This city, already of considerable extent, is destined, no doubt, to undergo a still further increase in wealth and population, not only from its contiguity to coal and iron, but from its admirable position at the head waters of the Ohio, and as the centre to which the canals and railroads of Pennsylvania and the adjoining states are directed. This and other towns, likely to spring up in the mining districts, cannot fail to add to the wealth of the state; while the agricultural districts will acquire additional value with the increased demand for provisions to supply the growing population.

The aggregate valuation of real and personal estate in Pennsylvania was $294,509,187 00; but

Realised wealth.

this value, owing to the returns being made upon a very low assessment, affords no true comparison with the values which have been given of the property in Massachusetts or in New York.

MARYLAND.

Amount of
debt and
liabilities.
THE actual debt and engagements of this state consist of loans raised or authorised to be raised for the following purposes : viz. —

For the tobacco inspection - - -	$48,000 00
For the expense of riots (indemnity stock) -	60,387 09
For the Washington monument - -	10,000 00
For the medical university - -	30,000 00
For the penitentiary - - -	97,947 30
For public improvements - - -	16,160,667 00

Making together $16,407,001 39

A large portion of the internal improvement debt, not being yet issued by the several companies in whose favour it has been created, may not for some time prove a charge upon the state. The total amount of debt actually chargeable with interest on the 1st December, 1838, was $7,995,334 39.

Form of
security,
and mode
of transfer.
A portion of the debt of this state is inscribed in the name of the holder in the books of the treasury at Baltimore, and may be transferred by him personally, or by his attorney; a part, more recently created, is in the form of bonds payable to bearer, which may, at the requisition of the holder, be exchanged for inscriptions in his name.

The portion of the debt issued up to December last was redeemable at the following periods : —

* $108,387 09 at the pleasure of the state.
   † 10,000 00, ditto, after three months' notice.
    30,000 00, ditto, after 31st December 1842.
   112,500 00, ditto, in 1844.
   225,000 00, ditto, in 1845.
   115,289 00, ditto, in 1846.
   220,220 00, ditto, in 1847.
   195,638 00, ditto, in 1848.
   300,353 00, ditto, in 1849.
    25,000 00, ditto, in 1850.
  ‡ 30,000 00 30th March, 1852, or to bear interest at 6 per
            cent.
  § 27,947 30 1st April, 1853, or ditto.
  § 20,000 00 at the pleasure of the state, in 1855.
  § 30,000 00, ditto, after 23d March, 1857.
  § 20,000 00, ditto, after 30th April, 1857.
   500,000 00, ditto, in 1859.
 3,000,000 00, ditto, in 1871.
    25,000 00, ditto, in 1878.
 2,500,000 00, ditto, after 4th June, 1886.
   500,000 00, ditto, in 1891.

_____

$7,995,334 39

The loans since issued or created are redeemable at various periods, from the 1st January, 1865, to fifty years from the respective dates of issue.

The loan of $500,000 00, redeemable in 1891, bears interest at 3 per cent. : $30,000 00 of that

  * Tobacco inspection and indemnity stock.
  † Monument stock.
  ‡ Medical university stock.   § Penitentiary stock.

redeemable in 1846, and $70,000 00 of that re-
deemable in 1847, making together $100,000 00,
bore interest originally at $4\frac{1}{2}$ per cent.; but the
rate was afterwards changed to 5 per cent., to
render the stock more marketable.

The penitentiary stock, redeemable in 1857,
and the loan of $3,000,000 00, redeemable in
1871, bear interest at 6 per cent. The loan of
$2,500,000 00, redeemable in 1886, originally bore
interest at 6 per cent., but a 5 per cent. stock, payable in London, has since been substituted for it.
The rest of the debt, whether for purposes of internal improvement or for miscellaneous objects,
bears interest at 5 per cent.

The loan of $2,500,000 00, above referred to,
forms part of a larger amount authorised to be
raised under an act, chap. 395. of 1835, in virtue
of which the above amount only had been issued
at the date of the treasurer's report. The act
contains a stipulation that the stock is not to be
sold at a less premium than 20 per cent., and that
the excess of the amount received above the par
value, should belong to the state. It was contemplated that this premium would pay the interest of
the debt for three years, and possibly contribute
something to the capital of the sinking fund * ; but,
as the loans could not be negotiated on the prescribed
terms, the legislature, in March last, passed an act
to permit the conversion of $7,300,000 00 6 per

---

* It seems originally to have been intended to apply the
premium to purposes of education.

cent. stock, being the whole amount authorised
under the act referred to, and including the sum
of $2,500,000 00, which had been pledged and
not sold, into $7,786,667 00 stock, bearing in-
terest at 5 per cent., the interest and principal to
be payable in London at the exchange of 4s. 6d.
per dollar. This stock, it is supposed, will be
disposed of on nearly as advantageous terms to the
state as the 6 per cent. stock would have been, on
account of the premium on the exchange. The
excess over $7,300,000 00 is still to be paid into
the state treasury.

The state pays the interest on its stock quarterly, on the first days of January, April, July, and
October: the several companies which the state
has aided by its loans agreeing to reimburse the
treasury for the amounts paid on their account.
The interest is payable at the treasury at Baltimore, excepting in the case of the bonds which
have been made payable in London. *

During the suspension of specie payments in Act making
1837, this state did not pay the interest on its dividends
payable in
stock either in specie or its equivalent, and, some specie.
of the holders refusing to receive depreciated bank
paper for their dividends, the treasurer, in December, 1837, reported the fact to the legislature. In
March, 1838, an act was, in consequence, passed,
which provides that the state treasurer shall cause
the interest on the state stock that shall hereafter

* On the bonds payable in London the interest is paid half
yearly only.

accrue to be paid " either in coin or its equivalent, in current bank notes, to be determined by the commissioners of loans by the price of coin in Baltimore on the quarter day." The act was also made retrospective.

Advan-
tageous po-
sition of
Maryland
for works
of internal
improve-
ment.

Several circumstances in the geographical position of this state have encouraged it to embark more deeply in works of internal improvement, in proportion either to the extent of its territory, or to its population, than any other state in the Union. Lying for a considerable distance along the two shores of the Chesapeake, it encloses the head waters of that magnificent estuary, and, gradually narrowing as it extends westward along the banks of the Potomac, it again widens after reaching Cumberland, and embraces one of the richest mineral districts in the United States. In mining countries the surface of the ground is usually sterile; but this favoured tract is scarcely less remarkable for its rich meadows and the general fertility of the soil than it is for its mineral wealth, while a mild and healthy climate enables the labourer to cultivate it under the most favourable circumstances.

Besides the advantages which Maryland thus possesses within itself, it occupies nearly a central position between the northern and southern extremities of the United States : its chief town, too, Baltimore, being situated on the western shore of the Chesapeake, is, by the deep indenting of that bay, brought nearer to the regions watered by the

Mississippi and its tributaries than any other city on the Atlantic coast.

While the proximity of the eastern and western waters in this state renders Maryland in some respects a place particularly adapted to connect them, the circumstance of the rich mining and agricultural districts lying near the sources of the Potomac, in the very track of the easiest route which the valley of that river affords, seems to hold out the prospect of a profitable return from any attempt to effect a junction at this place, before the great difficulty of crossing the Alleghany mountains need be encountered. The height of the mountains at this spot affords almost the only countervailing disadvantage.

The greater part of the sums borrowed by Maryland has been applied to take advantage of the fortunate combination of circumstances which has been described. Two of these, the Chesapeake and Ohio canal, and the Baltimore and Ohio railroad, are gigantic undertakings. The canal was the first attempted. By the plan originally contemplated, it was to commence at George Town, in the district of Colombia, and to proceed up the valley of the Potomac, by Harper's Ferry, to Cumberland, and was thence to be carried through the valleys of the Wells Creek and other rivers to Pittsburg on the Ohio, a total distance of $341\frac{1}{4}$ miles. The railroad was to commence at Baltimore, and, meeting the Potomac at the Point of Rocks, to proceed by Harper's Ferry in the same direction ; but by a judicial decision,

Nature of works undertaken by this state.

Chesapeake and Ohio canal, and Baltimore and Ohio railroad.

arising out of a dispute between the two companies on the subject of a prior right of the canal to certain parts of the route, the railroad company has been prohibited from ascending beyond Harper's ferry until the canal is finished as far as Cumberland. The railroad company, therefore, having completed the line from Baltimore to that point, are about to take up the route, where the part of the canal now in progress will terminate, at Cumberland, and carry it across the mountains to its final termination upon the track originally intended. It is probable that the companies will ultimately be content that each should confine itself to a separate part of the work, and blend their interests, instead of running on in their hostile career : in this manner, a series of canals and railroads may be formed similar to the Pennsylvanian line.

To render intelligible the pecuniary interest of the state in each of these works, it will be necessary to take a more detailed view of their respective progress.

Progress and expenses of Chesapeake and Ohio canal.
The project of the Chesapeake and Ohio canal was first entertained in 1820, and seems, more than any other work of the kind, to have been looked upon as a national enterprise. The central position of Maryland among the original states, and its local advantages, appear to have early pointed it out as the natural seat of the federal government ; but, as no state was to enjoy this privilege, a small district, called the district of Columbia, was ceded by Maryland and the adjoining state of Virginia, in which the city of Washington, and the dis-

trict towns of Alexandria and George Town, are situated.

A canal to unite the federal city with the rich districts of the west could hardly fail, therefore, to acquire a national character. Long before it was projected, General Washington, ever anxious to promote the welfare of the city which bore his name, and which he was desirous of rendering a capital of importance, had directed his attention to the improvement of the navigation of the Potomac, on the left bank of which Washington is built. As early as the 22d of December, 1784, commissioners on behalf of the states of Virginia and Maryland met at Annapolis on the subject, at which meeting General Washington presided.

When the idea of carrying a canal the whole distance from George Town to Pittsburg began to be entertained, the situation of president was filled by Mr. John Quincy Adams, a statesman who fully shared in the wish of his illustrious predecessor to promote the welfare of the federal city. At his suggestion, congress voted a million of dollars towards defraying the expenses of the canal, and granted a charter to execute it.   The town of Washington was authorised to raise a loan for a like sum, while George Town and Alexandria were each allowed to issue bonds for a quarter of that amount.   The state of Maryland subscribed half a million, and the state of Virginia, still affording her co-operation, appropriated two hundred and fifty thousand dollars towards an undertaking of so great an interest to both states : 6084 shares of one hundred dollars

188

CHAP.
VII.

each were taken by private individuals, thus raising the total subscription to $3,858,400 00.

The state of Maryland seems to have had recourse to a loan of $262,500 00 to provide part of this first subscription.* It afterwards subscribed a further sum of one hundred and twenty-five thousand dollars, for which a further loan to that amount was contracted.

In addition to the charter granted by congress, others were obtained from the legislatures of the states of Maryland and Virginia, as well as from Pennsylvania, in which last named state the work would terminate. On the 4th of July, 1828, being the anniversary of the declaration of independence, the first ground was broken with much ceremony by Mr. Adams. The work, however, proved much more costly than was anticipated: on the 4th of January, 1834, when 104 miles only had been completed, $3,707,263 00 had been expended, while the canal was far from having reached the coal and iron regions near the source of the Potomac, whence it was expected that a large portion of its revenue was to be derived.

When the first subscriptions were thus nearly exhausted, the state aided the company by a loan of two millions of dollars, reserving a right to convert its advance into the stock of the company on the completion of the canal to Cumberland, to

* A part appears to have been paid by making over to the company the state's share in the stock of the Potomac company, and a loan which it had made to the president and directors of that corporation.

effect which it was supposed that this sum would
be sufficient. In 1836 a statement was, however,
furnished to show that three millions of dollars
more would be required to complete this portion
of the work. Application was made to the general
government as well as to the district cities to join
in contributing this sum, but they refused to aug-
ment their appropriations. In fact, about this time
the right of the federal government to embark in
such undertakings began to be questioned, and the
district towns became unable even to meet the interest on the bonds which they had already issued.*

Under these circumstances the state of Maryland made the entire appropriation of the three
millions, on the assurance that this additional sum
was all that would be required. The state's share
in the stock of the company was thus raised to
$3,625,000 00.

In the month of March in the present year a
fresh statement was submitted to the legislature,
showing an available balance of funds in the hands
of the company, after paying the most pressing demands upon them, of $1,162,269 00; but showing
that a second sum of three millions of dollars would
be required to complete the canal to Cumberland,
and to render available to the state, to the general
government, and to the district cities, the large
sums which had already been expended in its construction.

* The federal government, under an act of the 20th May
1836, assumed these debts of the district cities, and from that
time has defrayed the interest and charges on them.

On this statement being submitted to the committee of ways and means of the state, the committee recommended that no further appropriations should be made, unless the general government and the district cities should surrender their interests in the work to the state of Maryland; but on this not being agreed to, after much discussion whether the further completion of the work should not be altogether abandoned, an appropriation has been made of $1,375,000 00, which will raise the state's share in the stock to $5,000,000 00, with a right reserved to claim in stock its advance of $2,000,000 00.

Progress of the Baltimore and Ohio railroad.

The scheme of a railroad began to be entertained in 1826, and the Baltimore and Ohio railroad company was incorporated by the legislatures of Maryland and Virginia in the February following: the legislature of Pennsylvania subsequently joined in the charter. The company is authorised to strike the Ohio at any place between Pittsburg and the mouth of the river Kennaway. The proposed line is longer, and passes over much higher ground, than had ever before been attempted; but neither the boldness of the plan, nor the difficulties attending its execution, prevented an immediate subscription of five millions of dollars from being entered into: of this, the state of Maryland and the city of Baltimore each subscribed half a million, and individuals the remainder. The road was finished to Harper's Ferry on the 1st of December, 1834, being a distance of about eighty-two miles, at an expense of nearly three millions of dollars.

Being prohibited by the injunction of the court from advancing at present beyond this point, the company applied part of its funds to the construction of a lateral railroad to connect the main line with the city of Washington. The state added a subscription of a second half million to this branch. These two subscriptions were paid for by contracting loans for $997,000 00 *; the difference to complete the million being paid by the premium obtained upon a portion of the stock. The state has since authorised the issue of an additional sum of three millions of dollars to be applied towards the completion of the main line. This grant was under the authority of the same act which, in 1836, appropriated a like amount to the Chesapeake and Ohio canal company; but, from the difficulty of effecting a sale under the prescribed conditions, no part of it has yet been issued.

Washington branch.

The state, at this time entering on a more extended system of public improvement, made appropriations by the same act of two millions of dollars to other companies which were then established in the state, or in contemplation at the time. These consisted of one million of dollars to the Eastern shore railroad company, and of half a million each to the Maryland canal company, and to the Annapolis and Potomac canal company.

Appropriations made to other works

* The loans contracted for the railroad appear to amount only to $981,189 00, but the sum stated above is on the authority of the last treasurer's report.

During the sitting of the next legislature, the last named company, however, released the legislature from the appropriation in its favour, on condition that the state would subscribe three hundred thousand dollars to the Annapolis and Elk Ridge railroad company ; while the Maryland canal company forfeited its share of the grant by failing to comply with the conditions of the law for the promotion of internal improvement, under which the several sums were appropriated. Although no part of the stock appropriated by this act, amounting, after the above substitution and deduction, to $7,300,000 00, has yet been sold, a considerable portion, as we have seen, forms a charge upon the state, from having been hypothecated by the companies.

The Baltimore and Susquehanna railroad is another work in which the state is interested. It had originally invested $100,000 00 in the stock of the company, and subsequently advanced a further sum of $1,252,000 00. By an act passed in the last session of the legislature, $750,000 00 more were appropriated to this company to release it from embarrassments into which it had fallen.

The state has likewise lately issued one million of stock, under an act to insure the completion of the Susquehanna and tide water canal. It had previously lent thirty thousand dollars to the president and directors of the Potomac company.

Details of debts contracted for these works.
The debt which the state has contracted or authorised, in order to subscribe for the stock of these different companies, appears to be as follows : —

State loan created	per act of 1826, ch. 229.	$30,000 00	
Railroad stock	per act of 1827, ch. 104.	256,189 00	
Ditto	per act of 1830, ch. 119.	100,000 00	
Ditto	per act of 1833, ch. 33.	500,000 00	
Ditto	per act of 1833, ch. 105.	125,000 00	
Canal stock	per act of 1827, ch. 105.	262,500 00	
Ditto	per act of 1833, ch. 239.	125,000 00	
State loan	per act of 1830, ch. 46.	350,311 00	
Ditto	per act of 1834, ch. 241.	3,000,000 00	
Ditto	per act of 1835, ch. 395.	2,500,000 00	
Ditto	per act of 1837, ch. 302.	500,000 00	

Amount chargeable with interest on Dec. 1. 1838 $7,749,000 00
There then remained to be issued
  under act of 1836, ch. 395 (to
  complete $7,300,000 00)   - $4,800,000 00
Add additional capital created on
  the substitution for this, of
  stock bearing interest at 5 per
  cent.   -   -   -   486,667 00
                                       5,286,667 00
Stock authorised by acts of the last session   - 3,125,000 00

                  Making a total of $16,160,667 00

    The state besides holds stock in the Potomac company, and in the Chesapeake and Delaware canal company; but it does not appear whether any debt was created to meet its subscriptions to the stock of these corporations.

    The Chesapeake and Ohio canal, which has proved so costly to the state, is a work on a most extensive scale. From Washington to Harper's Ferry, a distance of sixty-two miles, its width at the water line is sixty feet, and from Harper's Ferry to Cumberland fifty feet, and its depth

Description and prospects of Chesapeake and Ohio canal.

throughout six feet: the locks are 100 feet in
length and fifteen in width ; and the whole is executed in a manner which reflects much credit on
the skill and perseverance of those who have been
engaged in it. In August, 1838, 110 miles were
in actual use, and thirty miles more have since
been opened: the remainder of the line to Cumberland will, it is supposed, be finished in 1840,
and exertions are making to have it ready for the
anniversary of the 4th of July, in which case it will
have taken exactly twelve years to complete it. The
canal passes during the greater part of its course
through a rich agricultural region, abounding in
lime, lumber, and numerous other articles for trade
and transportation ; but it is not so much on these
sources that the state relies for a revenue, as on
the extensive trade in coal and iron which is likely
to spring up as soon as the canal reaches the
mineral region at the foot of the Alleghany mountains, when the most sanguine expectations are
entertained of its success; the president of the
company stating his firm belief, that the state's
share in the works will not only then discharge
all the interest it may have to pay on its loans,
but will defray the whole expenses of the government.

Baltimore
and Ohio
railroad.

The Baltimore and Ohio railroad was commenced in 1828, and completed to Harper's Ferry
in 1834 : it was, however, open for a part of the
distance in 1832 ; and the income, even at that
early period, more than defrayed the expenses.

The annual income and expenditure, for the first four years, were as follow : —

CHAP.
VII.

Year.	Income.	Expenditure.
1832	$183,053 21	$98,653 01
1833	191,673 92	83,880 75
1834	222,973 92	95,344 78
1835	263,368 10*	108,179 50

In the year 1836 the tolls amounted to $438,000 00, and the expenses, including a bonus to the state, to $290,000 00. In 1837 it was estimated that the receipts would reach six hundred thousand dollars.

The Winchester and Potomac railroad, in Virginia, which joins the Baltimore and Ohio railroad at Harper's Ferry, brings much traffic to it.

The lateral road to Washington was completed and opened for passengers in August, 1835, and has already been productive of sufficient revenue not only to pay the interest upon the cost of its construction, but to have largely contributed to the payment of the interest upon the state's investment in the main road. So beneficial has this branch proved, that the state's interest in the work, taken as one investment, now completely answers its purpose of affording a surplus, after payment of the interest on the debt incurred for its subscrip-

Of Washington branch.

* The income in 1835 was derived

From 97,758 passengers	-	- $93,540 22
From tonnage (72,634·11 tons)		- 169,827 88
		263,368 10

CHAP.   tions to the capital of the company.   This surplus
VII.   may be confidently expected to increase.*

In the construction both of the main line and the branch road considerable attention seems to have been paid to the permanent durability of the works ; and the whole appears to have been well executed, although, from want of experience, much unnecessary expense was at first incurred.   The curves on this railroad are so great (some of them having only 400 feet radius) as to render the speed attained on it very inconsiderable.

Eastern shore rail-road.   The Eastern shore railroad, from the northern part of the eastern shore to Pocomoke Bay, will be a work of considerable importance to that portion of the state.   This is the least populous part of the state ; and the population is decreasing in number, and less thriving in other respects than that of the western shore.

Annapolis and Elk Ridge rail-road.   The Annapolis and Elk Ridge railroad will connect Annapolis, the capital of the state, with the Baltimore and Ohio railroad.   This railroad is in progress.

* Upon the debt of $997,000 00 raised to meet the subscriptions, the state, up to 1st January, 1839, would, according to the treasurer's report, have paid for interest $251,928 34, while it would have received from the company, in interest and dividends, $252,717 79.   This includes a sum of $50,000 00, which was added as a bonus to the state's capital in the company.

In this calculation the state's subscriptions are considered as limited to one million of dollars to the main road and branch together, no part of the further advance of $3,000,000 00, authorised in 1836, having yet been issued.

The Baltimore and Susquehanna railroad is to extend from Baltimore to York, in the state of Pennsylvania, a distance of seventy-six miles. This work was for some time retarded, in consequence of the legislature of Pennsylvania having refused to allow the company to carry on the works within the limits of that state ; but that difficulty has been removed. As York is only eleven miles distant from Columbia, a railroad has been sanctioned, which, when finished, will unite this work with the Philadelphia and Columbia railroad, so as to form a direct railroad communication between Baltimore and Philadelphia, a distance by this route of 169 miles. This railroad will be important, as securing to Baltimore a part of the trade of the Susquehanna ; but the affairs of the company appear to be badly managed, and little regard seems to be paid by the directors to the obligations they have come under, as the treasurer of the state, in his last report to the legislature, had to communicate the failure of the company to furnish the treasury with the means of paying the interest on the debts of the state contracted for their use : a circumstance which he states to be the more unexpected and inexcusable, as, only three months before, the company had received from the treasury the large sum of $252,000 00. The assurances, however, which the treasurer states he received from the president and directors, of their unabated confidence that the profits of the work would soon enable them to fulfil their engagements, gave him reason, he says, to hope that their insolvency would be of short duration. A further advance has been made to free them from their temporary embarrassment.

The state is guaranteed for its advances by a prior mortgage on the property and revenues of the company. The city of Baltimore has subscribed and lent $950,000 00 to this undertaking.

Susquehanna tide water canal. The Susquehanna tide water canal, in March last, was about three fourths finished, and was expected to be completed in the course of the year. The town of Baltimore has subscribed $380,000 00 to the work. Under the Pennsylvanian charter, about one million and a half of dollars (including the above sum) were subscribed; and, on the passing of the Maryland charter, the whole stock of the Maryland company was subscribed for by the Pennsylvanian company, to insure one board of management. The management is said to be very good. Under these circumstances, it is more of a Pennsylvanian than a Maryland company.

The works in which this state is so largely interested may possibly hereafter repay it for the cost they have entailed on it; but it has doubtless embarked too deeply in works of internal improvement, and has injudiciously attempted to carry on too many at a time.

Sinking fund. A sinking fund has been established from premiums and other sources, which, on the 1st of December, 1838, consisted of

State 6 per cent. stock	-	-	$432,000 00
Ditto, 5 per cent. stock	-	-	378,172 30
Ditto, 3 per cent. stock	-	-	100,000 00

Stock in the bank of Baltimore - - -	6,300 00	CHAP. VII.
Stock in the farmers' bank of Maryland -	14,500 00	
Special deposit in the union bank of Maryland	32,407 85	

Making a total in stock and money of $963,380 15

The income of this fund is applied to the purchase of state stock. The addition made to it in the last year was $153,457 29, of which $47,249 21 was received in cash for dividends on the bank and state stock already invested in the names of the commissioners: $100,000 00 3 per cent. stock was added by the commissioners of loans: the remaining $6208 28 arose from various sources, including an addition to the special deposit in the union bank of Maryland, made by that bank itself.

There is a separate sinking fund for the discharge of the debt for the tobacco inspection, derived from the tobacco inspection revenue. $20,000 00 are also annually paid by the treasury in redemption of the indemnity stock.

The state besides holds stock, in nine of the State funds, &c. Maryland banks, to the amount of $528,966 66, and road stocks to the amount of $15,000 00. These funds, although not specially pledged by the state, would be available towards meeting its engagements, should other means be wanting. The state has likewise $175,000 00 in deposit, at the treasurer's credit, in the bank of Baltimore, on which it receives interest.

For some years past the revenue of the state Condition of the trea- appears to have been nearly sufficient to meet the sury.

CHAP.
VII.

Receipts
and pay-
ments in
1838.

demands of the treasury ; but in the last year the condition of the treasury does not present so favourable an aspect.

It appears, by the report of the treasurer, that the balance in the treasury on the 1st December, 1837, (when the last fiscal year commenced,) amounted to $80,364 52

That the receipts during the year ending 1st Dec.
    1837 amounted to   -   -   -   - 875,948 94

                              Making together 956,313 46
And that the payments out of the treasury in the
    same period amounted to   -   -   - 911,607 78

              Leaving the balance on the 1st Dec. 1838 $44,705 68

That balance was, however, subject to a variety of appropriations still uncalled for, amounting to $130,310 86; so that there was, in reality, a deficiency in the treasury at the close of the last fiscal year of $85,605 18, to which the treasurer states the probable cost of the present sessions ought to be added, which, if taken at his estimate of $70,000 00, would leave a charge on the receipts of the current year of $155,605 18.

The total receipts into the treasury being as above $875,948 94
The following incidental receipts should be de-
    ducted, to show the actual ordinary revenue of
    the state : — viz.
Revenue accrued before the year
    1838   -   -   - $25,541 29
Sums withdrawn from the deposit
    with the bank of Baltimore   -   50,000 00
Proceeds of the sale of 3 per cent.
    stock   -   -   - 252,000 00

Sums received from the Chesapeake and Ohio canal company for the railroad - - -	90,000 00	
Sundry repayments - -	594 72	
		418,136 01

Leaving for ordinary revenue $457,812 93

The whole payments for the year amounting to - $911,607 78
There should be deducted, in like manner,

Paid to the Baltimore and Susquehanna railroad company - -	$252,000 00	
The Eastern shore railroad company	30,000 00	
The Annapolis and Elk Ridge railroad company - -	60,000 00	
		342,000 00

Leaving 569,607 78
But, on the other hand, there should be added various appropriations made, but not yet called for, amounting to - - - 200,310 86

Making the ordinary charge $769,918 64

The ordinary revenue consisted of

Dividends on bank and road stocks - -	$34,103 66
Interest on deposit in the bank of Baltimore -	19,756 25
Auction duties - - - -	42,259 00
Licenses - - - -	65,515 90
State lotteries - - - -	18,225 44
Taxes for colonisation and for colonisation society	6,338 37
Taxes on plaintiffs and taxes in chancery -	3,390 07
Fines and forfeitures - - -	3,316 65
Tax on banks - - - -	17,872 25
Interest on personal accounts - -	1,876 80
State tobacco inspection in Baltimore - -	12,824 37
From the Baltimore and Ohio railroad company, for interest on the state's advance - - - $5,156 25	

For the state's one fifth of the receipts
on the Washington branch   -   - 38,537 09
                                                  ————— 43,693 34
From the Baltimore and Susquehanna railroad
company, for interest on the state's advance, and
premium to make the payment equivalent to
specie   -   -   -   -   45,300 00
From the Chesapeake and Ohio canal, for ditto   - 129,000 00
From the penitentiary, for interest   -   -   974 34
From the land office   -   -   -   6,848 64
From the eastern shore treasury   -   -   6,517 85
                                                  —————
                                              $457,812 93

The ordinary expenditure of the year was made
up of payments for
The legislature   -   -   -   - $73,345 26
The judiciary   -   -   -   - 38,156 11
Civil officers   -   -   -   - 14,397 77
The militia   -   -   -   - 5,350 64
Colleges, academies, and schools   -   - 18,562 57
Pensions to officers and soldiers of the revolution -   13,830 55
Public subscriptions, charitable donations, &c.   -   18,624 09
State colonisation   -   -   -   - 10,000 00
Interest on the public debt   -   .. $280,914 03
To make it equivalent to specie   -   16,733 39
                                          ————— 297,647 42
Indemnity 5 per cent. stock   -   -   - 20,000 00
State tobacco inspection at Baltimore   -   - 8,018 29
Miscellaneous expenses   -   -   - 51,674 98
                                                  —————
                          Total disbursements 569,607 78
Appropriated but not disbursed —
    Interest on the public debt   -   - $48,883 73
    Sinking fund   -   -   - 59,060 69
    Estimated cost of the present session   70,000 00
    Judiciary, civil officers, pensions &c.   22,366 44
                                          ————— 200,310 86

    Making the total ordinary expenditure $769,918 64

This large deficiency is accounted for by the treasurer, first, by the amount of revenue received having fallen considerably short of the amount anticipated, owing to the non-payment by the Baltimore and Susquehanna railroad company of the interest on the loan contracted on its account, and the want of means of the medical department of the Baltimore university and the state penitentiary to pay the interest on the loans raised for the use of those institutions * ; and, secondly, by the charges for the past year, on account of the legislature, the militia, the interest on the public debt, and for contingent and miscellaneous expenses, having greatly exceeded the estimated amounts, and the provision which the legislature had, in consequence, made for their payment.

The income for the present year is estimated at $446,825 00, (exclusive of any receipts from the Baltimore and Susquehanna railroad company, from

Estimated revenue and expenditure for 1839.

* The sums thus due, together with defalcations arising from the nonpayment of taxes, amounted to $52,540 19.

The loan for the medical school constitutes the oldest subsisting debt of the state. It was made irredeemable for thirty years, requiring the professors to pay the interest only: before one third of the time expired they failed to do so.

Four debts in succession have been incurred for the penitentiary, the directors being required to pay both principal and interest; but, before any of them have become redeemable, the institution has been declared unable to comply with its engagements. These instances afford strong proofs of the inexpediency of incurring debts for the use of institutions of which the chief purpose is not revenue, and especially of leaving the treasury to trust to such resources for the means of defraying the interest on its own engagements to the public creditor.

the medical professors of the university, and the penitentiary, as not to be relied upon,) and the expenditure at $478,234 36, which will increase the deficiency in the treasury to $187,014 54. Should the revenue not prove more productive than the estimate, recourse must be had to the deposit of $175,000 00 in the bank of Baltimore, which the treasurer considers will be sufficient, with such arrears as may possibly be paid in, to sustain the treasury till the 1st December, 1839.

Agriculture and commerce of Maryland.
The chief wealth of Maryland is derived from agriculture. Indian corn and wheat are the principal productions of the eastern shore, and these and tobacco of the western section of the state. Of 34,105 hogsheads of tobacco inspected in Baltimore, in 1835, 24,930 were the produce of Maryland. There are few manufactures in this state; but Maryland, though its trade has materially diminished, still ranks high as a commercial state. Baltimore, its commercial capital, has had a remarkably rapid growth. In 1750 a few houses only existed, built round the head of the bay; in 1790 its population was 13,503; in 1820, 62,738; and it now contains above 90,000 inhabitants. It has an excellent harbour, and formerly ranked next to New York and Boston in the amount of its shipping; but it now holds only the sixth place in this respect among the cities of the Union.

This is the first state in our progress southward in which slavery exists; but the number of slaves is inconsiderable, and is gradually decreasing.

Realised wealth.
There is no fixed mode in Maryland of ascer-

taining the value of the real or personal property in the state, so that no estimate on this subject can be relied on.

VIRGINIA.

By a statement rendered on the 5th of February, 1838, the public debt of Virginia at that time consisted of

The debt of the revolutionary war - -	$ 24,039	17
The war debt of 1812 - - -	319,000	00
The internal improvement debt - -	3,444,100	00
Making the total amount of actual debt	3,787,139	17
To complete the public works now in progress, engagements had been entered into which would require a further sum of - -	1,552,050	00
And the state had rendered itself conditionally liable to different corporations to the extent of - - - - -	1,322,900	00
Making the whole amount of debt and liabilities	$6,662,089	17*

The stock issued by this state is inscribed in the name of the proprietor, and is transferable at the state treasury by appearance in person, or by power of attorney.

The revolutionary debt, and the war debt of 1812, may be redeemed at the pleasure of the legislature.

The loans obtained for purposes of internal im-

* Considerable appropriations have been made within the last year; but I can give no correct details respecting them, not having seen the last treasury report.

provement are all irredeemable for twenty years from the date of issue. Power is reserved to the general assembly of not redeeming the earlier loans for a period of fifteen years after the expiration of the twenty years; but the period of redemption may not be delayed beyond the latter term. The later loans are redeemable after the expiration of twenty years at the pleasure of the assembly.

The following statement shows the years in which the right of redemption occurs, and the sum redeemable in each year: —

1840	$50,000 00	Brought forward	$1,499,000 00
1841	20,300 00	1851	38,000 00
1842	83,000 00	1852	130,000 00
1843	211,300 00	1853	27,000 00
1844	365,400 00	1854	186,500 00
1845	300,000 00	1855	305,000 00
1846	200,000 00	1856	116,300 00
1849	5,000 00	1857	1,136,300 00
1850	264,000 00	1858	6,000 00
Carried forward	$1,499,000 00		$3,444,100 00

Rate of interest, and when and where payable.

The debt of the revolutionary war bears interest at the rate of six per cent., that of the war of 1812 at seven per cent.

The following rates of interest are payable on the certificates of debt issued for purposes of internal improvement: viz.—

6 per cent. on	-	-	- $2,171,500 00
5½ per cent. on	-	"	25,300 00
5 per cent. on	-	-	- 1,247,300 00
			$3,444,100 00

The interest is payable at the treasury half-yearly, on the 1st January and 1st July.* CHAP. VII.

The purposes for which the internal improvement debt was created are as follow : —

Works on which the loans have been expended.

1. Improvements of the James River company prior to June 1835.

Subscription to the stock of the following companies : —

2. James river and Kanawha company.

3. Petersburg railroad company.

4. Winchester and Potomac railroad company.

5. Portsmouth and Roanoke railroad company.

6. Richmond, Fredericksburg, and Potomac railroad company.

7. Louisa railroad company.

8. Richmond and Petersburg railroad company.

9. City Point railroad company.

10. Dismal Swamp canal company.

11. Upper Appomattox company.

* The revolutionary debt, and the war debt of 1812, are held by the commissioners of the literary fund.

The internal improvement debt is held as follows : —

By the commissioners of the literary fund -	$ 584,583 33
By the board of public works - -	163,000 00
By the commissioners of the sinking fund -	52,900 00
By individuals and private corporations in Virginia - - - - -	510,916 67
By individuals and private corporations in other states - - - -	100,300 00
In England - - - -	1,867,400 00
In France - - - -	155,000 00
In Switzerland - - -	10,000 00
	$ 3,444,100 00

12. Chesapeake and Ohio canal company.

13. Rappahannock company.

14. Road from Price's turnpike to Cumberland Gap.

15. Road from the Ohio river to the Maryland line.

16. Road from Winchester to the Ohio.

The following statement will show the total amount of actual debt on the 3d of February, 1838, which had been contracted for each of these objects, the amount of certificates which the state had in each case still to issue to complete its engagements, and the amount which will have ultimately been expended on them.*

	Amount of Certificates of Debt already issued.	Amount remaining to be issued.	Total.
1.	$1,324,500 00	$2,500 00	$1,327,000 00
2.	780,000 00	1,210,800 00	1,990,800 00
3.	80,000 00	- -	80,000 00
4.	120,000 00	- -	120,000 00
5.	240,000 00	- -	240,000 00
6.	206,800 00	- -	206,800 00
7.	57,100 00	62,900 00	120,000 00
8.	114,200 00	85,800 00	200,000 00
9.	25,500 00	34,500 00	60,000 00
10.	16,500 00	- -	16,500 00
11.	7,000 00	20,700 00	27,700 00
12.	250,000 00	- -	250,000 00
13.	- -	13,350 00	13,350 00
14.	10,000 00	50,000 00	60,000 00
15.	- -	8,000 00	8,000 00
16.	212,500 00	63,500 00	276,000 00
	$3,444,100 00	$1,552,050 00	$4,996,150 00

* The figures in the first column correspond with those by which the works above enumerated have been indicated.

At the date of the report, the following items constituted the conditional liabilities of the state: —

Subscription to the Roanoke, Danville, and junction railroad company, dependent on subscriptions of three fifths of the stock by individuals, prior to 1st April, 1839 -   - $800,000 00

Subscription to the New Shanandoah company, dependent on subscriptions of three fifths of the stock by individuals, prior to 1st January, 1839   200,000 00

Baltimore and Ohio railroad company — assent of the company necessary to the conditions prescribed by the act — subscription not applied for - - -   -   - 302,100 00

Rivanna navigation company — not applied for - 10,000 00

Road from Beverley to Clarksburg, do.   - 8,000 00

Road from Ice's Ferry to Pennsylvania line, do.   2,800 00

$1,322,900 00

The improvements of James river early occupied the attention of this state. This river, scarcely inferior to the Potomac in utility and in the varied beauties of its scenery, rises in the Alleghany mountains. After passing in its course through the great valley of Virginia, and collecting the waters of that fine region, it emerges from the Blue Mountains at the Irish Falls, and, descending by a series of falls and rapids into the low country, becomes navigable at Richmond for vessels of 120 tons burden. At City Point, about sixty miles below this, and about eighty from the mouth of the river, it becomes navigable for vessels of 600 tons. The tide of the Chesapeake reaches to Richmond.

A series of short canals have been constructed to avoid the falls above the latter town, and one of more considerable extent round the Irish Falls. These works may be considered as the commencement of a much greater undertaking, intended to connect the waters of James river with those of the Great Kanawha, which, when completed, will afford one of the shortest and most direct lines of communication between the Ohio river and the Atlantic.

The Kanawha, the principal river of the western district of Virginia, has its navigation likewise interrupted by falls; but below what are called the Great Falls, at a short distance above Charlestown, and about seventy miles from its outlet into the Ohio, it becomes navigable for vessels of considerable burden.

It is at this point that it is proposed to effect a communication with the James river. By means of the canals round the falls above Richmond, already described, and those in the Blue Ridge, the James river has been made navigable, when the waters are high, as far as Covington; but, to render the object in view at all times attainable, a canal is now being made the whole way from Richmond to Covington, of which 150 miles to Lynchburg are far advanced towards completion. A railroad will connect Covington with the Great Falls of the Kanawha. To aid in this enterprise, which is under the management of an incorporated association, called the James River and Kanawha Company, the legislature, in January, 1835, authorised

a subscription, on the part of the state, of two
millions of dollars, or two fifths of the sum which
was required for the purpose. The state subscribed
a further sum of one million of dollars, as a shareholder, by making over the old improvements on
the river, which were valued at that sum, to the
company. Individuals and public institutions in
the state subscribed the remaining two millions of
dollars to complete the capital of five millions.
With these funds, it appears that the completion
of the work is now placed beyond a doubt. When
finished it will prove of great service to the state.

It would be tedious to trace, in detail, the
various railroads which have been enumerated
above as constituting works in which this state is
interested : a few only of the principal ones need
be described.

The Winchester and Potomac railroad has been
already noticed, in the account of Maryland, as extending from Winchester to Harper's Ferry, where
it is connected with the Baltimore and Ohio railroad by a viaduct over the Potomac. Though
only thirty miles in length, this work is important
as forming a link in a great contemplated chain of
communication with the southern states of the
Union.

The Richmond and Potomac railroad, extending
from Potomac Creek through Fredericksburg to
Richmond, a distance of seventy miles, forms the
first link in another line now almost completed,
which crosses the state from the Potomac to the
Roanoke. This portion was opened for traffic in

1836, and has been attended with great success. The Richmond and Petersburg railroad, a continuation of this line towards the south, is now in progress: the remaining portion from Petersburg to Blakely, in North Carolina, which completes the line, is already finished; but this work, which is one of the best constructed and best managed railroads in the country, seems to have derived no assistance from the state funds.

The Portsmouth and Roanoke railroad forms a second junction of the Roanoke and Chesapeake. This road was undertaken in order to restore to Norfolk the portion of the trade of the river Roanoke which the railroad last described was likely to divert from that town to Petersburg.   The Chesapeake and Ohio canal, in which this state is interested, and the Baltimore and Ohio railroad company, to which it is conditionally pledged, have been described under the head of Maryland.

Prospects
of these
under-
takings.
The returns to which I have had access, of the receipts of such of these works as are finished, are not sufficiently numerous, nor of sufficiently recent a date, to afford much evidence of their present financial condition, or of their future prospects; but a prudent restriction laid down by the legislature, in reference to subscriptions entered into by the state in behalf of such works as the general assembly may agree to patronise, affords considerable assurance to the holders of the state's engagements that the sums obtained in loans are safely applied.

Internal
improve-
ment board.
In order to organise a system of internal im-

provement, an act was passed by the assembly, on
the 5th of February, 1816, by which the different shares owned by the state in various turnpike and canal companies, and in two of the state banks, together with the accruing dividends, were vested in a corporation styled the Board of Works. The restriction referred to prevents this body, which is the sole dispenser of the state's grants, from subscribing to any proposed work until the necessary surveys and estimates have been made ; and it can only, after three fifths of the capital required for its execution have been subscribed by individuals, subscribe for the remaining two fifths.

In 1830, the permanent or inalienable fund under the control of the board amounted to $1,418,961 11 ; and what was called the disposable fund, or that acquired from the income of the fund, and which could be sold or invested in the stocks of newly formed companies, to $681,630 00, making a total of $2,100,591 11, of which $475,000 00 was unproductive of revenue.

On the 30th of September, 1835, the amount of the permanent fund had increased to $1,723,661 11, and the disposable fund to $1,499,823 49, making together $3,223,484 60.

The permanent fund at that time consisted of

Bank stock, James river stock, and loans, all productive of revenue - - -	$1,385,900 00
Stock in internal improvement companies, productive of revenue - - -	39,150 00
Stock in ditto, unproductive of revenue -	298,611 11
	$1,723,661 11

The disposable fund was invested as follows : —

In bank stock and loans, productive of revenue	$180,200 00
In ditto, unproductive - - -	50,000 00
In internal improvement companies, productive	230,575 00
In ditto, unproductive - - -	484,113 04
In stocks in railroad companies, productive -	120,000 00
In ditto, unproductive - - -	358,800 00
Cash in the treasury - - - -	76,135 45
	$1,499,823 49

Thus, of the whole amount, $1,955,825 00 was productive.

Interest charged on this fund. The interest on the internal improvement debt, with the exception of that on the subscription to the Chesapeake and Ohio canal, which is paid out of the public treasury, is charged to this fund.

This charge in the last year consisted of

6 per cent. on	$2,171,500 00	$130,290 00
5½ per cent. on	25,300 00	1,391 50
And 5 per cent. on	997,300 00	49,865 00
	Making in all	$181,546 50*

Interest charged on the treasury. The interest on the remaining portion of the debt is charged on the treasury. This in the last year amounted to

* The productive portion of the fund, which in 1830 amounted to $1,625,591 11, yielded a revenue in that year of $121,836 75. The present income, although the fund is so much increased, is stated only at one hundred and fifteen thousand dollars; but I have no means of ascertaining if it has really fallen to this, or whether the latter sum is erroneously given; nor have I been able to ascertain the present state of the fund, or whether it is fully adequate to the above charge. If necessary, the general revenue of the state is pledged for the deficiency.

7 per cent. on the war debt of 1814	$319,000 00	$22,330 00	CHAP. VII.
6 per cent. on the old military debt	24,039 17	1,442 35	
5 per cent. on the subscription to the Chesapeake and Ohio canal	250,000 00	12,500 00	

Making in all $36,272 35

The general revenue of the state for the year 1838 was estimated at $507,462 97, and the expenses for the same period at $437,181 92, which will leave a surplus of income over expenditure of $70,281 05. *State of the treasury.*

I have seen no other late statement of the financial condition of the treasury. The revenue for the year 1834 was $403,335 00, of which $291,581 00 was derived from taxes on land, slaves, horses, and carriages, and $101,283 00 from licences, making, with the balance of $185,221 00 in the treasury, at the close of 1833, a total of $588,556 00. The expenditure during the same year, exclusive of payments from literary and other funds, amounted to $472,337 00. Some of the principal items were as follow : — *Receipts and expenditure in 1834.*

General assembly - - - -	$90,141 00
Officers' salaries - - - -	78,815 00
Judiciary - - - -	22,625 00
Criminal charges - - -	32,240 00
Revolutionary half-pay claims - -	12,167 00
Transported and executed slaves - -	14,412 00
Public guard - - - -	19,225 00
Penitentiaries - - - -	23,911 00
Lunatic asylum - - - - -	34,500 00
General appropriations - - -	24,417 00

Virginia, the first in size, and, next to New York, the most populous state of the Union, is greatly *Agricultural produce of Virginia.*

CHAP.   diversified in soil and climate.   Here begin the
VII.   sandy unhealthy tracts on the eastern coast; but
the valleys between the ridges of the Alleghany
mountains are fertile and healthy.   West of the
mountains the climate is temperate, and the land
naturally most productive; but it is badly cultivated, being usually worked till exhausted, and
then left to recover from its own resources.   Tobacco was long the principal production of Virginia,
having been cultivated to the exclusion even of the
necessary supply of Indian corn; but the amount
produced in the eastern division of the state has
fallen off considerably on account of the exhaustion
of the soil, although its cultivation has been much
extended beyond the Blue Ridge.   Wheat in the
eastern part of the state has been substituted in its
room as an article of produce, and now forms one of
the chief exports of the state, Richmond being one
of the greatest flour markets of the country.   Every
portion of this state is traversed by fine rivers and
streams, affording great facilities for the transport
of its agricultural produce.

Commerce.   The trade of Virginia has greatly fallen off.
Before the revolutionary war, the imports and exports of this state were more than four times as
great as those of New York, and exceeded those
of all the New England states together.   By the
tables in the appendix it will be seen that it now
ranks very low in the scale of commercial enterprise.*

* In 1769 the imports of the colonies were as follow: —
Of Virginia   -   -   -   -   - £851,140

There seems no reason why Virginia should not
re-assume a higher position ; and the exertions now
making to improve its communication with the
Ohio may, probably, lead to this result. Few towns
situated so far from the sea possess greater commercial advantages than Richmond even now com-
mands: situated within reach of the tide of the
Chesapeake, on a river navigable for boats for 220
miles above the city, with fertile regions in the
background abounding in productions of the most
valuable description, there seems no reason why it
should not maintain a considerable commerce. *

Though agriculture has always been the chief
occupation of the inhabitants of this state, the
manufactures of Virginia are by no means inconsiderable in value or extent. The chief manufacturing establishments are at Wheeling. This town,
situated on the left bank of the Ohio, at the head
of the steam-boat navigation during the season of
low water, holds the second place in the state in

Of the New England states	-	-	- £561,000
Of South Carolina	-	-	- 555,000
Of Pennsylvania	-	-	- 400,000
Of New York	-	-	- 189,000

* The baneful tendency of slavery has no doubt contributed
to keep Virginia back ; but it must be recollected that it was
under the same circumstances in this respect that it rose to the
eminence it once enjoyed, and too much importance must not be
attached to this cause. The greater stimulus given to the cultivation of wheat, which may be cultivated by free labour, may,
perhaps, tend to gradually lessen this moral taint, of which traces
enough may be found, without seeking to aggravate its conse-
sequences.

CHAP.
VII.

respect of its population.   Like Pittsburg it owes its prosperity to the inexhaustible beds of coal that surround it, and to the easy channel of transmission which the Ohio affords for its manufactures.   The population of Wheeling in 1820 was 1567, and in 1836 it had reached 10,000 — in the latter year it contained 136 manufacturing establishments, producing, annually, goods to the value of two millions of dollars.   The trade of Wheeling is also extensive : in 1836 the number of the arrivals and departures of steam-boats was 1602.   It is, besides, the great thoroughfare from Baltimore to the Western states by the national road, on which eight daily stages are employed in the transport of passengers.

Realised
wealth.

The aggregate valuation of the real property of the state, which in 1818 was $206,893,978 00, is now estimated at 300 millions of dollars.   There is no mode of ascertaining the amount of personal property.

SOUTH CAROLINA.

Amount of
debt and
liabilities.

THE debt and engagements of this state consist of

The debt of the revolutionary war - -	$193,770 12
Loans for the construction of canals - -	1,550,000 00
Loan for rebuilding the city of Charleston -	2,000,000 00
Loan to the Louisville, Cincinnati, and Charleston railroad company - - -	2,000,000 00
Due to an individual creditor - - -	10,000 00

Making together $5,753,770 12

It does not appear from any documents I have seen in what form the stock exists, which has been issued for the construction of canals. The loan for rebuilding the city of Charleston, and that to the Louisville and Charleston railroad company, are in bonds payable to the bearer. The bonds of the latter are issued in the name of the company, the liability of the state, in this case, consisting in its having affixed its guarantee.

CHAP.
VII.

Form of
security
and mode
of transfer.

The principal of the canal stock is payable in Charleston : $800,000 00 of the amount is redeemable in 1840; the period when the remainder is liable to be paid off does not appear.

Where and
when re-
deemable.

The bonds constituting the two several sums of two millions of dollars are payable in London at the exchange of 4s. 6d. per dollar.

One half of the loan for rebuilding the city of Charleston is redeemable on the 1st July, 1858, and the remaining half on the 1st July, 1868. The loan for the Louisville and Charleston railroad is redeemable in 1860.

The interest on the several loans is payable at the respective places where the capital is redeemable : on $800,000 00 of the canal debt at six per cent., on the remainder of the debt at five per cent. : in the cases where the bonds are redeemable in London, at the exchange of 4s. 6d., the interest is payable at the same rate.

Rate of
Interest,
and when
and where
payable.

The loans which constitute the bulk of the debt have been contracted under such different circumstances, and, irrespectively of the credit of the state, rest upon such different securities, that it will

Objects of
loans.

Canal
loans.

be advisable to consider, in the case of each separately, the nature of the security taken by the state,
and that collaterally afforded to the public creditor.

The sums expended by this state in the construction of canals do not appear to make an
adequate return, the tolls upon the works in no
case paying the interest on the loans contracted
on their account. In many instances they do not
pay even the current expenses.

The chief work of this nature undertaken by the
state is the Santee canal, to connect the harbour of
Charleston with the Santee. This canal was completed in 1802, at the cost of $650,667 00. By
means of it, and of improvements which have
been made in the navigation of the Santee and
Congaree rivers, a water communication has been
established between Charleston and Columbia, the
seat of government in South Carolina.

Sinking
fund.

The state, which is the exclusive proprietor of
the bank of the state of South Carolina, has
pledged the capital of that institution, amounting
to $1,156,318 48, together with the accruing profits
as a security for the canal loans : by this means the
state stockholders are amply protected, notwithstanding the failure of the canals to produce a
revenue; for the accumulations of the annual profits
of the bank amounted on the 1st of October, 1836,
to $461,360 25, independently of the profits of that
year, which allowed $135,000 00 to be added to the
sinking fund. The sum now accumulated is more
than sufficient to redeem the sum of $800,000 00,
bearing interest at 6 per cent., which will be in

course of payment in 1840; and the institution continues to be prosperously conducted: although the president, in his report at the close of 1836, states, that the profits of that year were unusually great, and such as cannot be calculated upon for the future.*

CHAP. VII.

The loan for two millions of dollars for rebuilding the city of Charleston was contracted after the fire, which destroyed a large part of that town in April, 1838. †

Loan for rebuilding Charleston.

The money obtained was deposited in the bank of the state of South Carolina, as so much capital to be employed by the bank in accomplishing the object of the loan.

A description of the mode in which the money was directed to be advanced will best describe the nature of the security taken by the state. The president and directors of the bank were directed to advance, to the owners of lots on which the houses

Nature of security taken.

* Besides the sum of $135,000 00 added to " the sinking fund for the redemption of the 5 and 6 per cent. stock, and for the payment of the interest thereon," $20,638 73 was placed to the credit of a contingent account to meet sundry payments, and a sum carried to the account of profit and loss, being for bad debts of an old date.

In the amount of notes issued by this bank, a return is made of notes of a *less denomination than one dollar* of the aggregate value of $83,725 00 : most of the banks in the United States are prohibited from issuing notes of so small a denomination.

† This destructive fire broke out on the evening of the 27th of April, and raged with great fury till noon on the following day, laying waste 145 acres of the most populous part of the city. The amount of property destroyed was estimated at from three to four millions of dollars, of which about one half was insured.

CHAP.
VII.

were destroyed by fire, one half, in the first instance, of the assessed value of these lots *unimproved*, taking a mortgage on the premises, with bonds engaging that the sum advanced should be repaid in ten annual instalments, the first in three years from the date of the bonds : on proof of the faithful application of this first advance in the construction of *incombustible* buildings (which the law requires in future), the bank is allowed to advance an equal sum on the same conditions, and, finally, another equal sum, if necessary, upon proof of the faithful application of the two first — the parties having the premises insured, and depositing the policy with the bank for its security.

Sinking
fund.

The president and directors of the bank are required to keep a separate account of the accumulating profits which shall arise from the use of the two millions in this manner, and these are solemnly pledged and set apart by the law for the punctual payment of the interest and principal of the loan ; and when the profits on the original capital of the bank are released from the pledge they are now under to the stockholder of the prior loan, by effecting the discharge of the debt for canal purposes, they are, by " the act for rebuilding the city of Charleston," solemnly pledged and set apart for the payment of the interest on this loan, and its final redemption. The bank, by the endorsement of the bonds, gives also the guarantee of that establishment, and the city of Charleston by an ordinance of its council is bound to indemnify the state against any losses it may sustain by the non-fulfilment of their engagements by those who have received advances for rebuilding.

The engagement of the state to the extent of two millions of dollars to the Louisville, Cincinnati, and Charleston railroad company consists in its having affixed its guarantee to bonds to that amount issued by the company in their own name. This engagement will not be converted into an actual debt, unless the company fail in the punctual payment of the interest and principal.

The work contemplated by this company is the establishment of a railroad communication between the city of Charleston and the Ohio. The distance between Charleston and Cincinnati, in a straight line, is about five hundred miles. Several routes have been surveyed, by which the length of the railroad will be about six hundred; but no line seems to have been definitively fixed upon. A railroad called the South Carolina railroad already exists between Charleston and Hamburg, a town situated on the Savannah, opposite to Augusta, in Georgia: this railroad has been purchased by the company, and will be made use of as far as Branchville or Aikin. One plan is to carry the projected road from the former town to Columbia, the seat of government in South Carolina, and then up the valley of the Broad river into the state of North Carolina. After surmounting the Blue Ridge by inclined planes with stationary engines, the road would by this plan be carried down the valley of the French Broad river to Knoxville, in Tennessee, and thence through Cumberland Gap to Lexington, in Kentucky: from the latter city separate roads would proceed to Louisville, Cincinnati, and Maysville. The distance from Charleston to Cincinnati by this route would be 607 miles. If it should be thought advisable to take advantage of the whole extent of the South Carolina railroad, other lines, which are now in existence or under construction in Georgia, between Augusta and the Tennessee line at Rossville might be made available as far as the latter point; in which case the road would be carried on to the Ohio through Tennessee and Kentucky by a line further to the west than that described in the first route.

Notwithstanding some advantages which the latter route holds out, the one first described appears to be that contemplated by the company: as a charter has been obtained from the state of North Carolina, no part of the territory of which would be passed through if the more western line were adopted.

Charters obtained from different states.
The charters which have been obtained from Tennessee and South Carolina, as well as from North Carolina, confer very important privileges on this company, and among others, that of establishing a bank in connection with the railroad, which is likely to contribute essentially to the success of the work, as it is hoped that, by bringing successive portions of the road into use, the profits of the road and the bank together will be sufficient to afford from the beginning a dividend to the stockholders on the amount of their subscriptions. On the 1st of January, 1837,

the number of shares subscribed for was 43,332, representing a capital of $4,333,200 00 ; the charter contemplates the gradual extension of the capital with the progress of the road to the extent of twelve millions. The state of Kentucky has refused to concur in the charter of the company, or to allow it to exercise the privilege of banking within its jurisdiction, but it has accorded a right of way through its territory to the railroad.

The state of Carolina, in order to aid in this enterprise, authorised the raising of the loan referred to.

CHAP. VII.

Terms of loan from the state.

By the terms of the act conferring this authority, the comptroller of the state was allowed to pledge the faith of the state, as soon as half a million had been paid on the stock of the company, to the extent of one million of dollars, and on half a million more being paid on the company's stock, he was authorised to pledge it for a second million. As by the terms of this act the company, however, would be prevented from availing itself of any portion of the second million of the loan till the whole of the second half million of capital had been paid up, while its interests required that instalments should be received from time to time as funds might be required to carry on its operations, it was subsequently enacted that the comptroller should be allowed to affix the guarantee of the state to the company's bonds, when required to do so, provided a proportionate amount on the stock had been paid up. Under these conditions, about a million and a half dollars of the bonds of

the company, bearing the comptroller's endorsement, have already been issued.

The success of the South Carolina railroad holds
out a fair prospect for that of the greater work.
By affording the most northern outlet for the produce of the cotton-growing states, much of that of
Georgia, instead of being carried by the Chattahoochee to the ports in Florida or by the Savannah
to the town of that name, is already taken in preference by this railroad to Charleston.

This work, which was commenced in 1830,
was finished in September, 1833. For the six
months ending in October, 1834, the company
received for the carriage of passengers and cotton on the road $83,445 42; and by a statement
made on the 11th January, 1836, the receipts from
these sources, for the six months ending in December, 1835, had increased to $137,418 95, being as
follows : —

From 15,959 passengers - - - -	$53,819 66
For 21,231 bales of cotton - - -	83,599 29

The total income of the railroad for those six
months amounted to

	$141,630 47
While the expenses amounted to - -	93,838 47
Leaving for net income	$47,792 00

The South Carolina railroad, although thus
successful, had to contend with great disadvantages ; it was not only the first railroad attempted
in the southern states, but was, at the time it was
completed, the longest railroad that had been con-

structed in any part of the world; the distance CHAP. VII.
from Charleston to Hamburg being one hundred
and thirty-five miles and a quarter; so that the
projectors could derive little benefit from the experience of other works of a similar nature — the
whole work, too, which is a singular circumstance,
was executed by the black population. In addition to these drawbacks, the limited means of
the company caused the work to be executed in a
very imperfect manner. It is constructed of
wood with iron tracks: the superstructure is
generally supported on piles, which, in some of the
marshes which the road crosses, have been driven
to a great depth; in other parts these piles, being
left a considerable height above the ground, form
a substitute for embankments, which gives the
work in such places the appearance of a con-
tinuous bridge. When the limited means of the
original company have allowed it, embankments
have gradually been raised to afford a greater degree
of stability, but this even now has been only partially effected. The original cost of the road was
$904,500 00; but the filling up the spaces between
the piles, and other expenses, increased the cost,
up to the 31st October, 1834, to $1,336,615 09.
The present company have almost reconstructed
the whole work, two thirds of the purchase money
which has been paid, together with the expenses
which have already been incurred, having amounted to nearly two millions of dollars.

No sinking fund is appropriated by any act of the Sinking fund.
legislature for the redemption of the bonds of the

company, but it is intended to set apart 2 per cent. on the amount of the capital, out of the joint profits of the bank and the railroad, for this purpose. The capital of the company affords a guarantee for the security of the bonds, independently of the pledge of the credit and general resources of the state.

Financial condition of the treasury.

The annual expenses of this state seem to be kept within its income ; but I have been able to obtain no particulars respecting the details of the expenditure, or the sources from whence the revenue of the state is derived. The expenditure in 1833 amounted to $114,265 16.

Produce and commerce of the state.

The inhabitants of the interior of South Carolina are almost exclusively devoted to agricultural pursuits, and large quantities of cotton and rice are raised by their labour: the culture of the latter valuable and nutritious vegetable was introduced into South Carolina about the year 1694, and has contributed much to the prosperity of the state. The cultivation is carried on almost entirely by slaves, who in this state outnumber the white population.*

Although South Carolina, like Virginia, has fallen from the rank it once held as a commercial state, it has not only maintained its place better than the latter, but its imports and exports of late years have fallen off less than that of some

* In the low regions, where rice is chiefly grown, the proportion is as high sometimes as four or five to one : in the hilly regions, the whites are more numerous than the blacks ; and in the western districts, there are nearly three whites to one black.

of the northern states. The commerce of South Carolina is almost wholly centred in Charleston. This city, the largest in the United States, be- tween the Potomac and New Orleans, is advan- tageously situated about six miles from the sea, at the confluence of two rivers, which afford broad and deep basins on both sides of the town ; the harbour, however, is exposed to storms, which detract from its otherwise advantageous position. The shipping belonging to the state is very in- considerable. The property in this state is valued at $200,000,000 00.

CHAP.
VII.

GEORGIA.

THE state of Georgia, in the last session of the legislature, authorised a loan of one million and a half of dollars to complete the Western and Atlan- tic railroad. Under this authority bonds have been issued for about one third of the amount, which constitute the only existing debt of the state.

Amount of debt.

The bonds are expressed in sterling money, being for sums of 500l. each. The amount so issued is 100,000l. The bonds are made payable to the bearer, and are redeemable in London on the 1st day of September, 1868.

Form of security, where and when re- deemable.

Interest at the rate of five per cent. per annum is payable half-yearly in London on the 1st of March, and 1st of September.

Interest when and where pay- able.

The Western and Atlantic railroad, which will

Object of loan.

extend from Decatur across the Chattahoochee to the Tennessee river, near Rossville, will form a continuation of a line now being constructed, by an incorporated company, from Augusta to Decatur. When both are completed, an uninterrupted line of communication will be formed by means of these and the South Carolina railroad, between the Tennessee line and Charleston. The legislature of Tennessee has passed an act authorising its continuation through the territory of that state.

The length of the Western and Atlantic railroad from its southern termination to the Tennessee river will be one hundred and thirty-four miles; and its cost, according to estimates furnished to the legislature, about $2,580,000 00. The governor of the state, in his message of the 6th of November, 1838, states that the progress already made is satisfactory, and that one hundred miles are likely to be completed by the end of 1839.

Advantage
to the state,
and pros-
pects of the
work.

Great advantages may accrue to Georgia from this work, by its directing to its sea-ports the produce of the interior of the state, which, for want of such facilities as will be afforded by these railroads, has hitherto been carried by the rivers which flow into the Gulf of Mexico to the ports of Florida and Alabama; for as the risk and delay of transmitting goods round the peninsula of Florida will be entirely avoided by using this railroad, it is on this account likely, in most instances, to be preferred. As the Alleghany Mountains terminate in the northern part of Georgia, the difficulties which they and the Blue Ridge offer to the transport of the productions of the Western states to the northern Atlantic ports here disappear; a portion of the produce of Tennessee and Kentucky, or even of the southern parts of Indiana or Illinois, may, not improbably, therefore, seek an outlet also through this state.

Independently, however, of the favourable prospect which these circumstances hold out for the work undertaken by the state, an ample guarantee has been provided for the payment of the principal and interest of the state's loan, in the pledge which the legislature has made to the bondholder of the interest it possesses in different banks in the state.

The Central Bank of Georgia is the exclusive property of the state *; and the state in this and other banks holds altogether stock amounting to between three and four millions of dollars; the whole of which, with the exception of the dividends on a portion originally set apart for purposes of education, is pledged for the payment of the loan.

I have no details of the finances of this state, excepting for the year 1834: the expenditure for that year was $238,889 31, and the receipts, $245,505 06; but in the latter there is included

* In the reports of the banks of this state, the capital of the Central bank of Georgia was stated, on the 1st of January, 1837, at $2,410,950 00, but in a report subsequent to the suspension of specie payments it is stated at only $1,051,122 00 — at an intermediate period it is stated at $2,218,598 04 — the reason of the diminution is not apparent.

a loan of $100,798 07, but for which there would have been a large deficiency. As this loan has been since paid off, the general financial condition of the treasury must be more favourable than the solitary instance afforded by this year would indicate.

Produce and commerce of the state.
This state, the last settled of the British American colonies which constituted the thirteen original states of the Union, is, in point of extent as compared with the others, inferior only to Virginia; and, in the present political division of the territory, is surpassed only by that state and by Missouri.

The coast of Georgia is lined by a succession of low islands, divided from each other and from the mainland by wide channels or sounds, which are generally navigable, and afford a safe inland navigation along the shore. It is on these, and the neighbouring mainland, that the sea-island or long-staple cotton, so highly prized for the fineness of its fibre, is principally grown. Since the invention of Mr. Whitney's machine for clearing the upland cotton from its seed, the attention of the inhabitants of this state has been almost exclusively turned to the culture of the latter description of cotton, which, although it has never rivalled the sea-island cotton in quality, has greatly surpassed it in the quantity produced. Georgia ranks the third among the cotton-growing states, and in 1834 produced about one sixth of the whole quantity grown in the United States. The city of Savannah, whence a large portion of it is exported, is

advantageously situated for commerce, being accessible to large vessels from the sea, and com-
municating with the interior by the noble river of
the same name, on which it stands, which is navigable for steam-boats for a distance of 240 miles
above the city. Although the railroad from Augusta to Charleston, and the security of the inland
passage which it affords from the Savannah to that
city, have, of late, tended to divert much of the
trade thither, yet the city of Savannah, owing to
these advantages, is likely to maintain its place as
one of the most flourishing towns in the southern
states.

KENTUCKY.

THE debt of this state consists of bonds which
have been issued for the following purposes : —

As the state's subscription to the capital of the
   bank of Kentucky   -   -   -   - $1,000,000 00
As the state's subscription to the capital of the
   Northern bank of Kentucky   -   - 1,000,000 00
For internal improvements   -   -   - 2,635,000 00

              Making together $4,635,000 00

A further issue of bonds has been authorised to
provide the funds which will be required to complete the works now in progress, which will increase
the portion of the debt raised to carry on public
improvements, to $5,369,000 00, and the whole
debt to $7,369,000 00.*

* The governor, by an act passed in 1838, is authorised to
borrow, at a rate of interest not exceeding 6 per cent., any sum

Form of
security,
when and
where re-
deemable.

The bonds of this state are in all cases made payable to the bearer. Those issued as the state's subscription to the capital of the two banks are redeemable in New York in 1862.

The following table shows the period at which those issued for internal improvements are redeemable ; viz. —

$ 100,000 00	on the 25th May, 1865,	or any time after	20 years.
100,000 00	1st Aug., 1865,	ditto	25 years.
100,000 00	25th April, 1871,	ditto	30 years.
50,000 00	1st June, 1871,	ditto	30 years.
165,000 00	1st April, 1872,	ditto	35 years.
500,000 00	15th May, 1872,	ditto	35 years.
170,000 00	1st July, 1872,	ditto	35 years.
200,000 00	1st Oct., 1872,	ditto	35 years.
1,250,000 00	1st Monday in July, 1868.		

$ 2,635,000 00

The internal improvement bonds are likewise redeemable in New York. By an arrangement of the American Life Insurance and Trust Company, which became the purchaser of those redeemable in 1868, the principal of such bonds as are registered for that purpose is made payable in London, 90 days after they become due in America, at the exchange of 4s. 6d. per dollar, but the engagement of the state extends only to the payment at New York.

Rates of
interest,
and when
and where
payable.

The whole of the debt bears interest at the rate of five per cent., with the exception of $1,250,000 00, falling due in 1868, (being the

within the capacity of the sinking fund to pay the interest and ultimately to redeem the capital.

bonds bought by the American Life Insurance and Trust Company,) which bear interest at six per cent.

The interest on the portion of the debt raised for the state's subscription to the banks is paid by each establishment respectively out of the half-yearly profits which accrue on the state's share of the capital ; the excess of profit only over the amount of interest being paid into the treasury. The interest on the first and fourth of the loans issued for public improvements, as they stand in the foregoing table, is payable at Louisville, on the third at Lexington, and on the remainder, including the six per cents., at New York. The interest in all cases is payable half-yearly : on the five per cent. stock on the 1st of January and 1st of July, and on the six per cent. stock on the first Mondays in those months. By the arrangement of the American Life Insurance and Trust Company of New York, before referred to, the dividends on such bonds as are registered for payment in London are made payable there also, two months after they become due in America, at the rate of 6*l*. 3*s*. 0*d*. sterling for each coupon of thirty dollars.

The portion of the surplus revenue received by the state of Kentucky under the distribution act of Congress has materially lessened the immediate pressure of the debt upon the state treasury. The sum to which this state was entitled amounted to $1,611,976 52 ; but as three instalments only were paid, the sum actually received was $1,433,754 39.

By an act of the state of the 23d February, 1837, this money was ordered to be profitably invested : the profits arising out of one million of dollars were set apart to establish and maintain a system of common schools within the state, and those arising from the residue to form a sinking fund for the payment of the interest and for the redemption of the principal of the loans contracted by the state for purposes of internal improvement.

In order to effect a profitable investment of the capital, it was proposed that the state should apply $500,000 00, by subscribing for 5000 shares in the bank of Louisville, which were reserved for it under the charter of that institution; that five eighths of the residue should be applied to increase the state's share in the stock of the bank of Kentucky, and three eighths to add to its share in that of the Northern Bank. The act authorising these subscriptions required that the banks should agree to certain amendments being made in their charters ; but the bank of Louisville and the Northern Bank having refused to agree to the proposed terms, the bank of Kentucky alone received its proportion, viz. $583,598 37, which was added accordingly to the state's share in its capital.

The sums which would have passed to the non-consenting banks were paid to the commissioners of the sinking fund, who purchased with the amount $870,000 00 of the bonds issued for internal improvements, of which they are directed to hold $850,000 00 for the benefit of such common schools as should hereafter be established ; the remainder, viz. $20,000 00, they were to hold on account of the sinking fund itself.   Under this arrangement these sums constitute at present a debt due by the state to itself; for until a system of common schools is organised, which is not yet the case, no necessity will exist for the payment of the half-yearly interest on the first sum, and none will, at any time, be payable on the latter.

The sum, therefore, on which an interest of five per cent. is really paid by the state, is only $515,000 00, the annual charge being $25,750 00.

The greater part of the proceeds of the six per cent. loan not being immediately required, the amount has been deposited in the three banks of the state, which have agreed to pay interest at the rate of six per cent. on the money, so long as it shall remain in deposit with them : by this means, the rate of interest received being the same as that paid on the bonds, the amount really chargeable in the present year will be only $937,500 00 ; the interest on which being $56,250 00, the total charge for interest payable in this year will be $82,000 00.

In considering the application of the sums raised by this state, the portion which has been applied to banking purposes will be first adverted to.   The two banks which have benefited by the state's subscription to their stock are those which have been already alluded to, viz. the bank of Kentucky and the Northern bank of Kentucky.*

* The state has still authority to issue bonds, to subscribe, if it thinks fit, for the stock reserved for it in the bank of Louis-

Bank of
Kentucky.

The first of these, which is established at Louisville, was incorporated in 1834, and commenced business in April, 1835. The capital consisted originally of three millions of dollars, subscribed by individuals, and of one million by the state ; the state reserving the right to subscribe a second million, in order, ultimately, to make up the capital of the bank to five millions. It was in part of the state's subscription to this fifth million that the portion of the sum received under the distribution act of Congress was allotted to this bank, amounting, as we have seen, to $583,598 37. It has now been made imperative on the commissioners of the sinking fund, (to whom the excess of the dividends on the state's share beyond what is required to pay the interest on the bonds of the first million is paid over,) to invest this excess in the same way. From these several sources, the capital, on the 31st day of December last, amounted to $4,679,404 00.

Northern
bank of
Kentucky.

The Northern bank of Kentucky, which is established at Lexington, was incorporated in 1835, with a capital of three millions of dollars, of which two millions were subscribed by individuals, and one million by the state : — $2,895,685 00 had been paid up on the 31st December last.

The resources and liabilities of these banks on that day, as well as their respective conditions be-

ville ; but no notice has been taken of this in the enumeration of the state's engagements, as the state seems to have no intention of exercising the privilege.

fore and after the suspension of specie payments, will be seen in the Appendix.*

In comparing the statements of the condition of these banks, before and after the suspension, a great reduction in the amount of their circulation will be seen to have taken place in the interval. In the case of the Northern bank, this is clearly referable to the diminished amount of its loans and discounts, and of its investments in stock; but in the case of the bank of Kentucky the amounts of loans and other investments at the latter period are together greater than at the former. The reduction of the circulation in the case of this bank appears to have proceeded from its increase of capital, arising out of its acceptance of the provisions of the act to invest, in profitable stocks, the portion of the surplus revenue deposited with the state; the additional capital having been chiefly paid in its own notes, necessarily producing this result.

The great contraction of the circulation and business of the Northern bank seems to have been forced upon it by the withdrawal of deposits, while the bank of Kentucky was enabled to sustain its business, notwithstanding its diminished circulation, from an increase in the amount of its deposits, as well as by its augmented capital. The great pressure on the Northern bank was owing to the large amount which it held of the public deposits of the United States being at this time called for. †

* See Appendix, letter A A 1, &c.

† In examining the reports of these and other banks, regard must be had to the time of year at which the reports are made;

A great variety of documents have been published by a committee, appointed by the senate and house of representatives of Kentucky to investigate into the state of the banks, from which much useful information may be obtained; amongst other things, a detailed statement is given of the condition of each bank on the last day of each month, from the 1st of January to the 30th November, 1837, inclusive, at which latter date the investigation was closed.   At that time the bank of Kentucky, with a paid up capital of $4,597,410 76, had only $2,091,805 00 of notes in circulation, which is under 46 per cent. on the capital stock.   It had $754,484 55 in specie, which makes one dollar in specie to two dollars and 64 hundredths of notes in circulation.   Other banks were indebted to it in a greater sum than it was indebted to other banks; and its other liabilities, payable on demand, amounted only to $867,414 00.   It had

as this, in the case under consideration, will partly account for the diminished circulation of the banks in Kentucky. The produce of the Southern states being usually sent to market in the latter part of the year, the greatest advances are made by the banks at that time, they furnishing money to the trader on bills payable at the places to which the produce is sent: the returns take place in the early part of the year, when the money borrowed is repaid, and the business and circulation of the bank are reduced. The regular and fixed business of the banks in the Southern states may therefore be expected to increase in the autumn, and to be reduced in the spring. It will be necessary to bear this circumstance in mind, in forming a judgment respecting the situation of the several banks in this and other states, from the statements which will be given in the Appendix of the resources and liabilities of each at different times.

$1,225,853 66 of bills of exchange having less than
four months to run, and available within that time
to meet its circulation and deposits at call. It had
$1,420,100 00 of state and city bonds bearing in-
terest which could be converted into money in
case of emergency, and $4,844,331 40 of loans and
notes under discount, part of which could also be
made available if necessary. The condition of the
Northern bank was still better. It had a capital
paid in of $2,591,260 00, and $1,223,515 00 of
notes in circulation; in which respect it is nearly
in the same condition as the bank of Kentucky,
but it had $757,518 76 in specie, which is one
dollar in specie to one dollar and 61 hundredths
of notes in circulation. The amount due from
other banks was greater, also, in its case than the
amount it was indebted to other banks; and its
other liabilities, payable on demand, amounted only
to $534,001 37: it had $527,936 06 of bills falling
due within four months; $756,000 00 in state
bonds, and $2,410,614 65 in notes discounted.

The situation of the banks at the last return
was not so favourable; but the circulation when
compared with the capital stock paid in, and the
amount of specie in their vaults compared with
the notes in circulation, were still within what may
be deemed a safe and proper proportion. At the
former period, the committee seems to have fully
verified the validity of the resources set down, and
states, what is a creditable instance of good management, that the loans were distributed among a
large number of customers.

CHAP.
VII.

On 31st
Dec. 1838.

CHAP.
VII.

Rates of
dividends
declared.

The rates of dividend which have been paid by the banks since they commenced business are as follows : —

By the bank of Kentucky.		By the Northern bank.
On the 18th Jan., 1836	at 3½ per cent.	
On the 1st July, 1836	at 4 per cent.	at 4 per cent.
On the 1st Jan., 1837	at 4 per cent.	at 5 per cent.
On the 1st July, 1837	at 3½ per cent.	at 4 per cent.
On the 1st Jan., 1838 *	at 4 per cent.	at 4 per cent.

Contingent
fund.

Before any dividend is paid a contingent fund is required by the charters to be set aside, at the rate of twenty thousand dollars on each million of capital paid in. This contingent fund, together with the large capitals subscribed and paid up by individuals, afford to that extent an additional guarantee to the holders of the bonds which have been issued by the state on their account.

The charters of these banks contain regulations framed with a view to a judicious management of their affairs, and the institutions seem fully to have

* A bill was passed by this state to relieve the banks from the disabilities incurred by their suspension of specie payments ; removing, consequently, the impediment which their charter presented to the payment of dividends while the suspension existed. The facility of obtaining a relaxation of judicious rules is one of the evils of the interests of the state being too closely identified with those of its banking institutions. Among the reasons officially assigned for this dereliction from the stipulations of the charter, it is said that the state would otherwise have had no funds to pay the half-yearly interest on the state bonds issued for the bank, and that it required the tax and excess of dividends to pay the interest on the money borrowed for internal improvements.

answered the ends proposed by the legislature in their establishment.*

The system of internal improvements which has been adopted in this state consists in the construction of turnpike roads and railroads, and in improvements in the navigation of the principal rivers. The improvements on the rivers have been exclusively undertaken by the state; but the railroads and the turnpike roads, with the exception of four of inconsiderable extent, have been carried on in conjunction with incorporated companies.

Of these several descriptions of improvement, those which are directed to ameliorating the river navigation are likely perhaps to conduce more than the others to the prosperity of the state, although the largest expenditure has taken place in the construction of turnpike roads.

These roads are seventeen in number, besides the four alluded to in which the state is the sole proprietor: — in some of these the state is interested to the extent of one half of the sum embarked in them, and in others to the extent of two thirds.

These roads embrace a total length of $1083\frac{4}{100}$ miles, of which, on the 10th of October last,

	Miles.
The length finished was - - -	- 446·62
The length under contract and in progress	- 452·11
The length not yet under contract -	- 184·31
Total length as above	1083·04

* Among other salutary restrictions imposed by their charters, these banks are prevented from discounting a note after it falls due, although it remains unpaid ; they cannot therefore take the

The amount paid by the state on these up to the
   10th of October last was   -   - $1,444,091 00
The amount paid by individuals   -   - 1,207,612 00

                Making the total amount paid 2,651,703 00
The estimated amount which would be required
   to finish the part under contract was   - 1,207,957 27
And the amount required to finish the part not
   yet contracted for   -   -   - 1,437,227 32

     Making the probable cost when finished $5,296,887 59

The amount of tolls collected during the year
1838 was $81,236 00, although this appears not to
have been a full return : — the amount expended
for repairs during the year was $58,642 01.

Elaborate accounts of each road are given in the
reports of the Board of Internal Improvement;
but they may be described generally as branching
from Louisville and Lexington ; the two most
considerable ones extending from the former town
to the Tennessee line, which they reach, one at
Franklin, the other at Scottsville : — these two
lines are each upwards of 140 miles in length.

Railroads   The chief railroad in which the state is interested
is the Lexington and Ohio railroad, which is to
extend from Lexington to Portland on the Ohio.
The portion of this work from Lexington to Frankfort (twenty-eight miles) cost $544,798 00 : it has
been in successful operation for some years. The
part between Louisville and Portland, at the other
extremity of the line (three miles in length), is also
now open. A considerable portion of the interme-

notes of other banks otherwise than for cash ; the opposite practice has prevailed, and led to much abuse in other states.

diate part, between Louisville and Frankfort, a distance of sixty-six miles, is nearly completed. The cost of these sixty-six miles will be about one million of dollars. The state has subscribed to this work $200,000 00, and has in addition guaranteed the payment of the interest on the bonds of the company to the extent of $150,000 00.

The great Cincinnati and Charleston railroad will pass through this state; but no appropriation of the public funds has been made by the legislature to this work.

The rivers which have been the object of improvement by the state are, —

1. The Kentucky river.
2. The Licking river.
3. The Green and Barren rivers.
4. The Cumberland river, and some of minor importance.

The object of the state has been to render these rivers navigable by means of locks and dams. The following tabular statement, where the numbers refer to the above works, will show the sums which have been expended by the state on each up to the 10th of October, 1838, as well as the sum which it is estimated will be required to complete the work: —

	Miles now under contract.	Amount paid to 10th Oct., 1838.	Amount required to finish the part under contract.	Estimated amount when finished.
1.	92	$213,249 69	488,155 31	701,405 00
2.	51	21,725 50	469,774 50	491,500 00
3.	175	431,874 15	48,125 85	480,000 00
4.		4,500 00	26,500 00	31,000 00
		$671,349 34	1,032,555 66	1,703,905 00

The Kentucky is the principal river of the state :
it is formed by the junction of the north, south,
and middle forks, 257 miles before it falls into the
Ohio. The whole of the distance up to the point
where these streams unite, called thence the Three
Forks, will be rendered navigable for steam boats
of 150 tons burden. Five locks and dams are
being constructed, the average cost of which will
exceed a hundred thousand dollars; and there
being an abundance of the finest stone and timber
on the banks, this will be one of the most splendid
works of the kind in the Union.

In the Licking river navigation, it is designed to
extend the improvement from the mouth of the
river, which falls into the Ohio at a point just
opposite to Cincinnati, to West Liberty, a distance
of 231 miles.

The Green river takes a westerly course through
the state, and, after receiving the waters of the
Big Barren, flows with a deep and full stream into
the Ohio, into which it empties itself 180 miles
below Louisville. The improvements which commence at its junction with the Big Barren extend
up both the main and the tributary stream. The
Barren river branch of the improvement will extend to Bowling Green, 180 miles from the Ohio:
on the main stream the improvements will extend
to a point 275 miles from the Ohio, almost in the
centre of the state.

The improvements on the Cumberland river are
of a less important character, a small portion only
of the course of this river being included in Ken-

tucky, although it has both its source and its mouth within the state.

These improvements are well calculated to benefit the general interests of the state : the rivers which are the subject of them all run into the Ohio, and empty themselves into it at points far distant from each other. The Green river flowing from the centre of the state passes through a rich agricultural country well supplied with coal, and has thirteen counties bordering on it and its tributaries, containing more than 100,000 inhabitants. The Licking, the Kentucky, and the Cumberland have their sources beyond the agricultural district, in the heart of the iron and salt regions. Seven counties, containing a population of 70,000, border on the Licking, while the Kentucky waters in its course fifteen counties, with a population of not less than 170,000 : the noble river which receives these streams bounds the state for upwards of eight hundred miles.

The counties thus thickly peopled, and others contiguous to them, are chiefly agricultural, but several contain inexhaustible resources of coal, iron, salt, and lumber; articles which, from the want of facilities of transport, are now supplied from Ohio, Pennsylvania, and Virginia. Nothing but the want of these facilities could induce the inhabitants of Kentucky to have recourse to these states for their mineral stores, for the mines in Kentucky are very favourably situated, the strata of coal and iron ore being found in a position nearly horizontal, dipping just enough to permit the water to flow off, while the coal formation in this state is far distant from any other in the valley of the Ohio, except a portion of it which extends into Indiana.*

Sinking
fund.

The net receipts on the whole of the works of the state are made over to the sinking fund ; and as 446 miles of turnpike roads, advantageously laid out, are now finished, the commissioners entertain what appears to be a well grounded expectation, that the revenue derived from this branch of the public improvements will from the present time constitute a considerable item in the resources of this fund. Part of the tolls were applied in the last year to complete roads, when the amounts appropriated to them had not proved sufficient: this, of course, will not continue to be the case ; and the commissioners calculate that in the next year the revenue from the state turnpike roads may amount to $40,000 00.

The state is interested to so small an extent in railroads that these may be left out of consideration ; but the commissioners anticipate a material increase to the fund under their care, when the improvements in the river navigation shall be completed : the water power alone, it is thought, will let for $75,000 00 : but as the amount of tolls on

---

* The coal formation of the Upper Ohio (above the falls at Louisville) is very extensive, occupying the eastern part of Ohio, and the western parts of Pennsylvania, Maryland, and Virginia. The coal formation of the Lower Ohio embraces twelve counties in Kentucky, (most of which are in the Green river valley,) and thence extends across the Ohio river, up the valley of the Wabach in Indiana.

these streams will depend on many contingencies, no regular estimate can yet be made.

Besides the tolls which arise out of the improvements themselves, the state has set aside very ample sources of revenue to meet the interest on its loans, and the redemption of the sums borrowed. These consist, —

1. Of the excess of dividends over the amount required to defray the interest on the state's subscription to the capital of the bank of Kentucky, and the Northern bank of Kentucky.

2. Of the entire dividends on the portion which the state has subscribed towards the fifth million in the capital of the former bank.

3. Of the profits of the Bank of the Commonwealth, and of the Old bank of Kentucky, which are both the exclusive property of the state.

4. Of the proceeds of a tax on the capital of the joint stock banks in the state.

5. Of the dividends or investments made by the commissioners of the sinking fund in the stock of these banks.

6. Of the net proceeds of the penitentiary.

7. Of the excess beyond the sum of $10,000 00 of the ordinary revenue of the state over the ordinary expenditure.

The investments of stock hitherto made by the commissioners of the sinking fund in the different banks in the state consist of

1277 shares purchased in the bank of Kentucky.

400 shares in the Northern bank of Kentucky.

175 in the bank of Louisville.

The cost of these shares amounted to $174,781 49. The commissioners have also purchased, as before stated, twenty thousand dollars of the bonds issued for internal improvements. The board of the commissioners of the sinking fund, to whose care these funds are intrusted, was organised on the 20th of October, 1836; before that time the funds had remained in the hands of the treasurer of the state. On the 11th of January, 1837, the account was settled with the treasurer, when there appeared an available money balance, in the hands of the commissioners, of

	$24,473 83
The sums which have since been received amount to - - - -	1,173,138 14
	1,197,611 97
And the sums paid by the commissioners to -	1,136,332 48
Leaving, in the hands of the commissioners, at the close of 1838 - - -	$61,279 49

The following is the estimate of the revenue of the fund for the present year : —

The excess of dividends on the one million of capital in the bank of Kentucky - -	$35,000 00
The excess of dividends on the one million of capital of the Northern bank - -	37,500 00
Dividend on $700,000 00 of the fifth million of the bank of Kentucky - - -	59,500 00
Profits from the bank of the Commonwealth -	20,000 00
Profits from the old bank of Kentucky -	5,940 00
Tax on the capital stock of the bank of Kentucky ($4,700,000 00) - - -	23,500 00
Tax on the capital stock of the Northern bank ($3,000,000 00) - • -	15,000 00

Tax on the capital stock of the bank of Louis-
ville ($1,150,000 00) - - - $5,750 00
Dividends on 1277 shares purchased in the bank
of Kentucky - - - 10,854 50
Dividends on 400 shares purchased in the North-
ern bank - - - - 3,500 00
Dividends on 175 shares purchased in the bank
of Louisville - - - - 1,400 00
Profits from the penitentiary - - 7,500 00
Premium on sales of Eastern funds - 4,500 00
Dividends from roads, bridges, &c. - - 12,000 00

241,944 50

The estimated charge upon it consists of dividends on $515,000 00
at 5 per cent. - - $25,750 00
Ditto on $937,500 00 at 6 per cent. 56,250 00
Exchange to make dividends pay-
able at New York - - 3,000 00

85,000 00

Showing a surplus of - - - $156,944 50
Add balance in hand, 1st January, 1839 - 61,279 49

Which will make the surplus in the hands of the
commissioners at the end of the present year $218,223 99

This is taking a very low estimate of the amount
likely to be derived from tolls, and is independent
of any surplus that may accrue to the treasury
from the excess beyond the sum of ten thousand
dollars of the ordinary revenue of the state over
the ordinary expenditure, which has been stated
as one of the items constituting the sinking fund.
It appears possible, however, that about fifty thousand dollars more may in future be derived annually
from this source; for the estimate of the ordi-

nary revenue of the state for the year 1838 was
$300,000 00, while the ordinary expenditure of
the government for the same year was estimated
at $238,000 00, leaving a surplus of $62,000 00.
This estimate of the receipts into the treasury
was founded, however, on the probability that the
operation of two laws, which were then coming
into effect, would produce a large increase over
the amount of former years ; but until the result
be known, no great reliance, perhaps, ought to be
placed on so large an increase being obtained, for
heretofore the receipts and expenditure seem to
have been nearly equal in amount.*

Condition
of the trea-
sury.
The chief source of revenue which this state
possesses consists in a tax levied by the sheriffs
of $6\frac{1}{4}$ cents on every hundred dollars of taxable
property, comprising lands, town lots, slaves,
houses, and carriages : this tax is alone nearly
sufficient to defray the ordinary expenses of the
government.

The following items constituted the receipts
into the treasury in the year 1836, exclusive of
sums received from loans and from the sinking
fund : —

From the sheriffs	$139,381 00
From the clerks of court	24,281 00
From other sources	5,827 00
Making together	$169,489 00

* One of the laws referred to appropriates certain fines and
forfeitures to the payment of jurors ; the object of the other is
to render taxation more equal

The payments, exclusive of sums paid for internal improvements, and of the charges on the
sinking fund, were as follows : —

For the expenses of the legislature	-	- $19,999 00
For the executive and judicial officers		- 53,388 00
For the clerks of court, &c.	- -	- 21,484 00
For criminal prosecutions	- -	- 15,006 00
For slaves executed	- -	- 2,475 00
For charitable institutions	- -	- 24,166 00
For sundry appropriations and miscellaneous ex-		
penses	- - -	- 29,690 00

$166,208 00

Kentucky, which was one of the first of the new
states that was admitted into the Union, formed
part of the state of Virginia till the year 1792,
when, with the consent of that commonwealth and
of congress, it became an independent member of
the confederation. Though agriculture forms the
chief occupation of the inhabitants, this direction
being naturally given to the industry of the people
by the extreme fertility and productiveness of the
soil, yet this state is more actively engaged in
commerce than might be expected from its central
position and distance from the sea. Its chief
commercial intercourse is with the Western and
Southern states, through means of the Ohio and
the Mississippi. Louisville, the principal city in
the state, is situated on the former river, immediately above the falls : its position on one of the
bends of the river, which is here a mile wide, with
the islands and rapids below, is described as forming one of the most striking of the beautiful scenes

Commerce.

CHAP.
VII.

with which the Ohio abounds.*   In the year 1831 the mercantile transactions of Louisville were estimated at fifteen millions of dollars, and in 1836 at thirty-nine millions.   In the year 1800, the population of this town did not exceed 600.   In 1830 it had reached to 10,336 ; and in 1836 exceeded 20,000.

Amount of taxable property.

The increase in the general wealth of the state

* The falls of the Ohio are occasioned by an irregular ledge of rock stretching across the river : they are only perceptible at low water, the whole descent being but twenty-two feet, while the difference of level between the highest and lowest stages of the water is about sixty feet : when the river is full, they present, therefore, no serious obstruction to the navigation.   To obviate the inconvenience, however, at low water, a canal, called the Louisville and Portland canal, has been constructed round the falls ; which, though not apparently a work executed by the government, is deserving of notice as being, perhaps, the most important work of the kind ever undertaken.   The cross section of the canal is 200 feet at the top of the bank, fifty feet at the bottom, and forty-two feet deep, making its capacity about fifteen times greater than that contemplated for the Erie canal when its enlargement shall be completed : its sides are sloping and paved with stone.   The guard lock contains 21,775 perches of mason work, being equal to that of fifteen locks on the New York canals ; and three others contain 12,300 perches.   This canal is capable of admitting steam-boats of the largest class.   It is scarcely two miles in length, but, considering the quantity of mason work, and the difficulty of excavating earth and rock from so great a depth, together with the contingencies attending its construction from the fluctuations in the depth of the river, it is probably no over-statement, when it is said, that the work in it is equal to that of seventy or seventy-five miles of an ordinary canal.   In 1833, 876 steam-boats and 710 boats passed through the canal ; and in 1836, the number of steam-boats was 1182, and of smaller craft 260.

may be judged of by the progressive increase in the returns made to the auditor of the taxable property in the state. This, which in 1830 amounted to $103,543,638 00, by the last valuation amounted to $224,053,041 00.

TENNESSEE.

THE debt of this state consists at present of bonds to the amount of $500,000 00, which have been issued as part of the state's subscription to the capital of the Union bank of Tennessee, and of $1,000,000 00 issued to furnish part of the capital of the bank of Tennessee : a small sum, amounting, it would appear, to $289,166 66, has also been raised for the construction of turnpike roads and for the improvement of river navigation.

Amount of debt.

In founding the above two banks, the legislature, besides the purpose of affording facilities to commerce, had in view the establishment of a system of education, and through the means of the bank of Tennessee, further contemplated the carrying into effect an extensive system of internal improvements, which will lead to a considerable extension of the debt. The mode in which this object is to be effected, and the nature and extent of the improvements contemplated, will be explained in the observations which I shall have to make respecting the bank with which they are connected.

Object of loans.

Form of
security,
and when
and where
redeem-
able.

I have no information respecting the form in which the loans exist which have been raised for the construction of turnpike roads and for the improvement of the rivers, nor when they are redeemable.

The bonds which the state issued in payment of its share in the Union bank are payable to the bearer, and are redeemable at New York at the following dates; viz. —

$1,250,000 00 on the 18th October, 1847.
1,250,000 00 on the 18th October, 1852.
1,250,000 00 on the 18th October, 1857.
1,250,000 00 on the 18th October, 1862.

Those issued to raise part of the capital of the bank of Tennessee are likewise payable to the bearer, and are redeemable in New York at the office of the American Life and Trust Company on the 7th of May, 1868.

The New York company has undertaken to pay the principal, when due, in London at the rate of 4s. 6d. per dollar, on such portion of the stock as has been registered for that purpose; but the engagement of the state extends only to making the payment at New York.

Part of the stock raised for the construction of turnpike roads bears interest at the rate of five per cent., and part at six per cent.

The bonds issued for the Union bank bear interest at five per cent., which is payable, half-yearly, at New York. Those for the bank of Tennessee bear interest at six per cent. The interest on these also is payable at New York, half-yearly, on the

first Mondays in May and November, at the office
of the American Life and Trust Company. By
the engagement of that company the interest on
the bonds which have been made payable in London has likewise been made payable in the same
city, two months after it becomes due in New
York, at the rate of $109\frac{3}{4}$ per cent., or of 6l. 3s. 0d.
for each half-yearly warrant of 30 dollars.

The Union bank of Tennessee was established
by a charter, passed on the 18th of October, 1832,
with a capital limited to three millions of dollars,
of which shares to the amount of two millions were
subscribed for by individuals, and five hundred
thousand dollars by the state, the legislature reserving the right of increasing the stock of the
state at any future time to an amount not exceeding one million of dollars. There is no evidence
to show in what manner the stockholders paid for
their stock ; but by a statement of the funds on
hand a few days after the bank commenced business, it would appear that it must have been in specie
or in funds equivalent to specie : on the shares,
however, held by individuals, only $1,955,339 00
have been paid, so that $44,661 00 are still due
by stockholders, on their subscription for stock.

The original subscription of the state was paid
in state bonds, which were negotiated in Baltimore. Part of the proceeds appear to have been
lost by the failure of the bank of Maryland, but
the amount of the loss is not stated : whatever it
was, it was borne by the bank.

By a clause in the act of incorporation, the profits which arise on the stock owned by the state after paying the interest on the bonds, and the premium which was paid by the bank to the state for the privileges conferred by the charter, are appropriated to the establishment of common schools, with an authority to the state to subscribe the amount received to the capital of the bank : these sources had, at the date of the last return, produced $98,400 00.

The capital of the bank is, at present, therefore, composed

Of sums paid by individuals	- -	- $1,955,339 00
Of the state's subscription	- -	- 500,000 00
Of the premium and accumulation of profit	-	98,400 00
		$2,553,739 00

A part of the instalments received under the distribution act of Congress, amounting to $707,350 00 has been deposited with the Union Bank, on which the state receives an interest of five per cent. As this is not likely to be suddenly recalled it is available for all the purposes of capital.

Power conferred by charter.
The clauses in the charter which relate to the management of the business appear judicious : the bank may not purchase lands, but may advance money on mortgage of real property ; it may issue its own notes, but not in amounts below five dollars ; and its bills and notes issued may not at any time exceed twice the amount of the capital. In case of failure to pay on demand its engagements in gold or silver, the holder may recover interest from the time of such demand and refusal

at the rate of 10 per cent. The rates of interest
which the bank may take are limited to 6, 7, and
8 per cent., according to the length of time for
which the money is advanced.

The bank commenced business on the 4th of
March, 1833, and the profits have since been considerable. On the 1st of January, 1834, a dividend
was declared of 4 per cent. on the amount of capital
then paid up; and dividends at the rate of 8 per
cent. were paid every following half year till the
1st of January, 1837, when the half-yearly dividend was raised to 6 per cent.; but on the ensuing
July, specie payments having been suspended in the
mean time, no dividend was declared, nor was the
following one since paid; the interest on the state's
bonds has been paid out of the ordinary resources
of the treasury. The profits of the bank in the
mean time have been accumulating, and on the
3d of March, 1838, amounted to $394,720 37;
besides which, a contingent fund had been set
aside, out of former profits, which on the 1st of
January, 1837, amounted to $124,894 03.

Statements will be given in the Appendix of the
condition of this bank on the 3d of March, 1838,
as also before and after the suspension of specie
payments.*

The circulation of the Union bank, previous to
the suspension, was very high; and the institution
is one of those which particularly suffered from the
inconvenience which has been before alluded to, of

* See Appendix, B B 1, &c.

having made too large a proportion of it payable at distant places.*

On the 1st of January, 1837, it consisted of notes payable as follows; viz.

At New Orleans - - -	- $1,730,400 00
At Philadelphia and New York - -	154,395 00
Within the state of Tennessee - -	69,940 00
	$1,954,735 00

Between this time and the 1st of October, it was reduced by the large sum of $1,145,495 00, it having on the latter day consisted of

Notes payable at New Orleans -	- $576,345 00
Notes payable at Philadelphia and New York -	55,860 00
Notes payable within the state -	- 177,035 00
	$809,240 00

It is thus apparent that the whole reduction took place in the amount of the notes payable out of the state, the amount within the state having largely increased: by this means the circulation has been brought into a much more healthy state.

A great reduction, as a necessary consequence, took place during the same period in the amounts due by other banks; the notes withdrawn from circulation in New Orleans reducing the balances due from the banks in that city, at whose counters they were made payable. †   A committee of the

---

* See note at page 102.

† Banks with a large amount of circulation payable out of the state depend chiefly for the redemption of their notes on credits established by them with the banks in the places where

legislature appointed to investigate the condition   CHAP.
of the banks in this state after the suspension of   VII.
specie payments report favourably of the character of the debts due to this bank.

As the state's profits in this bank are applicable   Collateral
to purposes of education, there is, in this case, no   security of
                                                         bond
source for extinguishing the debt which the state   holder.
has contracted in order to subscribe to its capital ;
but the contingent fund and the large capital paid
up by individual shareholders afford a considerable
collateral security to the holder of the state's bonds.

The Bank of Tennessee was established under   Bank of
an act of the 19th of January, 1838, entitled " An   Tennessee.
Act to establish a state bank to raise a fund for
internal improvements, and to aid in the establishment of a system of education."

The capital of the bank is eventually to be five   Capital.
millions of dollars, to be composed of the common
school fund, of the proceeds of the sales of certain
lands, of the surplus revenue of the general government in deposit with the state, and of such additional sum to be borrowed as may be required to
complete that sum. This bank differs in an essential particular from the one the condition of
which we have just been considering, in its being
the exclusive property of the state, no part of the
capital being owned by individuals.

The internal improvement part of the bill pro-   Internal
                                                   improve-

---

the notes are made payable : this circumstance ought to be
borne in mind, or there will appear to be a greater disparity
than really exists between the amount of their circulation and
their specie.

ment
clauses.

vides that the state shall take half the stock in all the turnpike and railroad companies that may hereafter be authorised, and shall issue bonds for the amount whenever the other half shall have been taken by individuals, and a deposit of 15 per cent. paid by them: the state is to retain a lien upon the property of the subscribers until the sums they have subscribed are fully paid up, and also upon the works until they are completed.

The bill appropriates four millions of dollars for internal improvements, of which sum one million of dollars is to be expended in East Tennessee, one million six hundred thousand in Middle Tennessee, and one million in the Western district of the state.*

Of the above sum, six hundred and fifty thousand dollars are appropriated to the construction of the Hiwassee railroad, and the same amount to the Charleston and Cincinnati railroad.

This bank commenced business on the 23d of June, 1838, and on the 1st day of October published a statement of its affairs, which will be found in the Appendix.†

Prospects
of con-
templated
improve-
ments.

From so short an experience, no judgment can be formed of the goodness of its management. In the absence of a coproprietary, the security of the state bondholder will depend much on the judgment shown in the selection of the works which the state may hereafter assist. Of the two named

* $127,000 00 are appropriated to common schools and colleges.
† See Appendix, B B 3.

above as having already received appropriations, the Charleston and Cincinnati railroad has been already described under the head of South Carolina — the Hiwassee railroad, which is now in progress, will extend from Calhoun on the Hiwassee, to Knoxville, the principal town in East Tennessee.

As the eastern part of this state has only the choice, at present, for the transport of its surplus productions, of the long and tedious course of the Tennessee through Alabama, interrupted by several serious obstructions to its navigation, or the equally slow and difficult passage of the mountains by waggons, a communication with the eastern ports by an easier route would be here of great advantage ; but in the uncertainty which must attend the success of such an undertaking, and under the circumstance of the diversion of part of the profits of the bank to purposes unconnected with the security of the state's creditors, it becomes of much importance to investigate the condition of the state's resources.*

The information I can obtain in this respect is scanty, but so far as it goes, is satisfactory. The annual expenses of the state, exclusive of the expenditure for education and internal improvements, have usually fallen from thirty thousand to thirty-five thousand dollars below the amount of the

Condition of the treasury.

* The bonds raised for the Bank of Tennessee have the indorsement, and, consequently, the guarantee of the American Life Insurance and Trust Company — an institution of great wealth and character.

receipts into the treasury; although, in the year 1834, the date at which these details are given, the excess of the receipts over the expenditure was little more than twenty-two thousand, the receipts in that year having been $93,463 00, and the expenditure $71,243 00.

The property subject to taxation by law would, it would appear, produce a revenue far superior to that which is actually collected, were the laws enforced; the deficiency is attributed partly to the inefficacy of these laws, and partly to the state of the treasury not requiring the enforcement of them, there being usually a considerable surplus not appropriated to any specific purpose.

The amount and sources of the state revenue in 1834 were as follows: —

Tax on land	-	-	$23,190 00
Do. on town lots -	-	-	2,096 00
Do. on white polls	-	-	8,880 00
Do. on black polls	-	-	12,384 00
Do. on stud horses	-	-	33,72 00
Do. on pleasure carriages	-	-	1,091 00
Do. on law proceedings	-	-	8,769 00
Do. on conveyances	-	-	1,008 00
Do. on taverns	-	-	1,110 00
Do. on merchants	-	-	31,563 00

Total $93,463 00

Productive industry.

Agriculture forms almost the sole occupation of the inhabitants of Tennessee. A large proportion of the land is productive, and many of the valleys of East Tennessee, and much of the middle and western sections, are eminently fertile. Indian corn and tobacco are the principal productions of the state, but considerable quantities of tobacco, hemp, and wheat, are raised. Cotton thrives in almost every part, although the climate of Tennessee is not so well adapted for this plant as that of the more southern states — the crop is about 150,000 bales. The estimated value of the exports of this state is $8,000,000 00 ; the estimated value of real property about $150,000,000 00.

CHAP.
VII.

OHIO.

THE debt of this state consisted, on the 1st of January last, of

Amount of debt.

Loans for the state canals - -	-$ 6,430,000 00
For subscriptions to turnpike road, canal, and railroad companies - - -	2,252,615 00
Sum borrowed from the school fund - -	1,099,132 94
Other liabilities - - -	248,414 77
Making together	$10,030,162 71

The stock created for the construction of the state canals is inscribed in the name of the holder, and is transferable by appearance in person or by attorney ; the transfer books are kept at the office of the Manhattan Banking Company, in the city of New York.

Form of security.

The first loan made by this state for its canals, was contracted in 1825.

When and where re-deemable.

The sum borrowed in that year was -	-$ 400,000 00
In 1826 the sum borrowed amounted to -	- 1,000,000 00

In 1827 the sum borrowed amounted to   - 1,200,000 00
In 1828 to   -   -   -   -   - 1,200,000 00
In 1830 to   -   -   „   -   - $600,000 00

The principal of these sums, amounting to
$4,400,000 00, is redeemable at the pleasure of
the state any time after the 31st December, 1850,
and is payable in the city of New York. A portion
of the debt subsequently contracted on the same
account is redeemable after 1856, while a part
still more recently raised is not subject to redemption till 1860.

The canals for which these loans have been
raised are the exclusive property of the state.

In the session of the legislature of 1836–37, in
order to encourage private enterprise in works of
internal improvement, a law was passed, to the
effect that when one half of the stock of a turnpike road, or two thirds of that of a canal or railroad, should be taken by individuals, and the
object be approved of by those who have charge
of the public works of the state, the governor
should be authorised to subscribe in the name of
the state for the remainder. Under this law, the
state has become a coproprietor with individuals
and companies to the extent of $2,253,115 00, but
I have no information as to the form in which its
engagements exist for loans contracted for this
purpose, nor as to the time when the amounts are
redeemable.

Rate of in-
terest, and
where and
when pay-
able.

$550,000 00 of the loans raised for the state
canals bear interest at 5 per cent. ; the remainder,
as well as the debt due to the school fund, bears

interest at 6 per cent. The interest on the canal loans is payable half yearly, on the 1st of January and 1st of July, at the bank of the Manhattan company. I have no particulars of the rate paid on the loans for the state's subscription to works not exclusively of their own construction, nor of the place where such interest is payable.

The proceeds of the early loans of this state Applica-were applied to the construction of the Ohio canal tion of canal loans. and of the Miami canal from Cincinnati to Dayton, two works which have been undertaken and executed entirely at the public expense. Two other extensive works are now likewise in course of construction, unaided by private capital; viz. the Wabash and Erie canal, and an extension of the Miami canal from Dayton, to join the Wabash and Erie canal at Defiance. The federal government, however, has contributed towards the construction of these two important works by grants of public lands, by the sale of which it is thought that the whole expense may ultimately be defrayed, without the state incurring any permanent loans on their account.

In January, 1838, nine turnpike roads, three Of loans railroads, and two canals, had been approved of for works on joint by the board of public works, under the law of account. 1836–37; but I have been able to obtain little information respecting the several undertakings in which the state has thus become partially interested, or the prospects of the works.*

* One of the works in which, under this act, the state has a pecuniary interest, is the Mahoning and Beaver canal, intended

Works to
connect the
Ohio and
Lake Erie.

The object of the works which have been under-taken exclusively by the state has been the estab-lishment of canal communications between the Ohio and Lake Erie. No range of mountains, but only a slightly elevated ridge of highlands, separates the basin of the northern lakes from the valley of that river. This ridge attains its highest elevation towards the east, where it blends with the Alleghany chain: gradually sub-siding from this point as it extends westward, it becomes at length so little elevated above the level of the northern waters, that in high floods the Canadian settlers are said to have passed in boats from Lake Michigan into the channel of the Illi-nois, and down that river into the stream of the Mississippi. The descent of this ridge towards the south is so gradual, that in the state of Ohio the face of the country has the appearance of an extended table-land slightly inclined, so as to allow its superabundant water to be carried off into the Ohio by large but gentle streams. The descent towards Lake Erie is much more rapid, rendering the course of the rivers in that direction shorter and more precipitous.

The country so formed is well adapted in other respects for the construction of canals : the high-

---

to connect the Ohio canal at Akron, with the Beaver division of the Pennsylvania canal and railroad. The benefits which are likely to result from the completion of this work to the states engaging in it have already been pointed out in a note to page 168.

lands abounding in lakes and extensive marshes, being calculated to afford at all times an ample supply of water.

The Ohio canal, the only one by which the communication is already completed, leaves the Ohio at Portsmouth, and joins Lake Erie at Cleveland, a flourishing town, which owes its existence entirely to the traffic which the canal has occasioned. This work was commenced on the 4th July, 1825, and was completed in 1832. Advantage having been taken of the course of the rivers, the canal deviates considerably from a straight line, but it is thus carried in its course through several important towns. The length of the main line is 307 miles. There are several lateral branches. The most extensive is the Hockhocking, or, as it is generally abbreviated, the Hocking canal, down the valley of the Hockhocking to Athens. This is the extension of a branch to Lancaster, which was originally a private work, but has lately been assumed and enlarged by the state. Another branch extends to Columbus, the seat of government of the state. The Ohio canal reaches, at its highest point, 305 feet above Lake Erie and 499 above the Ohio at Portsmouth: the ascent and descent are effected by means of 152 locks.

The Miami canal commences at Cincinnati, on the Ohio: it also was begun in 1825, and was finished in the spring of 1829 as far as Dayton, a distance of sixty-five miles. The extension now in progress will carry it a further distance of 125

CHAP.
VII.

Cost of
these
works.

miles, to Defiance, where it will join the Wabash and Erie canal. The whole distance from Cincinnati to Lake Erie by this line will be 265 miles.

The cost of the Ohio canal was $4,244,539 00; that of the Miami canal, as far as Dayton, about $900,000 00. The two together, including a portion of the lateral branches of the Ohio canal, extending altogether a distance of 406 miles, cost $5,356,150 00.

Though executed, in proportion to the length, at less than one half of the cost of the Pennsylvania canal and railroad, the works in Ohio surpass those of the neighbouring state, both in execution and design, and rival even those of New York, from which state Ohio seems to have obtained its engineers: the greater facilities which the ground afforded in Ohio have no doubt favoured the construction of its canals at a lower cost.*

Extension
of the
Miami
canal.

The extension of the Miami canal to its intersection with the Wabash and Erie canal, and the construction of the latter now form the most important of the works carrying on by this state. These works were not authorised by the legislature

---

* The following table will show the comparative cost of the construction of the state canals in New York, Pennsylvania, and Ohio, as well as of the two principal private undertakings in Pennsylvania.

	Length.	Cost.	Cost per Mile.
New York canals	655 miles	$11,962,711 00	$18,264 00
Pennsylvania canal and railroad	709½	18,853,818 10	26,541 00
Ohio canals	406	5,356,150 00	13,192 00
Lehigh canal	46¾	1,546,095 00	33,071 00
Schuylkill canal	108	3,187,383 00	29,513 00

till 1835 and 1836, when the beneficial results to CHAP.
the public interests of the canals then executed VII.
had become apparent. The extension of the
Miami canal will be carried in a nearly direct line
from Dayton to Defiance.

The Wabash and Erie canal, which it there Wabash
joins, is intended to connect Lake Erie with the canal.
Ohio, through the valleys of the Wabash and the
Maumee. This work, which is being constructed
in concert with Indiana, will extend from La
Fayette on the Wabash, in that state, to Manhattan, near the mouth of the Maumee, a distance
of 187 miles : eighty-two only are within the territory of Ohio.*

The policy of the state being to dispose of as
little of the lands granted by congress as possible
until the works are finished and in use, much
exertion is being made to effect their completion,
and it is supposed that the whole may be in use
before the end of 1840.

* By the inconvenient system, so often adopted in the United
States, of establishing parallels of latitude as the boundary lines
of states, instead of following the rivers and natural features of
the country, the mouth of the Maumee was included in the
territory of Michigan, while the whole course of the river was
in Indiana and Ohio. The possession of the outlet of this river
became of great consequence when the operations of these
states, in regard to the canal, were likely to give a new importance to the spot, and a claim was in consequence raised to
this small tract on the part of the state of Ohio. The works
were for a long time suspended, while negotiations were pending,
and a hostile collision even was at one time threatened ; but, on
the admission of Michigan, in 1836, to the rank of a state in the
Union, the mouth of the Maumee was ceded to Ohio, and is
now included in its territory.

CHAP.
VII.

Tolls on
the Ohio
and Miami
canals.

The following table will show the amount of tolls collected on the Ohio and on the Miami canals, from Cincinnati to Dayton, since 1833.

	On the Ohio Canal.	On the Miami Canal.	Total on both Canals.
1833 - -	$136,092 70	$50,470 63	$186,563 33
1834 - -	159,977 23	50,040 99	210,018 22
1835 - -	180,977 41	51,917 00	232,894 41
1836 - -	206,864 91	51,110 52	257,975 43
1837 - -	292,836 10	62,933 40	355,769 50

In 1838 the sum collected amounted to $459,998 05: the increase in the last two years was owing in part to an increase in the rate of tolls, although largely attributable to the increased traffic.

The sum expended in repairs and new work on the Ohio canal, in 1837, amounted to $155,751 55; and that on the Miami canal, including large purchases of land to obtain water-power, to $85,635 96.*

The total expenses on the two canals, for the three years ending in 1837, including interest on the cost, were as follows: —

In 1835	-	-	- $309,891 47
In 1836	- . -	-	- 294,463 30
In 1837	-	- -	- 409,540 54

In 1838 the expenses on the canals were estimated at $435,656 00, which, assuming the interest on their cost at $355,000 00, would leave only $80,656 00 for repairs and superintendence, a sum which is probably under estimated.

* The expenditure during the same year on other state works amounted to $436,298 55.

It would appear, however, from this statement,
that the tolls received on these canals during the last year were likely to leave a surplus after paying the expense of repairs and interest, although, while other works are going forward which at present yield little or no return, the income derived from tolls to the canal fund hardly amounts to four per cent. on the whole sum that has been expended.*

The canal accounts are kept distinct from those of the general receipts and disbursements of the state.

Auxiliary funds are set apart for the payment of the interest on the canal debt, independently of the canal tolls. These arise partly out of sales of land granted by Congress, and partly out of a direct tax of two mills or $\frac{2}{1000}$ of a dollar on the assessment of property in the state. The proceeds of the sales of the school lands seem also to be paid over to the canal commissioners, to be used for canal purposes; and hence arises the debt of the state to the school fund, which has been included in the enumeration of the state's engagements.

Towards the construction of the Wabash and Erie canal, Congress granted the alternate sections of land to the distance of five miles on each side of

---

* I have not seen the original reports of the canal commissioners. The greater part of the statistical details given above is derived from an article on the state of Ohio, in the North American Review for July 1838. In this the estimated revenue of the two canals for 1838 is stated at $373,606 00, which, it will be seen above, has been much more than realised.

the canal, amounting to five sections or 3200 acres to each mile of its length. The principal part of these lands along the portion of the work in the territory of Ohio is retained by the state, and appropriated as a fund for the payment of interest and redemption of the debt; for which purpose, if a correct policy in the disposal of them is pursued, it appears there is little doubt they will be fully adequate. The state also holds certain lands granted in aid of the extension of the Miami canal.

These lands afford indirectly considerable security to the holders of the state's engagements for its canals, generally, as the tolls on the canals for which they were granted will be sooner set free, while the tendency of the works will be very much to enlarge the general business and wealth of the state.

In case of any deficiency in the canal revenues arising from these various sources, it is made imperative on the auditor of the state to levy the required amount by direct taxation, it being the acknowledged principle of the state that its loans are to be invariably secured by specific revenues, to be applied to the payment of both the principal and interest.

State of the treasury. In 1834, 17,819,631 acres of land were returned for taxation at an average value (excluding town lots) of little more than three dollars: this return seems still to be the basis of taxation for real property. The total property in the state subject to taxation in 1835 consisted of —

Lands (17,819,631 acres) including buildings	$58,166,821	00
Town lots, including houses, mills, &c.	- 15,762,594	00
Horses (262,291, valued at $40 each) -	- 10,491,640	00
Cattle (455,487, valued at $8 each) -	- 4,043,896	00
Merchants' capital and money at interest -	7,262,927	00
Pleasure carriages, (2,603) valued at -	" 199,518	00

Total $94,338,016 00

The increase since that time in the general property liable to taxation has been considerable : the portion of the taxes accruing to the state treasury from these sources in 1837 having amounted to $214,209 15. This, which formed about a seventh part of the whole sum levied on this assessment, with a tax on banks insurance companies and bridge companies, and taxes on certain trades and professions, was more than enough to defray the expenses of the state government; for the taxes above enumerated amounted to $48,378 07 and the whole receipts into the treasury derived from taxation, to $301,543 28, while the expenditure for the same year amounted to $274,071 40, leaving a surplus of $27,471 88; in 1836 the receipts from taxes amounted only to $205,922 44, while the expenses were $208,276 17.*

Besides these sums accruing from taxation, and which are applicable to the expense of the govern-

* Of the sum expended in 1837, $49,988 55 were to defray the cost of the legislature ; $23,070 53 for the salaries of state officers and judges ; and $28,380 53 for stationery and printing. Large sums are annually expended on the penitentiary and on public asylums.

ment, various other sums are collected and paid to the treasury. In a report of the standing committee on the currency, the total annual amount of money received by the auditor of the state is nearly as follows :

General revenue arising from taxation - -	$300,000 00
Ohio canal fund, arising from tolls and sale of public lands transferred to that fund - -	500,000 00
From sale of Wabash and Erie canal land -	300,000 00
For interest on surplus revenue deposited with the state - - - -	100,000 00
From sale of school and other public lands -	200,000 00
From tolls on national road - - -	40,000 00
Total $1,440,000 00	

The particular application of the latter sums does not appear : no part of the remaining taxes levied under the assessment passes through the state treasury, the amounts being appropriated to county and other purposes.*

* The taxes raised on the assessment of state property vary considerably in different parts of the state, but amount on an average to from 12 to 14 mills on the dollar ; the amount is appropriated in about the following proportions : —

For expenses of the state government -	- 2 mills.
For canals - - -	- 2
For schools - - -	- $2\frac{1}{2}$
For roads - - -	- 2
For sundries - - -	- 3
For towns and cities - - -	- $2\frac{1}{2}$

The property, however, is valued so low, that these taxes appear to be much higher than they are in reality. It is estimated that, on a real valuation, one mill and a half would be enough for all purposes.

This flourishing state, the first settlement of which was not made till 1788, already occupies in respect to the number of its inhabitants, the fourth place among the members of the Union. Its commercial facilities, arising out of its geographical position, are very great. Of the 75 counties of which it is composed, 14 lie upon the Ohio river, which in its windings bounds the state for 436 miles; while seven, which border on Lake Erie, possess a coast of upwards of 200 miles in extent. The great works which have been described, and others, the result of private enterprise, have given almost equal advantages to the interior districts. Canals now made or making pass through thirty-two counties, railroads through six, and macadamised roads through five; so that of the seventy-five counties into which the state is divided, there are only eleven which do not benefit from either natural or improved means of communication, and many even of these are traversed or bounded by rivers of inferior magnitude.

While its natural advantages and the industry of its inhabitants have thus secured for this state the benefits of an easy internal communication, its position is no less favourable for external commerce. The Ohio river affords a direct communication with all the country in the valley of the Mississippi, which requires much of its agricultural produce and of its manufactures; while, by means of Lake Erie, which has several good natural and artificial harbours, it communicates with Canada

and New York on the one side, and with the
country on the upper lakes on the other. The
shipping owned on Ohio in 1834 amounted to
9427 tons; in 1836 it had increased to 16,586 tons,
of which 10,036 were in steam-vessels on the
river, and the remainder, of which about one half
consisted of steam-vessels, belonged to the lake.
This statement does not include the numerous
river and canal boats, whose aggregate tonnage
would much swell the amount.

When the communication is completed between
the Ohio and the Pennsylvania lines, and still more
when the railroad is finished which is meant to
connect Cincinnati with Charleston in South Carolina, an additional stimulus will be given to the
industry of the state.

The completion of the latter work, by the importance it will confer on Cincinnati, is scarcely
of less interest to Ohio than it is to the states
whose territories it traverses. This city, which is
situated at the northern extremity of the line, is
the largest and richest town in the state, and more
extensive indeed than any other on the course of
the Ohio or Mississippi, between Pittsburg and
New Orleans. Its progress in wealth and rapid
growth are remarkable even in the United States.
Counting, in 1805, only 950 inhabitants, it already, in 1830, held the seventh place in point
of population among the cities of the Union. In
1836 it was estimated that the number of inhabitants exceeded 32,000, which would probably
assign it a still higher rank.

The soil of Ohio is very productive, and the climate temperate; and as slavery does not exert its demoralising influence upon society, the state presents great advantages to agricultural settlers. Numbers have in consequence migrated from the New England states, and have carried with them the industrious, orderly, and moral habits which so strongly prevail there. This state is in all respects one of the most flourishing of the Union.

LOUISIANA.

THE debt of this state consists of bonds which have been issued for the following purposes : —

To aid in the formation of banking companies	$18,354,000 00
To subscribe for stock in the New Orleans draining company - - -	50,000 00
As a loan to the New Orleans and Nashville railroad company - - -	500,000 00
For establishing an hospital - - -	125,000 00
For building the state house - -	100,000 00
For the heirs of Mr. Jefferson - -	10,000 00
Making a total of	$19,139,000 00

A further issue of four millions of dollars may be claimed by the Citizens' Bank of Louisiana, making the liabilities of this state to amount to $23,139,000 00.

The bonds granted by this state are in all cases made payable to the bearer.

In regard to those issued to aid in the formation of banking companies, the following statement will show the dates at which the several issues were made, the amount granted in favour of each institution, and the periods when the bonds are redeemable.

	Dates of Issue.	Amount.	Redeemable.
Bank of Louisiana - -	1st July 1824	$ 600,000 00	1st July 1844.
Do. - -	Do.	600,000 00	Do. 1849.
Mechanics' and Traders' Bank	1st May 1836	150,000 00	9th May 1853.
Planters' Association -	31st Dec. 1828	833,000 00	30th June 1843.
Do. - by act	7th March 1836	171,000 00	1st June 1848. *
Do. - -	1st May 1836	1,000,000 00	Do.
Union Bank of Louisiana -	1st Oct. 1832	1,750,000 00	1st Nov. 1844.
Do. - -	Do.	1,750,000 00	Do. 1847.
Do. - -	Do.	1,750,000 00	Do. 1850.
Do. - -	Do.	1,750,000 00	Do. 1852.
Citizens' Bank of Louisiana	1st Feb. 1835	1,600,000 00	1st Feb. 1850.
Do. - -	Do.	1,600,000 00	Do. 1859.
Do. - -	Do.	1,600,000 00	Do. 1868.
Do. - -	Do.	1,600,000 00	Do. 1877.
Do. - -	Do.	1,600,000 00	Do. 1886.
		$ 18,354,000 00	

The bonds issued as the state's subscription to the stock of the New Orleans draining company, are redeemable on the 1st of November, 1855; those to the Charity Hospital on the 1st May, 1858; and those issued as a loan to the New Orleans and Nashville railroad company, on the 1st of April, 1867.

Most of the companies in whose favour the bonds have been issued, have engaged to make the principal payable in London; but the engage-

* This amount was the unredeemed portion of a former issue to the Planters' Association, which became payable in 1838. By the act 7th March, 1836, the payment of these bonds and of those due in 1843 is postponed to the year 1848, and an exchange to other bonds authorised.

ment of the state extends only to the payment in New Orleans. Those assigned to the Union Bank, and that portion issued to the Planters' Association, which is redeemable in 1843, are made payable by those institutions at the exchange of 4s. 3d. per dollar; those issued to the Planters' Association in 1836, and those for the New Orleans draining company, are redeemable at 4s. 6d. Those issued to the Citizens' Bank are redeemable in London at 4s. 6d., excepting the first 1350 bonds of the different series (amounting to $3,000,000 00), which are redeemable in Amsterdam at the exchange of 1200 guilders for $444 44. $300,000 00 of those which have been issued to the New Orleans and Nashville railroad, are redeemable in London at the rate of 4s. 6d.; the remaining $200,000 00 of this loan were originally made payable at the Union Bank in New Orleans; but, by a subsequent resolution of the 14th of July, 1837, the principal is made payable at the Bank of America in the city of New York. The bonds issued to the Bank of Louisiana, those to the Mechanics' and Traders' Bank, and those to the hospital, are payable only in New Orleans.

The bonds issued to the different banking companies and to the New Orleans draining company, bear interest at 5 per cent., which is payable in London at the exchange of 4s. 6d., excepting on the bonds issued to the Mechanics' and Traders' Bank, the interest on which is payable at New Orleans, and on the portion of the stock issued to the Citizens' Bank, of which the principal has

Rate of interest, and when and where payable.

been made payable in Amsterdam ; the dividends on which are also payable in that city, at the same rate fixed for the principal, viz. 1200 guilders for $444 44. The state's responsibility attaches to the engagement to pay the dividends in sterling and Dutch money on the bonds issued to the banks.

The following are the dates at which the interests respectively fall due.

On the bonds granted to the Bank of Louisiana, and on those to the Planters' Bank, on the 1st days of January and July. On those to the Union Bank and on those to the Citizens' Bank, on the 1st of February and 1st of August.

On those to the Mechanics' and Traders' Bank, and on those to the Charity Hospital, on the 1st of May and 1st of November.

The dividends on the bonds to the New Orleans draining company are payable on the 1st of February and 1st of August at New Orleans, but not until three months afterwards in London. The bonds issued to the New Orleans and Nashville railroad company bear interest at the rate of 6 per cent., which is payable on the 1st of February and 1st of August. On the $300,000 00 of which the principal is payable in London, the interest has likewise been made payable there by the company at the exchange of 4s. 6d., two months after it becomes payable in New Orleans.

Loans raised for banks. Bank of Louisiana.

The first, in point of time, of the loans raised by this state to aid in the formation of banking companies, consisted of bonds to the extent of

$2,400,000 00, issued in payment of the state's CHAP.
subscription of two millions of dollars to the VII.
capital of the Bank of Louisiana; of these,
$1,200,000 00 have been paid off out of the profits
of the establishment, leaving an equal amount still
unredeemed.

A detailed account of this prosperous institution
having been already given *, it will be sufficient
in this place to refer to the statements in the Appendix, to show the nature of its liabilities, and
the manner in which its funds were employed
before and after its suspension of specie payments,
as well as at a more recent period. †

The Mechanics' and Traders' Bank is another Mechanics'
establishment for which the state has issued bonds and
in payment of its subscription as a shareholder Bank.
to its capital. The small stake which the state
holds in this bank, viz. one hundred and fifty
thousand dollars out of a capital of two millions,
renders the collateral security afforded to the holder
of the state bonds, by so large a capital, propor-
tionately great. The affairs of this bank will be
likewise detailed in the Appendix.

The capitals of the three remaining establish- Loans for
ments, which are what have been designated property
" property banks," have been entirely raised by banks.
the sale of state bonds. The nature of these in-

* See page 92. In the account alluded to, the second series
of the state bonds, amounting to $600,000 00, was referred to
as having been advertised for payment; since the account was
written, the payment has been effected.

† See Appendix C C, 1., &c.

stitutions has been already described and exempli-
fied in the account that has been given of the
Union Bank of Louisiana.*

Planters'
Bank.
The consolidated association of the planters of
Louisiana, commonly called- the Planters' Bank,
was established the earliest of the three, its charter
being dated in 1828. The capital of this institution was originally $2,500,000 00, raised by a like
amount of state bonds. These bonds are guaranteed by mortgages to the amount of three millions
on productive property in land and houses, worth
double that amount. Stockholders are allowed
to borrow to the extent of one half the amount of
their stock, but loans so obtained must be repaid
by yearly instalments to meet the payment of the
bonds by the bank. The state, on the full redemption of the bonds, is, in consideration of its
guarantee, to be admitted as a stockholder to the
extent of one million of dollars. Dividends are only
declared in proportion as the bonds are redeemed,
the profits until then being retained as a sinking
fund to meet the redemption of the bonds: the
charter to this bank was granted for twenty-five
years.

Union
Bank.
The Union Bank, and the Citizens' Bank, are
founded on the same principles. The capital of
the former was raised by the sale of state bonds
to the amount of seven millions of dollars. The
guarantee consists of original mortgages of the
stockholders to the extent of eight millions on
productive property worth double the amount.

* See page 97.

The profits realised by the Union Bank are to be divided between the state and the stockholders as each series of the bonds is redeemed, in proportion to the amount redeemed ; the interest of the state, in consideration of its guarantee, being one sixth. The charter of this bank, which was granted in April, 1832, expires in 1857. The Union Bank has eight branches in different parts of the state.

The nominal capital of the Citizens' Bank is twelve millions of dollars ; but bonds to the amount of eight millions only have been issued : the first three millions were sold in Holland.

Mortgages are pledged for the redemption of the bonds as they become due, to the amount of $14,400,000 00, on property worth upwards of $20,000,000 00.

The interest of the state in the profits of this bank is one sixth, as in the case of the Union Bank. The charter of the Citizens' Bank was granted in April, 1833, to continue for fifty years. This bank is authorised to establish eight branches.*

* The law granting the issue of the bonds actually in existence bears date only on the 30th of January, 1836 ; some delay having occurred, owing to the difficulty of disposing of the bonds in the form first proposed, by which they were to be issued in the name of the bank, and not of the state, as at present. Although bonds to the amount of eight millions of dollars have been issued to the bank, 3,600,000 remain unsold. To afford greater time for the disposal of these bonds, and at the same time to obtain the means of furnishing the stockholders of the bank with the loans to which they are entitled by law, the bank has issued post notes, bearing interest at the

CHAP.
VII.

Present
condition
of the
property
banks.

In 1834, the Planters' Association redeemed the first series of its bonds, amounting to $446,000 00.* The realised profits, however, at the time not amounting to this sum, it was necessary to take part from its capital. $171,000 00 more of the bonds being redeemable on the 30th of June, 1838, an act of the legislature was passed in March, 1836, to postpone the payment till the year 1848; the payment of the portion redeemable in 1843 was likewise postponed to the same time. On the 1st of May, 1836, a fresh issue of bonds took place to the extent of one million of dollars, but the amount of the outstanding bonds after this being only $2,004,000 00, they apparently must have been given in exchange for an equal amount of the bonds originally issued. The documents, however, which I possess do not clearly show the nature of these transactions.†

---

rate of $5\frac{1}{2}$ per cent., redeemable on the 1st days of February of the years 1841, 1842, and 1843. The bonds for $3,600,000 00 held by the bank are specially reserved to secure the payment of these post notes; the proceeds of the bonds, as sold, together with all profits and annual repayments on the loans to the stockholders being set apart for that purpose. The amounts of these post notes which had been issued on the 1st of October, 1838, were as follows: —

Due in 1841	-	-	- $423,000 00
1842	-	-	- 422,000 00
1843	-	-	- 423,000 00

* This amount should apparently be $496,000 00.

† The redemption of part of the first series of the bonds out of the capital of the bank seems to have been censured by the supreme court of the state, not only as being unfair to the

Although the framers of the Planters' Bank appear at the commencement to have been too sanguine as to its prospects of redeeming the debt originally contracted to establish it, the institution has proved very efficient, and its affairs have been, and continue to be, well conducted. Its capital being obtained at 5 per cent., while 8 per cent. is charged on the loans to which the shareholders are by law entitled, the employment of this portion of the capital affords a regular and steady profit.

The obligation, however, which the property banks are under to lend a portion of their capital on permanent loans, necessarily cramps their means of extending their circulation; and on referring to the tables in the Appendix, it will be seen that the liabilities in this particular of the three banks in question are of inconsiderable amount.

The situation of the Planters' Bank, at the time even of the suspension of specie payments, seems to have been one to which no censure can apply.* Its circulation, and the deposits of individuals on the 23d of January, 1837, constituting the only

---

creditors and customers of the bank, who have a claim to the preservation of the capital in its original integrity, but as having the effect of subjecting the shares of the stockholders to a greater proportion of the debts of the establishment than they had agreed to be bound for.

* See Appendix C C, 1., &c.

liabilities payable on demand, were then as follows : —

Circulation $385,605 00
Deposits   675,564 00
———————— Making together $1,061,169 00

There was, besides, due to it, from foreign banks,
the sum of $242,085 00. To meet these engage-
ments, the bank had in its vaults $325,846 00 in
specie, and held a large amount of bills of exchange,
of which $1,468,091 00 were due within fifty
days. This latter item, by making the weekly receipts of the bank to average $200,000 00, would
have apparently been sufficient to meet any drain
upon it in times even of the greatest distrust.

Profits real-
ised.
The other banks established on the same principle appear also at this time to have been in a
favourable position, and though more recently
established than the Planters' Bank, are making
greater progress in the accumulation of a fund for
the future redemption of the bonds issued on their
behalf.

The following statement will show the position
in this respect of the three establishments on the
23d of December, 1837, on which day there was—

At the credit of the state and the stockholders
of the Planters' Bank —

Profit realised, and considered as fresh capital - $300,000 00
Reserved fund, consisting of profits not yet applied as capital   -   -   -   -   174,856 00
                                                    —————————
              Total of profits realised $474,856 00

At the credit of the state and stockholders of the Union Bank —

As capital	-	-	- *$* 820,000 00
Reserved fund	-	-	1,091,406 00

Total of profits realised *$*1,911,406 00

And at the credit of the state and stockholders of the Citizens' Bank —

As capital	-	-	- *$*108,000 00
Reserved fund	-	-	- 331,470 00

Total of profits realised *$*439,470 00

It is true that the amount of protested paper held by the banks at this date was very considerable, but it was expected that a large proportion would be eventually realised.*

By a subsequent return on the 1st of October, 1838, the total of realised profits of the Union Bank and Citizens' Bank had advanced respectively to *$*1,967,019 00 and *$*494,656 00, but those of the Planters' Bank had fallen to *$*431,338 00; on the 3d of September preceding, the profits of this bank had been stated at *$*516,981 00. At these dates, the capital of the institution seems to have been still further reduced, as it is set down at *$*1,951,000 00; but no explanation is given of these circumstances. On the 31st of December,

* The total amount of paper held under protest by the Citizens' Bank was *$*176,527 00; that held by the Union Bank *$*819,648 00; and that held by the Citizens' Bank *$*120,599 00.

State of
banks
generally
in New
Orleans.

1837, the capital was stated at $2,532,000 00 : whether any further reduction of bonds took place in the mean time does not appear.*

The city of New Orleans, forming, as it does, the outlet and chief emporium for the produce of the vast tracts traversed by the Mississippi and its tributaries, necessarily requires, and can easily support, a large banking capital. Eleven establishments, besides those in which the state has a direct interest, are at present in existence.

In the early part of 1837, the affairs of the whole were subjected to the strict investigation of a committee appointed by the legislature, who reported that they found them, in the aggregate, in a sound condition ; and the readiness with which the enquiries were met, in all but two cases †, gives a favourable impression of the integrity with which their affairs are managed.

The paid up capital of these banks, on the 23d December, 1837, amounted to $39,943,832 00.‡

* Such facts as I have been able to collect with respect to this bank are given above as tending to elicit further particulars; they are not such in their present state as to warrant any conclusion being drawn with respect to the good or bad management of the bank.

† The Commercial Bank and the Orleans Bank refused to submit to any investigation, not wishing to admit such a precedent.

‡ Of this there was held in Europe - $ 20,725,080 00
In the state of Louisiana - - - 12,273,042 00
In other states - - - - 6,945,710 00
                                    _____
                                    $ 39,943,832 00

The total liabilities of the whole to the public amounted to $27,864,742 00, while the assets amounted to $72,712,463 00.

The immediate liabilities consisted of —

Circulation	-	- $4,397,960 00
Deposits	-	- 7,426,468 00
		$11,824,428 00

The specie in their vaults amounted to $2,729,983 00, bearing the proportion of about 60 per cent. to the circulation, and 23 per cent. to the immediate liabilities.

As the institutions with which the state is more immediately connected form part of this extensive system, it is satisfactory to see that banking is thus generally in a sound condition, and that the number of the banks does not appear to exceed the wants of the community.

The loans of this state, for purposes not connected with the establishment of banking companies, are so small in amount as to require comparatively few observations.

The New Orleans and Nashville railroad is to extend from New Orleans, or rather from the northern part of Lake Pontchartrain to Nashville, in Tennessee. When completed, it will be 564 miles in length ; but the portion within the state of Louisiana will be only about eighty miles. The bonds issued as a loan to this company are endorsed to the order of the Commercial Bank of New Orleans, and have the guarantee of that establishment.

New Orleans draining company.

Miscellaneous purposes.

Financial condition of the state.

Commerce.

The object of the New Orleans draining company is to drain the swamps between that city and Lake Pontchartrain by hydraulic machines, similar to those used in Holland. The extent of these marshes is about thirty-five square miles, and the profits of the company will be derived from the increased value which will be given to the land. The lands already drained, which have been reclaimed from a depth of several feet of water, are very valuable, and are under excellent cultivation : the sugar-cane is the principal production.

The security of the bonds for establishing the hospital, and of those for building the state house, depends entirely on the general resources of the state.

I have obtained no particulars respecting the financial condition of Louisiana ; but it is a state generally possessing extensive means.

The French, who were the first to explore and settle in the valley of the Mississippi, descended the river to its mouth in 1681 ; and, in the following century, the country, which received from them the name of Louisiana, was granted to the celebrated association, called the Mississippi Company, projected by John Law, in 1717. Though this scheme, so well known by the ruin which it spread among the first families in France, proved an entire failure to the projectors, it served to increase the population of the district in question, which from that time began to rise into importance. It was not, however, until it came under the rule of the United States, that Louisiana rose

to the high position in wealth and importance
which it now holds.*

The city of New Orleans is situated on the left bank of the Mississippi, about 100 miles from the sea by the windings of the river, though only about fifteen miles distant in a direct line from Lake Borgne, to the head of which bay vessels of moderate burden can come up. The Mississippi, by which alone vessels of larger size can approach the town, exceeds 100 feet in depth, and is about half a mile wide. This magnificent river preserves the same width, and nearly the same depth, to within a short distance of the sea, though on the bar there are only sixteen feet of water. The number of ships that load and unload at New Orleans is very great, the shipping that entered there in 1835 amounting to 357,414 tons. The shipping belonging to the port amounted in 1836 to 81,710 tons.

The value of native American produce exported from New Orleans greatly exceeds that from any other city in the Union ; the exports of that description from Louisiana amount to nearly one third of those of the whole country. With regard to its im-

* The name of Louisiana, previously to the year 1811, was given to the whole of that vast and ill-defined tract of country which was ceded by France to the United States in 1803, the part to which the name is now restricted having till that time been styled the Territory of Orleans. On this territory being admitted into the Union, it adopted the general name, when the remaining portion of the original Louisiana received the distinct names of Arkansas, Missouri, &c.

ports, this state falls far short of New York, but ranks next to it and Massachusetts. The population of New Orleans in 1830 amounted to 46,082, but in 1836 was estimated at 70,000. The principal agricultural products of the state are cotton and sugar; but the chief trade of New Orleans arises from its being the great emporium of the whole valley of the Mississippi and its tributaries; through means of which it enjoys a greater command of internal navigation than any other city in the world. The unhealthiness of the climate forms the greatest drawback to its prosperity.

INDIANA.

Amount of debt and liabilities. THE debts and engagements of this state consist of loans, raised or authorised to be raised for the following purposes, viz. : —

Raised for the state's subscription to the State
   Bank of Indiana   -   -   - $ 1,390,000 00
Raised for the Wabash and Erie canal   -   1,727,000 00
Raised or authorised to be raised under the
   internal improvement act   -   -   10,000,000 00
Authorised to be raised for the extension of
   the bank capital   -   -   -   1,100,000 00

          Making together $14,217,000 00

The state has, in addition, pledged its credit to the Lawrenceburg and Indianapolis railroad company for $500,000 00.

No part, however, of the last loan for the State

Bank having yet been raised, and about one half
only of the sum authorised under the internal
improvement act having been issued, the actual
debt of the state is little more than eight millions
of dollars.

The whole of the debt of this state consists of
bonds, payable to the bearer.

These are redeemable at a variety of times and
at various places. The sum for the state's subscription to the Bank of Indiana, under an act of
the 28th of January, 1834, was borrowed on a
credit of thirty years; but the principal may be
redeemed after twenty years from the 1st of July,
1836, at the pleasure of the state. The principal
of this loan is payable at the office of the Morris
canal and banking company in New Jersey, or at
their agent's in the city of New York.

One of the early loans for the Wabash and Erie
canal for $400,000 00, under an act of the 1st of
February, 1834, was raised on a credit of forty
years, from the 1st of January, 1835, but the principal may be redeemed after twenty-five years, at
the option of the state, either in full or by the payment of not less than 50 per cent. on each certificate at any one period. The principal of this loan
is payable at the Merchants' Bank in the city of
New York. Another sum of $500,000 00 for the
same canal, under an act of the 27th of January,
1836, was borrowed for fifty years, but with a
similar power reserved to the state to redeem the
principal after thirty years, from the 1st of January
in that year. The principal of this loan is payable

CHAP.
VII.

Form of
security,
and when
redeem-
able.

by the Morris canal and banking company at New Jersey, or at their agency in the city of New York. The loans under the general act for internal improvements are redeemable at a variety of dates from 1856 to 1866. The principal is chiefly payable by the Morris canal and banking company, or their agent in New York, but $1,700,000 00, redeemable in 1863, has been made payable in London at the exchange of 4*s.* 6*d.* per dollar.

Rate of interest, and when and where payable.
The bonds of this state bear interest in all cases at 5 per cent., which is payable at the places where the principal is redeemable ; but by an arrangement of the Morris canal and banking company, the interest on such bonds of the internal improvement loan as are registered for that purpose, is payable in London at the current exchange, three months after it becomes due in America. The interest on the bonds, the principal of which is payable in London, is paid at the exchange of 4*s.* 6*d.* per dollar.

State Bank of Indiana.
The State Bank of Indiana was established in 1834, and is the only bank within the limits of the state. Its capital on the 31st of October, 1837, was $1,847,125 00, of which the state held $865,000 00, and individuals $982,125 00. This capital appears to be insufficient for the growing wants of the state, and a committee, which was appointed to investigate into the condition and management of the bank, in a report dated the 29th of January, 1838, recommended an increase of state capital in its eleven branches to the extent of one hundred thousand dollars in each,

making together $1,100,000 00. As previous to the report, the capital of the bank amounted to $1,900,000 00, this increase, when effected, will raise it to $3,000,000 00. A loan has been authorised to provide the necessary sum.

The state's subscription, in the first instance, not absorbing the entire proceeds of the loan contracted for the purpose, a portion of the sum raised was lent to individual stockholders to enable them to pay for their stock, on their mortgaging to the state lands valued at double the amount of the loans : — the amount lent in this way at the date of the report was $255,009 05. For these loans, the stockholders pay interest to the state at the rate of 6 per cent. The premium received by the state on the loan, and the amount not absorbed in these two ways, appear to have been paid over to commissioners to form a sinking fund.

The committee, in their report, express an opinion that the act establishing the bank does not provide sufficiently for the exercise of a proper control by the state over the bank and its branches, and adduce an instance of great mismanagement in one of the branches, which by making large loans to stockholders with an understanding that the sums lent should not be called in, had greatly crippled its means of general usefulness. If the loans to these persons were on the security of their stock, which is not stated to be the case, the practice is one strongly to be condemned.

The committee, moreover, strongly and justly condemn the practice generally resorted to by the branches, of buying the notes of other banks at a discount; of their dealing in fictitious bills of exchange ; and of their risking large sums of money by deposits on interest, on the banks of other states. The committee, however, appear in some of their strictures to have formed incorrect notions of the functions of a state bank ; stating, that the object of a state in chartering such institutions, and contributing to their funds, is not to seek a profitable investment, but the public good ; they condemn, therefore, the principle that such a bank should look to profits rather than to the sustaining the enterprise and rewarding the industry of individuals. Such at least could not have been the motives of the state's co-proprietors in the institution ; nor by acting on such views, would a bank in the end be so likely to conduce to the good of the community, as if guided exclusively by the apparently more selfish principles of self-interest; and viewing the general condition of the bank at the different times at which it has published statements of its affairs, it will, so far as a judgment can be formed from these, notwithstanding the malpractices attributed to it, bear a favourable comparison with most of the banks in the United States, against which the same or similar practices may but too commonly be charged.*

* On the 1st of May, 1837, shortly before the suspension of specie payments, out of $4,219,280 15, due to the bank,

According to the statement of the president
of the bank, the average profit has been about 13 per cent. ; at the period of the suspension in May, 1837, the surplus fund amounted to $271,464 12; on the 31st of October it had reached $292,143 92. A statement of the affairs of the bank on the latter day, as well as its position on the 26th of November preceding, is given in the Appendix.*

The Wabash and Erie canal is the first under- Wabash
and Erie
canal. taking in this state for which a public loan was contracted. The portion of the work comprised within the limits of Indiana will extend from La- fayette to the Ohio state line, a distance of 105 miles, whence it is being carried down the valley of the Maumee, as has already been described under

---

$38,435 24 only, according to a statement of the president of the establishment, were in suspended debts, and no fears of the loss of any of the debts were entertained. The directors had not obtained loans beyond other men in business in similar cir- cumstances. More than $2,700,000 00 were lent to persons not stockholders; and the owners of about one half of the stock held by individuals were in debt to the bank less than one fourth of the amount of their stock. On a previous occasion, it was attempted by the president to ascertain what numbers of each employment or profession were then accommodated with loans, and it appeared that notes and bills had been discounted for 722 farmers, 339 merchants, druggists, and grocers, 272 mechanics, 134 produce and cattle dealers, 121 persons of the learned professions, 87 manufacturers, millers, and distillers, 27 innkeepers, and 266 persons whose employment was not ascertained.

* See Appendix D D, 1., &c.

the head of the latter state. As in the case of Ohio, alternate sections of the land along the line of the canal have been granted by Congress to the state of Indiana. The cost of the canal is estimated at $2,000,000 00; $220,000 00 have been already received from the sale of lands granted by the United States, and $367,833 00 are due on lands sold; the portion remaining unsold is estimated by the chief engineers of the state to be worth $1,808,396 00. It is intended to extend the canal from Lafayette down the valley of the Wabash to Terre Haute, a distance of 90 miles; and if the expectations of the engineers with respect to the value of the lands prove to be well founded, the sum realised will nearly complete this extension, which will carry the work along one of the richest valleys in the western country. Ninety miles of the main canal are already finished and in use, and fifty-five miles more are nearly completed.

Internal improvement board.
In January, 1836, a bill was passed by the legislature of this state, authorising a system of internal improvements which should embrace various public works to belong exclusively to the state, and to be constructed wholly at its expense. The act authorises the loan of $10,000,000 00 to be raised in such amounts as may be required. The construction of these works was confided to a board of public improvement; and the management of the internal improvement fund to a separate board of fund commissioners.

Part of this plan consisted in a series of canals

along the valleys of the great rivers of the state, many of which become unserviceable during a considerable portion of the year, owing to the lowness of the water. In connection with these lines of canals, the state proposed to construct several great overland routes of inter-communication, consisting, in part, of roads made on the principle of M'Adam, and in part of railroads.

The sum authorised to be raised was appropriated as follows : —

1. To the White Water canal, including a lateral canal or railroad, to connect with it the Central or White River canal - - $1,400,000 00
2. To the Central or White River Canal - 3,500,000 00
3. To the extension of the Wabash and Erie canal - - - 1,300,000 00
4. To removing obstructions on the Wabash - 50,000 00
5. To the Madison and Lafayette railroad - 1,300,000 00
6. To a turnpike road from New Albany to Vincennes - - - 1,150,000 00
7. To a turnpike road or railroad from New Albany to Crawfordsville - - 1,300,000 00

$10,000,000 00

It is by this bill, also, that the credit of the state for $500,000 00 is given to the Lawrenceburg and Indianapolis railroad company.

The cost of these works, which, as modified by a subsequent act, will comprise 840 miles of canal, 90 miles of railroad, and 335 miles of turnpike roads, will, it is supposed, be nearly twenty millions of dollars: about 400 miles of these improvements, embracing portions of each work, have been placed under contract, and are in progress.

The White Water canal will commence at Cambridge City on the National road, and be carried down the valley of the White Water river to Lawrenceburg on the Ohio, a distance of seventy-six miles. The bill provides for the subsequent union of the north end of this canal with the Central canal, at a given point in Delaware county.

The Central or White River canal is the most extensive of the works commenced under the Internal Improvement act. The part now in progress will pass from Indianapolis down the valley of the White river to Petersburg, and thence to Evansville on the Ohio, a distance altogether of 190 miles. It is intended to prolong the canal in a northerly direction from Indianapolis to a point on the Wabash and Erie canal near Peru, a distance, by the line surveyed, of about 120 miles. A cross canal, now in progress, from Terre Haute to the Central canal, near the mouth of Eel river, a distance of forty miles, will render the communication between the Ohio, at Evansville, and Lake Erie, complete, by means of the Wabash canal, should the northern section of the canal not be executed.

The works undertaken for improving the navigation of the Wabash river, consist in the removal of obstructions which exist above the mouth of the White river; a succession of rocks, bars, and islands, rendering the channel at this place crooked and intricate, and at periods of low water impeding the passage even of the river-boats. The state of Illinois has joined in this enterprise.

The Madison and Lafayette railroad, from Madison on the Ohio, through Indianapolis and Crawfordsville, to Lafayette on the Wabash canal, a distance of 160 miles, traverses a most important part of the state. The road from New Albany on the Ohio to Vincennes on the Wabash passes also through a central and important district : its length is about 104 miles. The New Albany and Crawfordsville railroad is designed to connect the Ohio with the Wabash and Erie canal, by a route nearly parallel with the Madison and Lafayette railroad, and of about the same length. The Lawrenceburg and Indianapolis railroad, which has received assistance from the state by the use of its credit, is ninety miles in length.

These works are all undoubtedly of great importance, but the anxiety of the inhabitants of the state, that, as all have equally contributed to the cost of the improvements, all should equally participate in the benefits, has forced it to commence too many at once, instead of adhering to one or two, and pushing them on to completion ; the consequence is, that very large amounts have been expended before any receipts have been obtained. The difficulty which the state has lately experienced in raising money has forced it to adopt a wiser policy ; and the lateral works are being abandoned, in order that the remaining funds may be exclusively devoted to the main lines.

The sum expended on the public works in 1837

was about $1,300,000 00. The total expenditure has now amounted to about five millions; a further sum of one million will complete 200 miles of the canal, forty-four miles of railroad, and forty-one miles of Macadamised road, which will then all yield income.

Auxiliary funds.

The interest on this sum, until the tolls on the public works become available, according to a statement made by one of the fund commissioners and the president of the state bank, has been provided for by taxation; but what particular tax, if any, is specially appropriated to this purpose, does not appear. Part of the interest, however, to the extent of $40,000 00 a year, has been paid out of a portion of the surplus revenue received by the state under the distribution act, the sum accruing under that act to this state having been made available for that purpose. The funds of the state set apart and applicable to the payment of the interest and principal of the internal improvement loan may be considered therefore to be, —

1. The tolls on the works themselves.

2. The tolls on the Wabash and Erie canal, when the loan on that account shall have been redeemed by the sale of the lands granted by Congress.

3. The sum received by the state under the distribution act, amounting to $860,254 44.

4. The bank stock of the state, which has likewise been appropriated to this purpose, when the

profits shall have redeemed the loans contracted CHAP.
by the state to pay for it. VII.

The property subject to taxation in this state is estimated at $75,000,000 00, which is considered a low valuation : the tax for the support of the state amounts to one twentieth per cent. of this, which is adequate to the expenditure of the government for state purposes. The aggregate receipts of the state for 1835 amounted to $107,714 00 ; and the expenditure for the same year to $103,901 00. I have no later particulars.

The inhabitants of this state are engaged almost exclusively in agricultural pursuits ; manufactures can hardly be said to exist. It contains no large towns, but thriving villages are scattered over its surface.

MISSISSIPPI.

THE debt of this state has been raised entirely for banking purposes, and consists of bonds issued — Amount of debt.

As the state's subscription to the stock of the
Planters' Bank of Mississippi - - $2,000,000 00
To form the capital of the Union Bank of Mississippi - - - - 5,000,000 00

Making together $7,000,000 00

The bonds granted by this state are made payable to the bearer. Those issued as the state's subscription to the Planters' Bank of Mississippi are redeemable as follows : — Form of security, where and when redeemable.

$125,000 00 on the 16th December, 1840.
 125,000 00 on the 16th December, 1845.
 125,000 00 on the 16th December, 1851.
 125,000 00 on the 16th December, 1856.
 500,000 00 on the 1st March, 1861.
 500,000 00 on the 1st March, 1866.
 500,000 00 on the 1st March, 1871.

$2,000,000 00

Those issued to form the capital of the Union Bank are redeemable as follows :—

$1,250,000 00 on the 5th February, 1850.
 3,750,000 00 on the 5th February, 1858.

$5,000,000 00

The principal of the last three series of the bonds issued to the Planters' Bank is redeemable at the Phœnix Bank in the city of New York.

The state engages to pay the principal of the remaining bonds issued to this bank as well as those issued to the Union Bank, in current money only ; but the Union Bank has engaged to pay those issued on its account in London, at the exchange of 4s. 6d. per dollar.

The bonds issued to the Planters' Bank bear interest at the rate of 6 per cent., payable, on the first four series, on the first days of January and July, and on the last three, on the first days of March and September : the interest on the latter is payable at the Phœnix Bank in New York, but by an arrangement of the Phœnix Bank, the dividends on such bonds as are registered for that purpose are payable in London at the current rate of exchange, subject to a deduction of 1 per cent. on the amount of the payment, which covers all charges, and includes the guarantee of bills remitted. The bonds issued to the Union Bank bear interest at 5 per cent., which is payable in London at the exchange of 4s. 6d. per dollar. The state concurs in and guarantees this arrangement.

The Planters' Bank of Mississippi was established by an act passed on the 10th February, 1830, and the bonds were raised under this and two supplemental acts. The capital in the first instance was limited to three millions of dollars, of which two thirds were reserved for the state, the remaining million to be subscribed for by individuals, to be paid for in gold or silver, or in the notes of the bank of the state of Mississippi. The state was authorised by the act to subscribe the capital of the literary fund and of other funds in the treasury, as part of its share of the capital of the bank, provided the dividend should be applied to the purposes originally intended in the creation of the funds. It was afterwards enacted that these items should be in addition to the capital of three millions of dollars; and the state's two millions were consequently made up by an issue of bonds to the full amount. The capital subscribed by individuals was also increased by a further sum of one million of dollars. By this means, the total capital of the bank on the 18th of April last amounted to $4,260,200 00.

A principal feature in the charter of this bank

is the permission it gives to hold real as well as personal property, provided the aggregate amount does not exceed six millions of dollars.

One half of the capital is directed by the act to be lent on mortgage. No notes of a lower denomination than five dollars may be issued, and the amount of notes issued may not exceed three times the amount of the stock and of the moneys in deposit in the bank. The bank is allowed to receive 7 per cent. on sums lent on personal security, and 8 per cent. on loans on mortgage. Permanent loans to directors are limited to six thousand dollars.

not attended to.

Some of these provisions have not been attended to ; and among them, the salutary one that the respective subscribers for stock should pay the amount subscribed in gold or silver or in the notes of banks of undoubted solvency, has not been enforced. While the state paid its share in actual capital, the two millions of stock subscribed for by individuals were paid, for the greater part, in their own notes, which remain uncancelled, having been renewed from time to time by the drawers ; nor has any portion of the capital stock been lent on mortgage security, a deviation from the charter which defeats one great object in the creation of the bank, which was the promotion of the agricultural interests of the state.

Situation of its affairs.

The Planters' Bank refused all scrutiny into its affairs, when a commission was appointed to examine into the condition of the banks of this state ; but statements of its situation at two periods, viz.

on the 27th of April, 1837, and on the 18th of CHAP.
April, 1839, have been published, and will be found VII.
in the Appendix.*

At the latter date, the portion set aside to the
credit of profit and loss amounted to $1,321,351 24,
and a profit realised in discounts is not included
in the amount. The sum under discount is however very large, and the portion designated as
being in suit amounts to $643,368 39. The im-
mediate liabilities of the bank, if in these be included the items of " bills and cheques payable,"
seem greatly disproportionate to its means to meet
them ; and an item of " bonds payable," to the
extent of no less than $2,233,333 33, shows the
bank to have resorted to a means of raising funds
which is not creditable to a moneyed institution.†

The act to incorporate the Union Bank of Mis- Union
sissippi was passed in the last session of the legis- Bank.
lature, with a view to remedy the disordered currency of this state, where the banking institutions
have been in general very badly conducted.

The capital of this bank is limited to fifteen
millions of dollars. Like the property banks of
Louisiana, it is based on landed security, on the
pledge of which the state has issued bonds to the
extent of five millions of dollars, which form its
active capital. It remains to be seen how far it

* See Appendix E E, 1., &c.
† The legislature having transferred the stock held by the
state in the Planters' Bank to the Mississippi railroad company,
the capital of the latter company now affords a collateral security to the holder of the state's bonds.

CHAP.
VII.

Bad condi-
tion of the
banks in
this state.

may answer its proposed end, no sufficient experience having yet proved the goodness of its management.

The banking capital of this state seems already
to be far beyond the wants of the inhabitants, the
increase in late years having been very considerable.

On the 1st of January, 1836, there were five
banks in the state, with a nominal capital of about
twelve millions of dollars, and less than nine millions actually paid up. On the 15th of February,
1838, the governor, in his veto message to the
legislature refusing to incorporate another bank
whose charter had received the sanction of the
two houses, assigns, among other reasons for refusing his consent to the bill, that there were then
twenty-four banks in existence, with nominal
capitals amounting to $62,512,000 00, of which
$18,884,340 00 were actually paid up; and that
when the Union Bank and others then recently
chartered should have come into operation, the
banking capital of the state actually paid in would
exceed forty millions. Most of the banks being authorised to issue notes to the extent of three times
the amount of their actual capitals, they would thus,
he observes, as it is, have the power of inundating
the state with a circulation which could not maintain its value, and which would injure the planters
and the commercial interests by the evils of a fluctuating and depreciated paper currency. This evil,
however, seems already to exist in the state; its

notes in January, 1838, having been in other states
at a discount of 20 per cent.

The efforts of Governor M'Nutt to correct the abuses which, in the banking institutions, are undermining the prosperity of the state, seem to have met with little favour from the legislature; as on the day following the rejection of the above bill another was presented to him, to " authorise the bank to issue post notes and for other purposes" to which he likewise affixed the executive veto.* In his message on this occasion he pertinently observes, that " borrowing money does not pay debts; — it merely substitutes one creditor for another; the debt remains to be paid out of the produce of the soil."

The resources of this state derived from the
soil are considerable; and, if the inhabitants would learn wisdom from experience, are such as might soon relieve them from their prostrate condition.

A large portion of the southern part of this state is comprised in the great sand plain of this region, and the western border, on the Mississippi, consists chiefly of swamps, marshes, and lagunes; but the higher parts consist of a gently waving country of great productiveness.

Tobacco and indigo used to be the chief productions of Mississippi, but they have for some time ceased to be cultivated, the attention of the plant-

* The Planters' Bank has issued post notes, however, to a large extent.

ers being almost exclusively directed to the production of cotton. Manufactures have scarcely
any existence in this state.

Natchez, the principal city in the state, though
380 miles from the mouth of the Mississippi, carries
on a considerable direct trade with foreign countries and the northern ports, as large ships can
come up to the town; its river and inland trade
is, however, more extensive. The population in
1837 was estimated at 6000.

ILLINOIS.

Amount of
debt and
liabilities.
THE debt of this state consists of stock issued
or authorised to be issued for the following purposes : —

For the establishment of banks	- -	$3,000,000 00
For the construction of the Illinois and Michi-gan canal	- - - -	500,000 00
For internal improvements	- - -	8,000,000 00
For other purposes	- - -	100,000 00

Making together $11,600,000 00

Form of
stock, and
when and
where pay-
able.
The whole of the debt is in the form of bonds
payable to the bearer; but the internal improvement stock is the only part respecting which I
have been able to ascertain any precise particulars.
Part of this is issued under an act of the 27th of
February, 1837, and part under a supplementary
act which was passed on the 4th of March following, authorising the commissioners to subscribe

$2,000,000 00 of additional stock to the State
bank of Illinois, and $1,400,000 00 to the Illinois
bank of Shawneetown.   The bonds issued under
the supplementary act form what is called the
bank and internal improvement stock. Both descriptions of bonds are redeemable at the bank of
the United States at Philadelphia, or at its agency
in New York, at the option of the holder ; those
of the internal improvement stock under the first
act at any time after the 1st day of January, 1870,
at the pleasure of the state, and those of the bank
and internal improvement stock under the supplemental act at any time after the 1st of January,
1860.   The interest on both descriptions of stock
is at the rate of six per cent., and is payable half-
yearly on the first Mondays of January and July,
at the bank of the United States, or at its agency
in New York.   The bank and other loans of the
state bear interest at the same rate.

CHAP.
VII.

Rate of in-
terest, and
when and
where pay-
able.

By a statement published on the 8th of January,
1838, it appears that the active capital of the
state bank of Illinois consisted of $3,515,000 00,
of which $2,100,000 00 were owned by the state,
and $1,415,000 00 by individuals : a real estate
fund of $500,000 00 has to be added to this,
making the whole capital $4,015,000 00.

State bank
of Illinois.

Among the liabilities of the state bank there
is an item of $2,842,601 34, which appears to be
additional capital belonging to the bank and its
branches ; but as I have no particulars of the
manner in which the sum obtained by the sale of
the $3,000,000 00 of bonds which were issued for

314   ILLINOIS.

CHAP.
VII.

Bank of
Illinois at
Shawnee-
town.

banking purposes was applied, nor of the position of this bank beyond what its published statements show, the account I can give of it is very imperfect.

The capital of the bank of Illinois at Shawnee-town, by a statement made up on the 6th of January, was $658,050 00, of which $500,500 00 appear to be owned by the state, and the rest by individuals. Of the sum owned by the state $400,000 00 had been recently added under the authority of the act allowing the commissioners of the internal improvement fund to subscribe from its funds to increase the capital of the two banks. The bank at Shawneetown, at the date of the return, still held $400,000 00 of the bank and internal improvement stock issued for this purpose, and the state bank $1,765,000 00. The latter bank held the whole of the Illinois and Michigan canal stock. The commissioners appointed to investigate into the state of the bank of Illinois at Shawneetown, in January, 1837, give an excellent account of its condition, and of its management during the twenty years it had been in existence; and the published statements of both institutions present their affairs in a very favourable light.*

* See Appendix, letter F F, 1., &c. Among the assets of the state bank the sum of $2,740,983 06 is included under the head of state banks and branches; which, if the corresponding sum on the other side of the account denotes capital, must denote the employment of that capital at the branches: but no details being given, no judgment can be formed of the position of the affairs of the bank at these branches; both sums, however, may be a mere nominal matter of account.

The stock owned by the state in these banks, which amounts to about half a million of dollars more than the amount of the bonds issued in payment of it, together with the dividends upon it, is pledged for the punctual payment of the interest and the redemption of the $3,000,000 00 of bonds when they shall become due.

This state at an early period conceived the project of connecting the river Illinois with Lake Michigan by means of a canal, and a board of commissioners was appointed in 1823 to explore the route and estimate the cost. Little, however, seems to have been done, except obtaining a grant from Congress until the session of 1835–6, when an act was passed to authorise the construction of the canal. Under this act authority was given to raise a loan of $500,000 00, which is the only loan that has been contracted for this work.

The general system of internal improvements is under the management of a distinct board from that which has the superintendence of the Illinois and Michigan canal. An act to establish and maintain the general system of improvements was passed on the 27th February, 1837. It provides two boards, one to manage the fiscal arrangements, the other to superintend the construction of the works : it is under this act that authority was given to the fund commissioners to raise a loan of eight millions.

Before entering on a detail of the works provided for under the general improvement act, the resources of the Illinois and Michigan canal fund

CHAP.
VII.

Sinking fund.

Works undertaken by this state.

Illinois and Michigan canal.

will be taken into consideration, this canal being
quite distinct from the other improvements of the
state.

This great work, in which considerable progress
has been made, will extend from near Peru, below
the lower rapids of the Illinois, up the valleys of
that river and the Des Plains, and across from the
latter to a point on the Chicago river, about five
miles from its mouth.

The total length of the canal, including a navigable feeder which will connect it with the rapids
of the Fox river, will be 100 miles and 28 chains,
to which, if the length of the Chicago from the termination of the canal to the mouth of the river be
added, it will give upwards of 105 miles for the
entire length of the navigable line.

That such a work should be projected by so
young a state is a proof of great enterprise, especially if the difficulties presented to its execution
by the nature of the ground be taken into consideration. Although no great height has to be sur-
mounted, the waters of the Lake and the Illinois
being almost blended in high floods, yet, from the
Chicago to the Des Plains river, a distance of
more than twenty miles, a substratum of solid limestone is found only a few feet below the surface of
the ground ; it has been necessary to cut through
the whole of this, to the depth of from seven to
twenty-eight feet, for the width of the canal, which
is thirty-six feet at the bottom and sixty on the
surface. The expense of this cutting is estimated

at four millions of dollars, and the cost of the whole work at $8,654,337 00.

Congress, however, came forward, at an early period, in aid of the undertaking, and by granting each alternate section of land for ten miles in width along the line of the canal, contributed largely towards the means of executing it. This grant was passed in 1829, and in 1836 sales had been realised, producing $1,395,911 08 : 270,182 acres at that time remained unsold, which were estimated to be worth twenty dollars per acre.

The appropriations which have been made by the board of internal improvement extend to a variety of undertakings, and exceed already the amount authorised to be raised by loans.

These appropriations may be classed as follows : —

For improvements in the navigation of rivers -	$ 400,000 00
For the improvement of the national road -	250,000 00
For the central railroad - - -	3,500,000 00
For the South Cross railroad - -	1,750,000 00
For the Alton and Terre Haute railroad -	1,250,000 00
For the Northern Cross railroad - -	1,850,000 00
For the Warsaw and Bloomington railroad -	1,050,000 00
And for the benefit of those counties through which no railroad is made at the cost of the state - - - -	200,000 00
	$10,250,000 00

The latter sum is to be laid out in the improvements of roads, bridges, and other public works, at the discretion of the counties themselves. The improvement of the national road, and the special

CHAP.
VII.

appropriation to the counties, were to be provided for out of the first loan. Other clauses of the act regulate the mode of proceeding which the commissioners are to adopt; and as soon as five miles of any line of railroad is completed, they are required to place engines upon it, to give facilities of transport, and to establish tolls.

Improve-
ments of
rivers.

The contemplated improvements in the navigation of rivers consist in the ameliorating the channel of the Wabash, a work undertaken in concert with Indiana, which has been referred to under the head of that state, and in the removal of obstructions in the beds of the Illinois, the Rock river, the Kaskaskia, and the Little Wabash.

National
road.

The national road, which passes through this state, has been already incidentally referred to. Beginning at Baltimore, it traverses the whole of the United States in a westerly direction : leaving the state of Maryland at Cumberland, it crosses a corner of Pennsylvania and Virginia, passing through the flourishing town of Wheeling in the latter state. Entering Ohio at Ganesville, it passes through Columbus, the capital of the state, and thence across Indiana through Indianopolis, to the border of Illinois. Here the road, assuming a south-westerly course, passes to Vandalia, the present capital of the state.* From Vandalia its course westward is not yet determined on, but it will probably cross the Mississippi at Alton or St. Louis, and be continued to Jefferson city, in the

* Vandalia is to be the seat of government till 1840, after which it is to be removed to Alton.

state of Missouri. Its course in Illinois, from the CHAP.
VII. eastern side of the state to Vandalia, is ninety miles in length; but it is not yet in use. The width of the road, as laid out, is eighty feet.

The railroads to which sums have been appro- Railroads. priated intersect every part of the state. The Central railroad is to extend from the junction of the Ohio and Mississippi, through Vandalia and Peru, where it crosses the river Illinois at the southern termination of the Michigan canal, to Galena at the northern extremity of the state, a dis- tance of 457$\frac{1}{2}$ miles. Although the point at the junction of the Ohio and Mississippi is annually overflowed, the great natural importance of the site has suggested the idea of making this the southern extremity of the railroad; and it is in contemplation to build here a town of considerable magnitude, secured from inundation by levels or embankments. The future city has already re- ceived the name of Cairo.

The other railroads of the state intersect this line in various places : three of them cross the state in its entire breadth from the Mississippi to the Wabash.

The most southern of these, called the South Cross Railroad, extends from Alton to Mount Carmel. A second line diverging from this at Edwardsville is to extend to Shawneetown on the Ohio. These two lines including a short cross road will be 318 miles in length.

The Alton and Terre Haute railroad commences also at Alton, and proceeds to the Indiana state line at Terre Haute in a north-easterly direction through Shelbyville and Paris: the length of this work is about 160 miles.

The third and most northerly line which crosses the state is the Northern Cross railroad, extending from Quincy on the Mississippi to the state line of Indiana in the direction of Lafayette: the length of this is about 220 miles. The last work to which the state has made an appropriation, viz. the Warsaw and Bloomington railroad, joins these towns, passing through Peoria.

Amount expended.
Considerable progress has been made on the Northern Cross railroad, on which more than four hundred thousand dollars had been expended before the end of the year 1838. The total sum expended on these different railroads to that time amounted to $728,125 00.

Auxiliary funds.
The lands granted by the general government to aid in constructing the Illinois and Michigan canal are pledged for the redemption of the canal bonds; and the two banks, towards the capitals of which the commissioners of the internal improvement fund have been authorised to subscribe a portion of their funds, guarantee the ultimate redemption of those constituting the bank and internal improvement stock. The dividends on the state's share of this stock, after paying interest on the bonds, are applied towards the payment of the interest on the internal improvement loan.

The sums further appropriated to the payment of the interest on the loan for internal improvements and its final liquidation, consist, —

1. Of all rents of water power, and tolls arising from the works when constructed.

2. Of the proceeds of all donations of lands from the general government (excepting those specially pledged for the canal), or from individuals and corporations.

3. Of a portion of the surplus revenue received by this state under the distribution act of Congress.

4. Of such appropriations as may from time to time be made out of the revenue of the state.

No property, excepting land, is taxed by this state for state purposes. All lands, without regard to soil or improvements, are taxed alike, one cent and a half per acre.*

The annual revenue of the state was estimated in 1831 at $50,000 00; the ordinary annual expenses did not then exceed $28,000 00. Any surplus has usually been expended upon internal improvements. The whole annual disbursements for salaries to the executive and judicial officers amounted, in 1831, to $14,000 00, and the expense of the legislature to $8000 00. I have no later particulars of the financial condition of the treasury. A considerable revenue appears to be derived from a per centage on the value of lead produced in mines belonging to the state.

The Indians and French had long been accus- tomed to procure small quantities of ore from the

* All lands sold by the general government are exempt from taxes for five years.

CHAP.
VII.

valuable mines in this state, but it was not until 1822 that the process of separating the metal from the ore was regularly practised. From that time, up to the end of 1835, 70,420,357 pounds of lead were obtained, and upwards of 13,000,000 pounds have been smelted in one year; but the business having been overdone, the produce has since been considerably less. This statement includes the produce of Wisconsin territory as well as that of Illinois. Formerly the government received 10 per cent. in lead for rents, but it is now reduced to 6 per cent.

Population.

This state contains a great extent of fertile land, and the industry of the inhabitants is devoted entirely to agriculture : there are but few large towns in the state. Chicago, which has sprung up with the canal, is said to contain about 8000 inhabitants. The population of Alton is estimated at 2500. The general population of the state is increasing with astonishing rapidity. In 1835 it contained 272,427 ; since which time it is said to have considerably more than doubled.

ALABAMA.

Amount of debt.

BONDS have been issued or authorised by the legislature of this state for the following purposes : —

For the establishment of the bank of the state of Alabama at Tuscoloosa, and its branches, under various acts prior to the suspension of specie payments, authorising in all   -   - $7,600,000 00

As the state's subscription to the Bank of Mobile, under act of 10th January, 1835 *   - $ 600,000 00
For the relief of the bank of the state and its
branches, under an act 30th June, 1837,
legalising the suspension of specie payments   5,000,000 00
To extend the capital of the bank of the state
and its branches, under an act of the 23d December, 1837   -   -   -   -   2,500,000 00

Making together $15,700,000 00

The allotment of the capital to the bank of the
state of Alabama and its branches prior to the late
act was as follows : —

To the bank at Tuscoloosa   -   - $ 600,000 00
To the branch bank at Mobile   -   -   3,000,000 00
To the branch bank at Montgomery   -   -   1,500,000 00
To the branch bank at Decatur   -   -   1,500,000 00
To the branch bank at Huntsville   -   -   1,000,000 00

$7,600,000 00

Of the bonds to which the bank and its branches
were entitled under this allotment, the bank at
Tuscoloosa put into circulation one hundred
thousand dollars only, leaving five hundred thousand unissued: the branch at Mobile has in like
manner seven hundred thousand dollars unissued
of its original bonds, and the branch at Montgomery six hundred and eighteen thousand, re-

* The act authorises the issue of $740,000 00 as the state's
subscription to the capital of this bank, but the stockholders
refused to give the state more than 6000 shares, so that bonds
to the extent of $600,000 00 only were issued, although the
bonds, in reciting the act, state the larger amount.

Form of
security,
and when
and where
redeem-
able.

ducing the amount really issued on account of the state bank and its branches under the original grants to $5,782,000 00.

Of these, three hundred thousand dollars are redeemable not earlier than the first Monday in May in the year 1852, and the remainder not earlier than 1863. The bonds issued as the state's subscription to the Bank of Mobile are redeemable, part in 1859, and part not earlier than 1866: those constituting the capital of the bank of the state and its branches are payable in New York; those for the Bank of Mobile are made payable by the state in London, at the exchange of 4s. 6d. The bonds for the relief of the bank being, as will be presently explained, for a temporary purpose, were made payable at New York at the pleasure of the state at any time after two, four, and six years, in equal proportions: those issued to the branch at Decatur have been made payable at the end of these periods absolutely, in London, at the exchange of 4s. 6d.

The bonds issued under the act of 23d of December, 1837, are made payable by the state, in 1858, in sterling money. A small amount only of the last two loans has been negotiated.

Rate of in-
terest, and
when and
where pay-
able.

One hundred thousand dollars, which form part of the original capital of the bank of the state, bear interest at the rate of 6 per cent., as do the bonds issued under the bank relief bill; the rest of the loans of the state bear interest at 5 per cent. The interest on the loan for the Bank of Mobile, and on that to extend the capital of the bank, are payable by the state in London at the exchange of 4*s*. 6*d*. per dollar. The interest on the other loans is payable in New York, excepting on that portion of the loan under the bank relief bill, which was allotted to the branch at Decatur; the interest of which, as well as the principal, has been made payable by that branch in London.

The interest on $3,500,000 00 of the loan constituting the original capital of the branch banks, which is made payable by the state at the Phœnix Bank at New York, has been made payable by that establishment in London at the exchange of the day, three months after it becomes due in New York.

The bank of the state of Alabama, and its several branches, are the exclusive property of the state. Though nominally forming one institution, the branches act independently of the parent establishment at Tuscoloosa, and of each other.

The parent establishment commenced business in March, 1825. The branch bank at Mobile was shortly afterwards established, and that at Montgomery in 1832. The capital of the parent bank, independently of the sum raised by a sale of state bonds, consists of several distinct state funds which have been invested in it: these are the university fund; the three per cent. fund, being the proceeds of sales of the public lands given to the state for objects of internal improvement; and the revenue fund, being the surplus of the ordinary sources of the revenue of the state. These funds, which, in 1832, amounted together

CHAP.
VII.

Bank of
the state of
Alabama.

to $571,538 00, had, on the 7th of November,
1837, been increased, by gradual additions, to
$1,117,248 45, and were then as follows: —

University fund	-	- $282,016 34
Three per cent. fund	-	431,075 56
Revenue fund	-	- 404,156 55

$1,117,248 45

This sum, with the addition of $100,000 00
raised by the sale of the state 6 per cent. bonds,
made the total capital of the parent bank on
that day $1,217,248 45, and the capital of the
Condition
of, up to
1836.
bank and branches $6,899,248 45. The State
Bank and its branches appear to have been very
successful until the period of the embarrassments
of 1836. One hundred thousand dollars had been
paid annually out of the profits for some years previously to that time for the support of the state
government, under an act to abolish direct taxation
in the state : the residue of the profits, after deducting all expenses, and the annual interest on the
original capital borrowed, had been allowed to accumulate and form a sinking fund. This surplus on
the 1st of October, 1836, amounted to $1,303,634 02,
besides which, a large sum had been set aside to
meet contingencies. At this time, the institution
began to suffer from the revulsions of trade and
the general derangement of the monetary affairs
in the United States, to which Alabama, by a wild
spirit of speculation, had largely contributed.

Considerable profits accrued to the bank from
its operations after the period referred to, the sum

carried to the credit of the sinking fund on the 1st of October, 1837, being $557,053 25; besides which, a considerable sum was set aside to add to the contingent fund, while $70,000 00 were appropriated under an act of the legislature to defray the expenses of a war against the Creek and Seminole Indians; an item which will ultimately be repaid by the federal government.

The profits during this period would have appeared even larger than this, had it not been that on an amount of debt the time of repayment of which was extended under the bank relief bill the discount was not charged as usual in advance, but was to be retained, to be added to the profits, as the sums were repaid.

A large portion of the profit resulting from the business during this period of commercial distress may, however, have been swept away, if any considerable portion of the amount owing under the head of suspended debt should have proved, or may still prove, to have been ill secured. In a minute statement on the subject, which was submitted to the legislature towards the end of 1837, the amount of bad and doubtful debts is stated at $619,542 00, of which $109,272 00 are stated as bad, and $510,270 00 as doubtful: of the whole amount of bad and doubtful debts $340,910 00 were owing to the branch at Mobile. The suspended debt is, however, in reality, much larger. On the 9th of October, 1837, by a return from the branch at Mobile, the amount of notes then under protest at that establishment alone was $1,334,350 77, and the

CHAP.
VII.

Suspended debt.

CHAP.
VII.

amount of bills of exchange under protest was $2,162,887 81, making the total amount of suspended debt $3,497,238 58. This sum, however, included $655,000 00 due from the Bank of Mobile and the Planters' and Merchants' Bank of Mobile, arising out of cheques drawn by those institutions on New York which had been dishonoured : as there was little doubt that these sums would be eventually paid, this would so far reduce the amount of suspended debt.

Relief bill.

In the embarrassment produced by the loss of the control over so large an amount of the active funds of the bank in this and the other branches, which, though not to the same extent, were similarly situated, the relief bill, already alluded to, was passed.

This act, which is entitled " An Act to extend the time of indebtedness to the bank of the State of Alabama and its branches, and legalising the suspension of specie payments of the same, and for other purposes," has had the effect of greatly diminishing the account of suspended debt, but chiefly by retransferring the amount from this account to the discount account, the bank, under this act, having been compelled to discount new notes of the drawers of protested bills, in satisfaction of their debts ; the directors, with the new note, taking such additional security as the parties could give in the way of pledge either of real or personal property.

The time for the payment of the debts due to the banks was extended by the act to certain fixed periods, the repayments being required to be made in three annual instalments ; viz. 25 per cent. the first year, and 37½ per cent. in each of the two succeeding ones.

Under this act the banks were obliged to extend, not only all debts actually due, but all obligations, whether in the form of bills of exchange or otherwise, which were then running to maturity. Every debtor obtaining an extension of his debt, under this act, if it amounted to upwards of two thousand dollars, was excluded from obtaining any further loan or accommodation in discount until the whole of his debt should be discharged ; but any person having a debt extended for a less sum than two thousand dollars was entitled, by the act, to apply for accommodation to make up his debt to that sum ; and the banks were required to lend a like amount to all parties not already debtors to the bank, on their applying for it, and giving notes payable in one, two, and three years, such parties procuring at the same time two good and sufficient securities to guarantee the payment.

To supply the place of the funds locked up by this measure, and to supply additional resources, the state issued bonds to the respective banks to be sold at their par value, redeemable after two, four, and six years. By the twenty-second section of the act it is provided that the annual repayments made to the bank by the persons obtaining relief under the act should be applied to the redemption of the bonds thus authorised to be issued, and that the bonds, when so redeemed, should be cancelled, and the circulation based upon them no longer be allowed to remain outstanding. Although a considerable portion of the debt, the payment of which has been deferred under this act, was secured in a way satisfactory to the directors, it is admitted that the securities, in some instances, were insufficient, being the best only that could be obtained ; and when it is considered that many of those which were supposed good may turn out to be otherwise, and that many of those really good at the time may, under the varying circumstances of things, be no longer so at the end of three years, it can hardly be doubted that much loss will accrue before the debts thus extended by the act are finally liquidated. The commissioners appointed by the legislature to investigate the condition of the banks at this time strongly insist on the probability of extensive losses, and condemn the idea that the state should trust to those institutions, for some time to come, as a source of revenue.

The act referred to contains some salutary provisions for the future management of the banks and the proportion to be observed between their issues and their specie ; but the provisions of the original charters, had they been attended to, would have sufficed to have preserved the institutions from the embarrassments which have come upon them ; the constitution of the state providing that no bank should owe at any time more than twice the amount of its capital, nor should commence operations until one half of the capital stock subscribed for should have been actually paid in gold or silver. To give additional facilities to the state bank and its branches, an act, authorising the issue of $2,500,000 00 bonds to extend their capital, was passed in the December following.

The Bank of Mobile was instituted at an early period; but the state has only become interested in it since the 1st of January, 1836, having then subscribed for the portion of the capital reserved for it under the terms of the charter : the surplus profits made up to that time were divided among the then existing shareholders. This bank is liable to many of the charges of mismanagement which have been brought against the state banks; but the state possessing only two fifths of the capital, the remaining three fifths, or $900,000 00, are liable for the $600,000 00 bonds issued by the state in payment of its subscription, and guarantee to that extent the bondholders.

Statements of the position of these different banks will be given in the Appendix.*

I have no late details respecting the financial position of this state.

The principal agricultural production of Alabama is cotton, of which a larger quantity is grown than in any other state of the Union, excepting perhaps in Mississippi, which in 1834 produced an equal quantity.

Alabama has also a considerable foreign trade, for which it is well situated, as although possessing a sea-coast of only sixty miles in a direct line, this short space embraces Mobile Bay, one of the deepest and most important inland basins in the Gulf of Mexico, while by means of the river Mobile which empties itself into this bay, and its numerous

*See Appendix, G G 1, &c.

Financial
position.

Trade and
shipping.

tributaries, almost every part of the state has a ready outlet for its produce. A scattered French and Spanish population has existed round the shores of Mobile Bay for more than a hundred years, a French military post having been established on the present site of the town of Mobile at an early period in the last century; it is scarcely, however, twenty-five years since the settlement of white persons, to any extent, was commenced in this state. Its progress, owing to the rapid increase of the cotton trade, has therefore been remarkable, the population of the city of Mobile having in 1836 amounted to nearly 10,000. The shipping belonging to the port in that year amounted to 11,765 tons, of which 5097 tons were employed in steam navigation.

MAINE.

Amount of debt.

THIS state has borrowed $554,976 00, and is therefore included among the states which have outstanding debts, although its situation, in this respect, differs from that of the other states, inasmuch as no part has been borrowed for objects affording a profitable return.

The stock of this state is transferable by the holder; but it does not appear in what form it exists, nor when it is redeemable.

Rate of interest, and when and where payable.

The interest is at 5, 5¾, and 6 per cent. That on $235,000 00 is payable annually at Boston; that on the residue is payable half yearly at the state treasury.

Part of the stock was raised for the establishment of an insane hospital, part for primary schools, and a portion, as if to turn corn laws into burlesque, has been created to allow the state to pay a bounty on the growth of corn.

The stock of this state is to be redeemed, under the direction of the legislature, by the sale of public lands, from debts due to the state, or otherwise, as may be deemed expedient.

Individuals are indebted to this state on their notes for the sale of lands to the amount of $326,721 00.

The climate and soil of this state being little favourable to agriculture, the attention of the inhabitants has been chiefly directed to navigation and fisheries. Only two states, New York and Massachusetts, possess a greater amount of shipping; and these, with Louisiana only, exceed Maine in the amount of tonnage entered and cleared annually.

CHAP. VII.

Objects of loans.

Means of repayment.

Commerce and shipping.

MISSOURI.

This state has issued bonds to the extent of $2,500,000 00, under an act entitled "An Act to charter the Bank of the State of Missouri," which was approved on the 2d of February, 1837.

The bonds are payable to bearer on the 1st of May, 1863, at the Bank of America, in the city of New York.

The interest is payable at the same place on the 30th of April and 30th of September, at the rate

Amount of debt.

Form of security, and where redeemable.

Interest, when and where payable.

CHAP.
VII.

Condition
of the bank.

Condition
of the
country.

of $5\frac{1}{2}$ per cent., or in London at the rate of 4s. 6d. per dollar.

I have no details respecting the form or constitution of this bank. Its active capital on the 30th of December, 1837, amounted to $607,398 00 ; a general statement of its affairs, on that day, will be found in the Appendix.*

The soil, generally, of this state, is fertile ; and the alluvial tracts in the vicinity of the Missouri and its tributaries are in the highest degree so. This river flows through the state for a distance of 600 miles. The Osage, the most important of the tributaries, flows through some of the most fertile parts for an equal distance, while the Mississippi washes the eastern border of the state for a distance, by the windings of the stream, of about 470 miles. No region possibly in the world surpasses Missouri in the variety and abundance of its mineral wealth : the lead ore yields from eighty to eighty-five per cent. of pure metal, and, by a more careful process than the rude ones which are now had recourse to for separating the metal from the ore, might be made to yield considerably more.

The inhabitants, however, have been slow to turn these advantages to account. Consisting for a long time of French colonists who removed to the western shore of the Mississippi after the peace of 1763, when the French claims, to the country east of that river, were abandoned, the original settlers resembled more their Canadian countrymen than

* See Appendix, H H 2, &c.

the active, enterprising inhabitants of the United States. Large numbers of the latter have since emigrated to its fertile regions, and the population of the principal towns consists now chiefly of the newer settlers. St. Louis, the principal, and indeed the only considerable town of Missouri, is situated on the right bank of the Mississippi, 1350 miles above the Gulf of Mexico, and nearly in the centre of the Great Valley. It was founded by the French in 1764, but in 1820 contained only 4598 inhabitants ; the number is now estimated at above 14,000. The landing-place is convenient, and the water, close to the shore, is deep enough for the largest class of Mississippi steam boats, which are of 500 tons burden. The abundance of coal in the neighbourhood, and the wealth of the mines, at no great distance, joined to its advantageous position on the river, will probably render this, at no distant period, a city of considerable importance.

ARKANSAS.

THE debts of this state consist of bonds issued for the following purposes : —

To establish the Bank of the state of Arkansas $1,000,000 00
To establish the Real Estate Bank of the state
   of Arkansas   -   -   -   - 2,000,000 00
$3,000,000 00

CHAP.
VII.

Amount of debt.

A small portion only of the bonds have yet been negotiated. The state having reserved to itself a credit with the Real Estate Bank to the extent of fifty thousand dollars annually is authorised to issue additional bonds for all moneys so received. On the 19th of December, 1837, bonds for one hundred thousand dollars had in this manner been issued, making the total debt of the state at that date $3,100,000 00.

The bonds of this state are payable to the bearer.

Form of stock, and when and where payable.

It is not stated when those issued to the bank of the state of Arkansas are redeemable. Those to the Real Estate Bank are redeemable on the 26th of October, 1831 ; and those issued under the annual credit to which the state is entitled, in ten years from their respective dates.

Rate of interest, and when and where payable.

The whole of the bonds of this state were originally at 5 per cent. interest ; but by an act passed on the 19th of December, 1837, those issued to form the capital of the Real Estate Bank, were authorised to be exchanged for bonds bearing interest at the rate of 6 per cent. The bonds which had been issued up to that time on the state's annual credit remain at 5 per cent., but the bonds issued for all future sums so obtained are to be at 6 per cent.

The interest is payable on the 1st of January and July.

Bank of the state of Arkansas.

The bank of the state of Arkansas is established at Little Rock, and is the exclusive property of the state. It commenced business on the 12th of

June, 1837; but specie payments being suspended
immediately afterwards, its business has been very
limited.

Its capital, at the commencement, consisted,
1st, of $100,000 00, which had been obtained for
bonds then sold; and, 2dly, of $286,156 49, being
part of the surplus revenue deposited with the state
under the distribution act of congress; there were
also deposited with it, but whether as capital or
otherwise does not clearly appear, $26,725 00,
being the five per cent. fund arising from the sale
of public lands, together with the Seminary Fund,
and the Saline or Salt Spring Fund, amounting
together to $223 80, making a total available
capital of $413,105 29.

The report of the bank on the 6th of November
showed a clear profit of $8,460 28, after paying
$7,972 87 for the expense of outfit. The report
of the President states the difficulties they had had
to encounter in the deranged state of credit, and
the skill and caution evinced in the early management of the bank augurs well for its future prosperity. On the 1st of January, 1838, the net
profits amounted to $11,822 11. At this time a
further sale of $200,000 00 had been effected,
raising the active capital to $613,105 29.*

* The United States' government became the purchaser of
both the sums of stock issued on account of this bank,
$100,000 00 having been purchased on account of the com-
missioners of Indian affairs, and $200,000 00 on account of the
Chickasaw orphan fund. A further purchase of $500,000 00
Arkansas stock has been made by the federal government since

A statement of the general affairs of the bank at the latter date will be found in the Appendix.*

The Real Estate Bank was incorporated in 1836, with a charter, to be in force for twenty-five years: it is founded on the principle of the property banks in Louisiana, the state having required the pledge of mortgages to the amount of $2,250,000 00, on property worth double the amount, to secure the $2,000,000 00 bonds issued to form the capital. The charter requires the stockholders to be citizens of the state; and so great was the demand for shares, that $4,106,200 00 were immediately subscribed by sixteen counties only, out of thirty-six which are comprised in the state. The difficulty, however, of establishing titles and other causes reduced the amount, and in the end there was no excess beyond the sum required; but the securities obtained are said to be very ample, a few cases only of equitable titles having been admitted where they were known to be good. Stockholders are entitled by the charter to a credit equal to one half of the amount of their shares; but the whole of the discounts and loans of the bank may not exceed twice the amount of the capital and realised profit. Many other salutary

---

the account in the Appendix was rendered, but in which loan does not appear. This was the investment of a legacy to the United States, left by Mr. James Smithson of London, to found a literary institution at Washington. These instances afford a proof of the estimation in which the security of state stock is held in America.

* See Appendix, Letters I I 1. &c.

regulations are laid down for the management of the business.

The state does not in consideration of its guarantee become a shareholder as in the case of the Property Bank of Louisiana, but is to receive the sum of five thousand dollars annually, for the term of ten years, and is entitled to an annual credit as before mentioned of fifty thousand dollars, to be repaid in ten years from the date of borrowing. The sum of five thousand dollars is to form part of the revenue of the state, to be applied towards the payment of its annual expenditure. The remainder of the profits is to accumulate until the full payment of the bonds of the state and of the engagements of the Bank, and to be divided only at the end of the charter among the shareholders.

Arkansas, like Missouri, is rich in minerals, but consisting chiefly of low grounds, interspersed with numerous lakes and swamps, does not present an equally favourable surface with the latter to the agricultural labourer. As yet there are no lines of road secure from the interruptions of frequent and protracted inundations, but the state is traversed or bordered by several of the largest rivers in the United States: the Mississippi bounding its eastern limit for more than 350 miles, while the Red River, flowing through the south-western corner, renders this part of the state accessible to steam-boats. The river from which the state derives its name forms, however, the great channel of internal communication, traversing the whole breadth of the state

Condition of the state.

through its centre, by a very winding course of 530 miles, and being navigable during the greater part of the year far above the western limit of the state.

Arkansas contains no considerable towns. Little Rock, which is the capital of the state, and the chief city, contains only 1500 inhabitants.

MICHIGAN.

Amount of debt.

THE debt of this state consists of stock raised or authorised to be raised for the following purposes : —

For internal improvements -	- $5,000,000 00
To be lent to railroads - -	- 120,000 00
For the university - - -	- 100,000 00
For the state penitentiary - -	- 20,000 00
To defray the expense of the controversy with Ohio - - - -	- 100,000 00

Making together $5,340,000 00

Form of security, and when and where redeemable.

The stock issued for public improvements is in the form of bonds payable to bearer; the principal is redeemable on or after the 1st of January, 1863, in gold or silver, at the Morris Canal and Banking Company's office in New Jersey, or at their agency at New York. The interest is at the rate of 6 per cent., and payable at the same places on the 1st of January and 1st of July: by an agreement with the Farmers' Loan and Trust Company of New York, the dividends may be received in London at the exchange of 4s. 1d. per dollar.

The stock raised to assist private railroads by
loans of money bears interest also at 6 per cent. ;
but no further particulars appear respecting this
or the loans raised for the state, for purposes unconnected with public improvements.
The chief works contemplated by this state consist of three lines of railroad across the peninsula.

1st. The southern railroad from the city of
Munroe to New Buffalo. The length of this will
be 178 miles, the estimated cost $1,509,645 00.

2d. The central railroad from Detroit to the
mouth of the Saint Joseph. This work was originally undertaken and commenced by a private
corporation in 1836 ; the length of the line is 191
miles, and the estimated cost $1,751,547 00.

3d. The northern railroad from Huron to the
navigable waters of the Grand River; length, 201
miles ; estimated cost, $1,409,015 00. Various
canals are also contemplated as well as improvements in the navigation of the principal rivers.
Surveys have been made, and it is found that the
whole improvements, including the above railroads,
embrace a distance of 1109 miles : the estimated
cost is nearly eight millions of dollars. At the
beginning of the present year $888,300 00 had
been expended. Twenty-eight miles of the Central Railroad from Detroit to Ypsilante are finished,
but this is the only work sufficiently advanced to
make any return. In the first ten months that
this portion was open $81,604 00 was received in
tolls ; 28,751 passengers had been carried upon it ;
9,792,415 pounds of merchandise, and 15,050 bar-

rels of flour. This statement is favourable, but the
state appears to be attempting too much.

A board of commissioners has been created to
superintend the public improvements, and to raise
the sums that are required.

Internal
improve-
ment fund.
An internal improvement fund has also been
created and placed under its management. The
following sums had been placed to this fund on
the 1st of January, 1838 : —

From the surplus revenue received under the dis-
    tribution act of Congress   -   -   - $286,751 00
From 5 per cent. to which the state is entitled on
    the sale of public lands   -   -   - 151,800 00
                                                    _____
                                          $438,551 00

The tolls on the public works are pledged for
the payment of the principal and interest of the
loans contracted for their construction. The loans
to railroads are guaranteed by the pledge that has
been made of the roads to the state, but I have no
particulars respecting them : certain lands belonging to the University are pledged for the
loans for that object. The interest on $100,000 00
issued to defray the expense of the controversy
with Ohio on the subject of the right to the outlet
of the Maumee river is paid by a direct tax for
that purpose.

Condition
of the state.
In point of fertility this peninsula is not surpassed by any tract of equal extent in the world :
in the southern part particularly there are alluvial
lands of great extent, with rich vegetable mould
of from three to six feet in depth ; and although

the northern part has been less perfectly ex- CHAP.
amined, and appears to be much more hilly and VII.
rugged than the south, it contains a large proportion of excellent land. The face of the country is
represented as being exceedingly beautiful. The
population of Michigan is almost entirely composed of emigrants from New York and the
New England states, and from Great Britain.
There are about 4000 French, the descendants of
the original white settlers of this region. Detroit,
the principal town of Michigan, was long a strong
military post of the French : in 1837 the population amounted to 8323. In 1820 there was but
one steam-boat on Lake Erie ; and in 1836 thirty
steamers of the largest class were running between
Detroit and Buffalo ; of these, seventeen, with an
aggregate tonnage of 2080 tons, belonged to Detroit, where there were also owned eighty-four sail-
ing vessels of 5147 tons. This state may be destined
to hold a high position among the United States ;
but, in the mean time, the works undertaken have
involved it in a debt which is disproportioned to
the number and resources of the inhabitants.

TERRITORY OF FLORIDA.

ALTHOUGH this portion of the United States has Amount of
not yet been admitted as a state into the Union, debt.
it has at different times issued bonds on the authority of the Governor and Legislative Council
of the territory.

The purposes for which these bonds have been issued, and their amounts, are as follow : —

To form the capital of the Union Bank of
   Florida   -   -   -   -   - $3,000,000 00
To increase the means of the Southern Life
   Insurance and Trust Company   -   -   400,000 00

Making together $3,400,000 00

Form of
security,
and when
and where
redeem-
able.
The bonds of this state are payable to the bearer. The first issue of these to the Union Bank consisted of one million of dollars, which are redeemable as under : —

$250,000 00 in 1858. $250,000 00 in 1862.
250,000 00 in 1860.   250,000 00 in 1864.

The second issue consisted of bonds redeemable as follows : —

$500,000 00 on the 1st January, 1862.
500,000 00 on the 1st January, 1864.
500,000 00 on the 1st January, 1866.
500,000 00 on the 1st January, 1868.

The Union Bank has undertaken to redeem the bonds of the second issue in London, at the exchange of 4s. 6d. per dollar. The bonds of the Southern Life Insurance and Trust Company are issued in the name of the company, the territory merely affixing its guarantee ; these, also, are redeemable in London on the 1st of August, 1865, at an exchange of 4s. 6d.

The interest on the bonds issued to the Union Bank is payable on 1st January and 1st July ; on

those of the first issue in current money, and on
those of the second issue in London, at the exchange of 4*s*. 6*d*. The dividends on the bonds of the Southern Life Insurance and Trust Company are payable in London on the 1st April and 1st October, at the exchange of 4*s*. 6*d*.

The Union Bank of Florida was established under
a charter granted on the 12th of February, 1833, to continue for forty years. The capital was limited at first to one million of dollars, with power to extend it to three millions, after the bank should have been one year in operation.

This establishment being a property bank, the capital has been raised entirely by the sale of bonds issued by the territory, which are guaranteed by mortgages on real property to at least the same amount; two thirds of the mortgages were allowed at first to be on unimproved lands : but the increase in the value of property has been so great, that the property thus mortgaged to the bank is said now to be worth nearly three times the sum for which it was originally pledged.

The charter is framed on the model of those of the property banks in Louisiana, but some of the clauses are less strict; as in the instance of unimproved lands being admitted to form part of the original security for the bonds. Shareholders, too, in the Union Bank of Florida are entitled to a credit or loan equal to two thirds of the amount of their stock.

After paying the expenses of the establishment, and the interest on the bonds by means of which the capital was raised, the profits must, by the terms of the charter, be allowed to accumulate, till the surplus shall equal the amount of the bonds; after which the profits are to be divided equally between the territory, in consideration of its guarantee, and the shareholders; but on the expiration of the charter the whole capital is to be divided among the shareholders.

The Union Bank commenced business on the 16th of January, 1835, and on the 1st of January, 1838, the profits, after paying interest on the bonds, and all expenses, amounted to $100,524 90, the capital up to that time being only one million of dollars : a further sum of $20,000 00 was reserved as interest on suspended debts. Specie payments having before this been suspended throughout the Union, the amount of protested bills held by the bank was at this time $334,822 93, besides which the bank held a considerable number of bonds and notes in suit.* The profits during the year ending on the 1st of January, 1839, are said to have been very large, the sinking fund on that day being stated to have exceeded $300,000 00; but I have seen no detailed statement of the affairs of the bank at so late a period, nor any account of what proportion of the suspended debt was considered as likely to be ultimately available.

The Southern Life Insurance and Trust Company. The Southern Life Insurance and Trust Company partakes of the nature of a banking institution; but has power besides, under its charter, to

* See Appendix, Letters K K 1. &c.

insure lives, to grant and purchase annuities, dependent either on lives or otherwise, and generally to enter into all contracts in which interest on money and the duration of life are involved. Another characteristic of this institution, in which it differs from all others to which the aid of public credit has been extended, is the authority which the company has to receive money upon trust, and to accept and execute the trusts of whatsoever description they may be, upon which the money is lodged.*

The capital stock of the company, which is answerable for the due execution of the trusts committed to its care, is to be two millions of dollars, with a power reserved to increase it to four millions ; but the capital paid in on the 8th of January, 1838, was only $500,150 74. The whole of the capital is directed to be invested in bonds, secured by unincumbered real and personal estate within the territory of Florida, of double the value in each case of the sum so secured ; which bonds are to bear interest at the rate of eight per cent.

To enable the company to make loans beyond the amount of their capital, they are authorised to issue certificates which must be redeemable within the term of the charter ; and the faith of the territory is pledged by the act of incorporation to

* Institutions of this description are not unusual in other parts of the Union, especially in the state of New York, where there are several in a very prosperous situation. The Southern Life Insurance and Trust Company is the only one, however, for which any state or territory is in any way responsible.

guarantee the same, provided the amount of certificates issued does not exceed the debts placed
under mortgage to the company, on which mortgages the territory reserves a prior claim.

This arrangement affords to the holders of these
bonds all the security usually provided for bonds
which form the capitals of property banks; while
they possess, besides, the security of the paid-up
capital of the institution.

Another novel feature in the security afforded to
the holders of the bonds of this company, over that of
those issued in favour of other banking institutions,
is the existence of a sinking fund independent of
the common profits made by the establishment :
for the amount of the certificates being secured on
mortgages paying 8 per cent. per annum, the company has engaged to remit the whole interest on
the mortgages, as received, to England, to be applied, in the first instance, to the payment of the
interest on the certificates, and the residue as a permanent and accumulating sinking fund. By this
means a portion of the certificates will be yearly
redeemed; and the dividends on the portion so
redeemed, as well as the annual appropriation, are
to be successively applied to the cancelling of
fresh certificates. A statement of the affairs of this
institution will be found in the Appendix.*

Condition
of the ter-
ritory.
By direction of an act of Congress, a convention
has been appointed for the purpose of framing a
constitution for Florida, which will probably become a state in the course of the year 1840. In

* See Appendix, Letters K K 1. &c.

extent of territory it will rank the sixth in the Union. The whole of Florida belongs to the low sandy region, which constitutes a feature already repeatedly referred to in describing the southern states : no part rises more than 200 feet above the level of the ocean : a great portion, especially towards the south, is still unexplored, excepting along the coast. The soil and climate are well adapted for the growth of the sea island as well as the short staple cotton, and the agricultural productions of the southern states generally. The coast offers some good harbours, particularly the Bay of Pensacola, and as this is an advantage not frequently occurring on the coast of the Gulf of Mexico, it gives Florida commercial advantages which its contiguity to Mexico and the West Indies may render very important. I have obtained no financial particulars respecting this territory, or the states which have been last described.

P. S. — The legislative council of Florida has likewise pledged the faith of the territory for the payment of the principal and interest of bonds to the amount of $500,000 00, issued by the bank of Pensacola. The act which guarantees these bonds provides for an extension of the capital of the bank, on condition that the bank should construct a railroad from Pensacola to Montgomery, and, further, pledges the territory to endorse additional bonds, to the extent of $10,000 00 per mile, for every mile of railroad when finished, until the whole is completed : the distance is 156 $\frac{46}{100}$ miles, and the estimated cost $2,432,099 57. The bonds hitherto issued are redeemable in 1860, and bear interest at the rate of 6 per cent. The interest is payable in America, on the first days of January and July, or, by requisition, in London, three months afterwards. The condition of the bank of Pensacola by which the bonds are issued, will be seen in the Appendix.

CHAP. VIII.

AGGREGATE OF STATE DEBTS. — PROBABLE NECESSITY OF
TAXATION TO PAY THE INTEREST. — PROBABLE CONDUCT
OF THE STATES UNDER THESE CIRCUMSTANCES. — INFLU-
ENCE OF DEMOCRATIC PRINCIPLES. — DURABILITY OF THE
UNION. — CONCLUSION.

CHAP.
VIII.

Aggregate
of state
debts.

THE statements in the last chapter exhibit in a
strong light the impulse which the policy of the
several states of the Union has given to the industry of the citizens, by raising funds, on the
credit of the state, to be applied to works of public
utility.

At the end of the year 1835, the debts of the
separate states already amounted, in the aggregate, to more than sixty millions of dollars, the
greater part of which sum had been expended
in a productive manner; between that time and
the middle of 1838 an addition of no less than
$108,423,808 00 was either made to this amount,
or authorised to be raised, and the sum since
added is considerable, the aggregate amount of
state debt now exceeding $ 183,000,000 00.* Of
the amount raised or authorised from 1835 to 1838,
about forty millions were appropriated to the establishment of banks, and about sixty-eight millions
to works of internal improvement.

Probable
necessity
of taxation
to pay the
interest.

As the average profits of banking in the United
States considerably exceed the interest paid by
the states on the bonds which they have issued in

* See Appendix, Letter N.

payment of their shares, or for the establishment of the banks in which they are interested, there will usually be found, in this source, a sufficient fund for the payment of the interest and final liquidation of the bonds raised for this purpose, if the banks are managed with common prudence ; but an attentive consideration of the facts adduced can scarcely fail to show the probability that many of the works undertaken by the states, to facilitate internal communication by means of canals and railroads, will fail to yield a revenue sufficient to keep the works in repair, and to pay the interest on the loans raised for their construction.

In all these cases, as well as where the finances of the state, from being too much mixed up with banking institutions, and dependent upon them, may be deranged by injudicious management of the banks, auxiliary funds will be required to sustain the credit of the state, or, if these do not exist, recourse must be had to taxation.

In the case even when auxiliary funds have been set apart, they are not, as we have seen, in all cases adequate to the required purpose ; or, if ample at present, they are, in many instances, derived from sources which are in themselves uncertain. The time, therefore, will probably come, and seems now to be approaching, which is to determine whether, in case of a partial or total failure of the expectations of the projectors of the various schemes on which the states have entered, those states so circumstanced will be willing to uphold their credit by submitting to taxes levied

for the express purpose of providing for engagements entered into by their legislatures, and whether they will be willing to go to the extent that
may be necessary for this purpose.
Where sufficient data have been obtained, an
attempt has been made, in the last chapter, to
show the ability of the several states to meet the
demands that may possibly be made upon them ;
and in some cases that point has been satisfactorily
established : but as the ultimate security of even
the greater part of the loans may have finally to
rest on a system of taxation, not only the means,
but the probable disposition of the inhabitants to
submit to taxation, ought to be taken into consideration, in an attempt to exhibit the degree of credit
which should attach to these engagements.

Probable
conduct of
the states.
The general anxiety shown by the people of the
United States to control their rulers, by making
them dependent on their will for the supplies
necessary to carry on the government, has already
been alluded to ; but no disposition seems ever
to have been shown, on the part of the legislatures,
to impede, by withholding supplies, the fulfilment
of engagements which may have been entered
into either by themselves or by their predecessors.
The conduct of the several legislatures which have
successively composed the general congress has indeed been the reverse of this in a remarkable degree ; and all the documents emanating from the
legislatures of the separate states indicate that a
strong feeling is entertained of the inviolability of
such engagements.

Though, in estimating the future by the past, there is great reason, therefore, to believe, that a determination to adhere strictly to their engagements is still likely to characterise the people of the several states, yet the effect of the continued and rapid strides which democratic principles are making in the United States may have too important consequences to be altogether overlooked in the present inquiry.

Until late years, the middling classes, which in all free countries constitute the most important section of the community, enjoyed in the United States a practical importance in no degree inferior to that of the corresponding classes in this country. Possessed of wealth, of talent, and of station, they were able to exert the influence which these ought ever to command in the selection of their representatives in the national councils ; but the subjugation of this important and respectable class to the numerical force of the majority, in the wealthiest states of the Union, at the period of the elections in 1834, evinces the power which the dangerous right of universal suffrage is calculated to confer on those who are little fit to judge of the true interests of the state, and most open to the influence of uncontrolled feelings.

The growth of popular opinion, in the worst sense of the word, in the United States, and the influence it has had in over-ruling the wiser and better principles advocated by the more enlightened portion of the citizens, have been lamentably shown in the little power which the executive has been proved to possess on all points where it has been opposed by popular clamour, which, whether expressed throughout the Union generally, or in a detached portion of it, has, in the end, always proved victorious.

The continuance of slavery, and still more the unnecessary recognition of it in Missouri, on that state being admitted into the Union; the want of power in the local governments to protect the abolitionists at New York, or the Roman Catholic establishment at Boston; and the inability of the general government to confirm the decisions of the supreme court in cases of the violation of treaties with the Indians *; the yielding to the Carolina tariff question, and the abolition of a national bank, though the clamour in the first of these instances had common sense in its favour, and, in the other,

* In a former chaper (at page 28.), relying on the authority of Mons. de Tocqueville, I made a statement respecting the smallness of the sums paid to the Indian tribes for the abandonment of their lands, which requires to be corrected and modified. The payment there stated to have been made to the Quapaws for the relinquishment of twenty-nine millions of acres, is said to be four thousand dollars. Having since had an opportunity of referring to his original authority, viz. Morse's Report on Indian Affairs, I find the sum paid was four thousand dollars, in goods and merchandise, besides an annuity, also payable in goods, of one thousand dollars; but what more materially alters the features of the case, and which is not stated by de Tocqueville, is the small number of the tribe, which consisted only of 476 individuals. The locality of the Quapaws is stated in the same chapter as having been originally to the east of the Mississippi, while the territory ceded was between the Arkansas and the Red Rivers. The name of the tribe is, in the chapter alluded to, erroneously printed Quassaw; and Chactan has also been printed for the Chactas or Choctaw tribe.

was sanctioned by the head of the government,—
are all proofs of the supreme authority of the popular voice when the feelings of the people are
excited.

The effect which this prevalence of democratic
principles may have in the case before us is very
evident ; for, should the states be obliged hereafter
to have recourse to taxation to defray the interest
on their loans, it will not, probably, be till the
different undertakings for which the loans were
raised will have been rendered unpopular by want
of success ; and although it does not follow that
the people, under these circumstances, will refuse
to submit to the necessary sacrifice, their adhering
to their engagements cannot be so confidently depended upon as it might be if the legislative bodies
were returned by classes more directly interested
in the maintainance of the financial integrity of the
states.

In deprecating, however, the dangerous tendency
of democratic principles, it must be borne in mind
that the direction of the bias which this power will
give to the course of events will depend on the
character of the people who exercise it ; and as, in
the supposed instance, the question is a simple
one, of whether the states will act honestly or
fraudulently, much will depend on the prevalence of religious principles among them ; for no
views of expediency, however far-sighted, or even
principles of national honour, can, under the supposed circumstances, be relied upon. To what
extent, therefore, religious feelings prevail in the
United States, and are likely to form a principle

of action, must be a question of deep importance, if viewed only in connection with the subject under discussion ; for in deciding whether, in times of difficulty, the states will keep good faith with their creditors or not, the existence, of such an influence or of an opposite one must infallibly be found to throw its weight into one side of the balance or the other.

Being without the means of forming an opinion on this subject, and wishing neither lightly to admit the existence of this feeling among the inhabitants of the United States, nor lightly to deny it, I shall content myself with pointing out the importance of it.*

A subject connected with it, the dissemination of education, comes more within the scope of statistical inquiry ; and the great attention paid to the subject, especially in the northern states, may be affirmed as likely, if it be well directed, to enhance the better parts, and remedy some of the defects, of the American character.

The judicious policy of the federal government in promoting education has been already referred to ; and this appears to be no accident of time or place, but to be based on one of the fundamental principles of the constitution, it having been declared, in an ordinance passed in 1787, that, " reli-

---

* No legislative provision is made for the support of religion in any of the states, it being left entirely to the voluntary choice and good will of the people : in the state of Massachusetts the constitution, however, compels all the citizens to belong to some religious society, or to pay for the support of some religious teacher, though it allows them to support whatever society or sect they may choose to attach themselves to.

gion, morality, and knowledge being necessary for
good government and the happiness of mankind,
schools and other means of education shall for
ever be encouraged."
It was in pursuance of this wise and benevolent
policy, that, on the formation of the new states,
grants of land were made by the general government to constitute funds for the support of public
schools, and that in most of the other states provision has been made, by assessments or other
means, for the same purpose. Education, however, in the United States, can hardly be said to
have advanced in a manner proportionate to the
views of the enlightened framers of the ordinance
of 1787, as, although considerable progress is now
making in many parts of the Union, there are
parts where the children receive hardly any, or at
best a most superficial, education.*

* Different states vary very much in this respect. The New
England states have always been distinguished for their excellent
system of common education ; and Massachusetts probably contains a larger proportion of well educated persons than any
other equal portion of the globe. In the state of New York
great attention has been paid, of late years, to the subject, and
in 1832 507,105 children were educated at the public expense.
In the adjoining state of Pennsylvania, notwithstanding the
benevolent views of its founder, education is very limited.
Though scarcely inferior in wealth and population to New
York, the number of children educated in like manner in Pennsylvania, at the public expense, in 1832, was only 23,592, while
out of 331,380 children returned by the census of 1830, only
150,000 at that time received education at schools of any sort.
In the southern states the thinness of the white population
renders the formation of district schools almost unattainable
among this class ; while, with a lamentable policy, the educa-

Another question deserving of attention is the probable durability of the Union, and the effect which a dissolution of it would have upon the means of the several states to comply with their engagements.

The first part of the question has often been discussed, and the great and increasing extent of the Union been adduced as a cause likely to effect a dismemberment. By the gradual extension of the western limit, as new people and new states spring up beyond the Mississippi, the political centre becomes constantly displaced, and the city of Washington, once the centre by position of the Union, as it still is the site of the federal government, becomes more and more inconveniently situated. Again, by the accession of newer and more extensive states, the older ones lose their comparative importance, and sink in power, not owing to any retrograde movement on their part, or even to their standing still, but solely to the greater ratio of progress in which the newer states are advancing.

These two circumstances are not only hurtful to the pride of the older states, but are calculated to give them a distaste for the continuance of a system productive of such mortifying results.

On the other hand, there is so much to connect the interests of the north with those of the southern and western portions of the Union, and each

---

tion of the blacks is forbidden under severe penal enactments, so that the minds, as well as the bodies, of this unhappy race seem doomed to remain in a state of equal subjection.

of the latter with the other, that less importance need attach to these reasons. Not only a common language, one of the strongest ties that can bind mankind together *, but a common way of thinking on all important matters, and even common prejudices, as De Tocqueville justly observes, unite the inhabitants of this vast continent; but it is probably their mutual dependence on each other in their commercial relations that is above all likely to secure a maintenance of the Union. The most striking feature in the commercial position of the south is the extent to which cotton is grown. The demand for this article, both in the New and the Old World, is so great as to render its cultivation in those states which are suited to its growth more profitable to the landowners than that of any other description of produce. The southern states are, on this account, almost entirely dependent on the interior and north-western states for their supply of provisions. The cotton and other products of the south are usually shipped from New Orleans or the southern Atlantic ports; but the returns of manufactured goods, owing to the easier communication between England and New York, are sent almost exclusively to the latter port, and thence find their way by means of the Erie canal, and the Ohio and Mississippi, to the agricultural

* On the admission of Louisiana as one of the states of the Union, it was made a condition that all its laws should be promulgated, its records preserved, and its judicial and legislative written proceedings conducted in the language in which the laws and the judicial and legislative written proceedings of the United States are now published.

and producing districts of the west and of the south. Were this system interfered with by internal barriers, and custom-house duties, (an almost necessary consequence of a rupture of the Union,) this state of things, so conducive to the prosperity of the whole body of the states, would have an end. Many other reasons might be adduced to show the great interest which the states have in the maintenance of the Union; but they have been repeatedly urged by writers of reputation, and need not here be repeated.

Effect of dismemberment.

In the event of the dismemberment of the Union, were such a step, contrary to their best interests, to be taken by the states, it is scarcely possible to suppose that it would fall back into its original integral parts, or that each state would form a separate or entirely independent republic. It is more probable that clusters of states, according to their local position and interests, would form themselves into separate confederations; but, as even this is not likely to take place until, in the course of time, they shall have acquired sufficient strength and consistency to stand alone, it does not appear that the rupture of the Union would be attended with further injury to the credit of the states, than by entailing an additional expenditure upon them, to provide for the means of defence against the aggressions of rival states, from the necessity of which, under the present constitution of things, they are exempt.

Character of the inhabitants.

Before concluding these general remarks, it ought to be observed that the business-like habits of the people of the northern states are calculated to inspire confidence in their engagements; and living in a country where almost every one is employed in some profitable pursuit, and where idleness or an expensive appearance must be injurious to credit, it is likely that their general character for industry and thriftiness will be maintained until greater advances at least have been made in the realisation of wealth, when luxury and its demoralising consequences may interfere to deteriorate it.

In the southern states the same general character is not wanting; but there are many causes, amongst which may be enumerated the more easy means of acquiring wealth, the moral degradation which the system of slavery stamps both on master and slave, the effects of an enervating climate, and the carelessness which often accompanies the uncertainty of life in the unhealthy marshes of the south, which all conspire to promote reckless habits, to loosen moral restraints, and thus greatly to modify the more favourable character which the inhabitants of the north have earned for themselves, and such distinctions should not be lost sight of in forming an estimate of the credit to which the different states are severally entitled: a too great proneness to engage in rash speculation is, however, a fault equally chargeable against the inhabitants of all parts of the Union.

On a review of the whole subject, we have seen Recapitu- the conduct of the states collectively in respect of lation. former loans, and their punctuality in discharging

them : we have seen the physical condition of the
country, and the well-founded prospects of still
greater resources being derived hereafter from
the improvement of the vast territory yet to be
cultivated : we have seen their prudent manner of
managing their affairs, both in the frugal expenditure in the civil government generally, and in
the application of their loans ; and in a country
in which the population so rapidly increases, it
must be borne in mind, that if recourse must be
had to taxation to defray the interest on their
debts, the greater the number to assist in paying
it, the lighter will be the burden upon each : we
have seen, lastly, the general enterprising and industrious character of the people.   Such are good
ingredients towards the establishment of national
credit ; and a considerable degree of confidence
is due on these grounds to the engagements of
the states generally.   In the case of the northern
Atlantic states, Massachusetts and New York
may be looked upon as entitled to the highest
place in the scale.   We have here realised wealth,
an extensive trade, old established institutions, and
a people to whom the general good character given
to the citizens of the states more particularly
applies.

Conclu-
sion.
In instituting a comparison between the newer
northern and the southern states, it may, perhaps,
be affirmed that, although the latter are richer,
and possess more present means of meeting their
engagements, the northern states contain the elements of a more enduring prosperity.

POSTSCRIPT.

SINCE the preceding sheets were sent to the press, intelligence has been received of the banks of Pennsylvania, and of those of almost every other part of the Union, with the exception of New York and Massachusetts, having again suspended specie payments. This cannot be attributed to a recurrence of the same causes which led to the suspension of the same establish-- ments in May, 1837; no new speculations on too extensive a scale having been entered into: it proves, rather, that the return to specie payments was premature. The unsound state to which the currency of the different states had been reduced, by the banks having had recourse to an issue of post notes, to replace the portion of their capital which had been rendered unavailable by the exchange of protested paper for promissory notes payable at a distant period, has been mentioned as rendering it doubtful whether the institutions, which had had recourse to this means of obtaining funds, could long continue to pay in specie, and the error of the system has now been made apparent.*

The present embarrassment has, indeed, been more general than could at that time have been anticipated, and is partly dependent on other causes, among which the undue extension of the operations of the United States' Bank, and its departure from the legitimate principles of banking, are the most prominent.

The difficulties of this and other institutions in the several states can scarcely fail for a time to have a prejudicial effect on the commerce of the country, and to prove more or less injurious to the immediate prospects of some of the undertakings for which the loans of the states have been raised; but the remedy though severe will turn out to be an efficacious one, if it causes the banks, generally, to revert to better principles, and trade to be restored to a sounder condition.

---

* See page 102.

The difficulties of the several banking institutions cannot, however, permanently check the progress of the states in the acquirement of wealth, nor dry up the prolific sources from whence they derive it. The states whose financial affairs are most mixed up with banking institutions may, indeed, be embarrassed by the derangement which continued mismanagement may occasion, and may have to resort to other sources, or to taxation, to defray their expenditure, and provide for the interest on their loans ; but having, in the course of these observations, sufficiently alluded to the condition of the states that were so cirumstanced, I do not, on the whole, see any cause from recent events to add to what I have already said on the subject.

A subject which has been recently mooted, and not noticed in the preceding pages, may be here adverted to, as affording an opportunity of recording the opinion of Mr. Daniel Webster on the general subject of the engagements of the several states, and no one has better opportunities of forming one. On the question of the legal and constitutional power of the states to contract loans either at home or abroad being submitted to him for his opinion, in consequence of doubts which had been entertained on the question, he addressed the following letter to Messrs. Baring, Brothers, and Co., through whom, though they never entertained a doubt themselves on the subject, the question was put, with the view of establishing the point on the highest authority : —

"London, 16th Oct. 1839.

"Messrs. Baring, Brothers, and Co.

"Gentlemen —I have received your letter, and lose no time in giving you my opinion on the question which you have submitted for my consideration. The assertions or suggestions to which you refer, as having appeared in some of the public prints, had not escaped my notice.

"Your inquiry is 'whether the legislature of one of the states has legal and constitutional power to contract loans at home and abroad?'

"To this I answer, that the legislature of a state has such power ; and how any doubt could have arisen on this point it is difficult for me to conceive. Every state is an independent, sovereign, political community, except in so far as certain powers, which it might otherwise have exercised, have been conferred on a general government, established under a written constitution, and exerting its authority over the people of all the states. This general government is a limited government. Its powers are specific and enumerated. All powers not conferred upon it still remain with the states, and with the people. The state legislatures, on the other hand, possess all usual and ordinary powers of government, subject to any limitations which may be imposed by their own constitutions, and with the exception, as I have said, of the operation, on those powers, of the constitution of the United States. The powers conferred on the general government cannot, of course, be exercised by any individual state ; nor can any state pass any law which is prohibited by the constitution of the United States. Thus no state can, by itself, make war, or conclude peace, nor enter into alliances or treaties with foreign nations. In these, and in other important particulars, the powers which would have otherwise belonged to the state can now be exercised only by the general government, or government of the United States. Nor can a state pass a law which is prohibited by its own constitution. But there is no provision in the constitution of the United States, nor, so far as I know or have understood, in any state constitution, prohibiting the legislature of a state from contracting debts, or making loans, either at home or abroad. Every state has the power of levying and collecting taxes, direct and indirect, of all kinds ; except that no state can impose duties on goods and merchandise imported, that power belonging exclusively to Congress, by the constitution. This power of taxation is exercised by every state, habitually and constantly, according to its own discretion, and the exigencies of its government.

" This is the general theory of that mixed system of government which prevails in America. And as the constitution of the United States contains no prohibition or restraint on state legislatures, in regard to making loans, and as no state constitution, so far as known to me, contains any such prohibition, it is clear that, in this respect, those legislatures are left in the full possession of this power, as an ordinary and usual power of government.

"I have seen a suggestion, that state loans must be regarded as unconstitutional and illegal, inasmuch as the constitution of the United States has declared that no *state shall emit bills of credit.* It is certain that the constitution of the United States does contain this salutary prohibition; but what is a bill of credit? — It has no resemblance whatever to a bond, or other security, given for the payment of money borrowed. The term 'Bill of Credit' is familiar in our political history, and its meaning well ascertained and settled, not only by that history, but by judicial interpretations and decisions, from the highest source. For the purpose of this opinion, it may be sufficient to say, that bills of credit, the subject of the prohibition in the constitution of the United States, were, essentially, paper money. They were paper issues, intended for circulation, and for receipt into the treasury as cash ; and were sometimes made a tender in payment of debts. To put an end, at once and for ever, to evils of this sort, and to dangers from this source, the constitution of the United States has declared, that 'no state shall emit bills of credit, nor make any thing but gold and silver a tender in payment of debts, nor pass any law which shall impair the obligation of contracts.' All this, however, proves, not that states cannot contract debts, but that, when contracted, they must pay them in coin, according to their stipulations. The several states possess the power of borrowing money for their own internal occasions of expenditure, as fully as Congress possesses the power to borrow in behalf of the United States, for the purpose of raising armies, equipping navies, or performing any other of its constitutional duties. It may be added, that Congress itself fully recognises this power in the states, as it has authorised the investment of large funds, which it held in trust for very important purposes, in certificates of state stocks.

"The security for state loans is the plighted faith of the state, as a political community. It rests on the same basis as other contracts with established governments ; the same basis, for example, as loans made to the United States under the authority of Congress; that is to say, the good faith of the government making the loan, and its ability to fulfil its engagements. These state loans, it is known, have been contracted principally for the purpose of making railroads and canals ; and in some cases, although I know not how generally, the income or revenue expected to be derived from these works is directly and specifically pledged for the payment of the interest and the redemption of the debt, in addition to the obligation of public faith. In several states, other branches of revenue have been specifically pledged, and in others very valuable tracts of lands. It cannot be doubted that the general result of these works of internal improvement has been, and will be, to enhance the wealth and ability of the states.

" It has been said that the states cannot be sued on these bonds. But neither could the United States be sued, nor, as I suppose, the Crown of England, in a like case. Nor would the power of suing, probably, give the creditor any substantial additional security. The solemn obligation of a government, arising on its own acknowledged bond, would not be enhanced by a judgment rendered on such bond. If it either could not, or would not, make provision for paying the bond, it is not probable that it could, or would, make provision for satisfying the judgment.

" The states cannot rid themselves of their obligations otherwise than by the honest payment of the debt. They can pass no law impairing the obligation of their own contracts — they can make nothing a tender in discharge of such contracts but gold and silver. They possess all adequate power of providing for the case, by taxes and internal means of revenue. They cannot get round their duty, nor evade its force. Any failure to fulfil their undertakings would be an open violation of public faith, to be followed by the penalty of dishonour and disgrace ; a penalty, it may be presumed, which no state of the American Union would be likely to incur.

" I hope I may be justified, by existing circumstances, to close this letter with the expression of an opinion of a more general nature. It is, that I believe the citizens of the United States, like all honest men, regard debts, whether public or private, and whether existing at home or abroad, to be of moral as well as legal obligation ; and I trust I may appeal to their history, from the moment when those states took their rank among the nations of the earth, to the present time, for proof that this belief is well founded ; and if it were possible that any of the states should at any time so entirely lose her self-respect, and forget her duty, as to violate the faith solemnly pledged for her pecuniary engagements, I believe there is no country upon earth — not even that of the injured creditors — in which such a proceeding would meet with less countenance or indulgence than it would receive from the great mass of the American people.

" I have the honour to be,

" Gentlemen,

" Your obedient Servant,

(Signed) " DANIEL WEBSTER."

APPENDIX.

A.

THE American dollar contains $371\frac{1}{4}$ grains of pure silver, or 416 grains of standard silver.

The American eagle of the old coinage, previous to the 31st of July, 1834, contained $247\frac{1}{2}$ grains of pure gold.

The eagle of the new coinage contains 232 grains of pure gold.

The British sovereign, on leaving the mint, contains $113\frac{18}{1214}$ grains of pure gold, and, according to the mint valuation of the United States, is worth $4 $87\frac{7}{120}$.

In commercial dealings, $4 $44\frac{4}{9}$ has long, however, been assumed as the par of exchange on England, making the dollar equivalent to 4s. 6d.

This practice began when the Spanish pillar dollar was in circulation, which was then nearly of this intrinsic value, the market price of gold compared with that of silver being less then than it is at present.

While different standards existed in the two countries, the standard in the United States being at that time silver, the true par necessarily varied with every variation in the relative proportion of the value of gold to that of silver. It was estimated by Mr. Gallatin, writing in 1829, at 7 per

cent. above the nominal par, and at the time of the passing
of the gold bill, and for some time previous, it was about
1 per cent. higher, or at 8 per cent. premium. It was
with reference to the change that had taken place in the
true par, that by an act of Congress, of the 14th of July,
1832, the value of the pound sterling in calculations for
duties was fixed at $4 80 instead of $4 44$\frac{4}{9}$ as before.

By the passing of the gold bill, on the 28th of June,
1834 (which was to take effect from the 31st of July
following), the true par became about 9$\frac{7}{10}$ per cent. above
the old nominal par; and gold being by that act constituted the standard of the United States, as it is of England, this proportion will remain unaltered so long as the
respective coins of the two countries remain of their present weight and fineness.

The rate of exchange varies according as the balance
of payments between the countries may be on one side or
the other.

The United States generally receive more in goods
and merchandise from England than they send produce in
return, and the exchange, owing to this and other circumstances, is usually above the real par; but it will be seen
by the accompanying table that in 1834 the exchange fell
to 2 per cent. discount, or to 10 per cent. below the real
par. The drain of specie at this time from England to
the United States, rendered profitable under these circumstances, has already been referred to. In 1837, during
the suspension of specie payments, the exchange rose to
22 per cent. above the nominal, or 14 per cent. above the
real par.

TABLE showing the highest and lowest Rates of Exchange at New York on London, at 60 Days after Sight; and the Price of Sovereigns, in each Year, from January, 1825, to 1st May, 1838.

Years.	Exchange on London.		Premium and Price of Sovereigns.	
1825	$4\frac{3}{4}$	to 11 pm.	$2\frac{1}{2}$ to 10 pm.	
1826	$7\frac{1}{2}$	12	6	$11\frac{1}{2}$
1827	$9\frac{3}{4}$	$11\frac{3}{4}$	$8\frac{1}{2}$	11
1828	$9\frac{3}{4}$	$11\frac{1}{2}$	$8\frac{1}{2}$	10
1829	8	10	7	9
1830	6	$9\frac{1}{2}$	4	9
1831	$6\frac{1}{4}$	11	5	10
1832	$7\frac{1}{2}$	$10\frac{1}{2}$	$6\frac{1}{2}$	$9\frac{1}{4}$
1833	5	$8\frac{3}{4}$	$4\frac{1}{2}$	$8\frac{1}{2}$
1834	2 disct.	$7\frac{1}{2}$	2 disct. 8	
1835	$6\frac{1}{2}$ pm.	10	$4 84	$4 $85\frac{1}{2}$
1836	$6\frac{3}{4}$	10	4 84	4 86
1837	$7\frac{1}{2}$	22	4 84	5 $47\frac{1}{2}$
1838	$4\frac{1}{2}$	$10\frac{1}{2}$	4 85	5 06

B.

AMOUNT of the Debts of the separate States assumed by the Federal Government at the Close of the Revolutionary War.

Names of States.	Amount of Debt assumed.
New Hampshire	$ 282,595 51
Massachusetts	3,981,733 05
Rhode Island	200,000 00
Connecticut	1,600,000 00
New York	1,183,716 69
Pennsylvania	777,983 48
New Jersey	695,202 70
Delaware	59,161 65
Maryland	517,491 08
Virginia	2,934,416 00
North Carolina	1,793,803 85
South Carolina	3,999,651 73
Georgia	246,030 73
	$18,271,786 47

C.

AMOUNT of unredeemed Debt, both foreign and domestic, as it stood on the 31st of December, 1794.

Foreign debt - - -		$13,745,379 35
Funded domestic debt, viz.		
1. Arising from original domestic debt, viz.		
Stock bearing present interest of 6 per cent. - -	$17,912,138 01	
Future - - -	8,538,228 97	
Interest at 3 per cent.	12,275,347 55	
2. Arising from state debts assumed.		
Stock bearing present interest at 6 per cent. - -	7,908,374 19	
Future - - -	3,940,608 96	
Interest at 3 per cent.	5,994,115 70	
3. Arising from balances to creditor states.		
Stock bearing present interest at 6 per cent. - -	2,345,056 00	
Future - - -	1,172,528 00	
Interest at 3 per cent.	703,516 80	
		60,789,914 18
Unsubscribed debt - - -		1,561,175 14
Total of unredeemed debt		$76,096,468 67

D.

APPORTIONMENT among the several States of the Surplus Revenue remaining in the Treasury on the 1st of January, 1837, (reserving $5,000,000 00) according to the Number of electoral Votes for President, agreeably to the Act of Congress, 23d June, 1834.

States.	Electoral Votes.	Amount to be deposited.
New Hampshire - -	7	$892,115 71
Massachusetts - -	14	1,784,331 43
Rhode Island - -	4	509,780 41
Connecticut - -	8	1,109,560 81
New York - - -	42	5,352,694 28
Pennsylvania - -	30	3,823,353 06
New Jersey - -	8	1,019,560 81
Delaware - - -	3	382,335 31
Maryland - - -	10	1,274,451 02
Virginia - - -	23	2,931,237 34
North Carolina - -	15	1,911,676 53
South Carolina - -	11	1,401,896 12
Georgia - - -	11	1,401,896 12
Vermont - - -	7	892,115 71
Kentucky - - -	15	1,911,676 53
Tennessee - -	15	1,911,676 53
Ohio - - -	21	2,676,347 14
Louisiana - - -	5	637,225 51
Indiana - - -	9	1,147,005 92
Mississippi - -	4	509,780 41
Illinois - - -	5	637,225 51
Alabama - - -	7	892,115 71
Maine - - -	10	1,274,451 02
Missouri - -	4	509,780 41
Arkansas - - -	3	382,335 31
Michigan - - -	3	382,335 31
		$37,468,859 97

E.

SITUATION of the Bank of the United States on the 1st of January, 1833.

The claims against the bank were:

Notes in circulation - -	- $17,459,571	79
Public and private deposits -	- 13,547,517	95
Debt to the holders of the funded debt of the		
United States for principal and interest -	6,723,703	16
Unclaimed dividends - - -	76,529	84

Amounting to $37,807,322 74

Its resources were:

Specie - - - -		$8,951,847	60
Notes of state banks -	- $2,291,655 04		
Balances due by state banks -	1,596,252 08		
		3,887,907	12
Funds in Europe, and foreign bills of exchange		3,190,225	43
Real estate - - -	-	3,036,241	52

Debts due by individuals; viz.

On notes discounted -	- $43,626,870 32		
On domestic bills of exchange	18,069,043 25		
		61,695,913	57
Mortgages, &c. -	" -	103,330	75

Making $80,865,465 99
From which deduct the claims as above - 37,807,322 74

Leaving an excess of $43,058,143 25

Viz. $35,000,000 00, being the original capital, and $8,058,143 25 of surplus, or realised profits.

F.

STATEMENT of the Number and Condition, at different Intervals, of all
the Banks in the United States.

Date.	No. of Banks.	Capital.	Loans and Discounts.	Specie.	Circulation.	Deposits.
Jan. 1. 1811	89	$ 52,601,601	- - -	$ 15,400,000	$ 28,100,000	- - -
1815	208	82,259,590	- - -	17,000,000	45,500,000	- - -
1816	246	89,822,422	- - -	19,000,000	68,000,000	- - -
1820	308	137,110,611	- - -	19,820,240	44,863,344	$ 35,950,470
1830	330	145,192,268	$200,451,214	22,114,917	61,323,898	55,559,928
1834	506	200,005,944	324,119,499	- - -	94,839,570	75,666,986
1835	558	231,250,337	365,163,834	43,937,625	103,692,495	83,081,365
1836	567	251,875,292	457,506,080	40,019,594	140,301,038	115,104,440
1837	634	290,772,091	525,115,702	37,915,340	149,185,890	127,397,185
1838	663	318,148,643	489,110,526	35,064,051	118,216,683	85,306,349

G.

PUBLIC LANDS.

THE quantity of public lands disposed of from the earliest period of sales in 1787, up to June 30th, 1820 (when the credit system ceased), was 13,649,641·10 acres, and the net amount paid by purchasers up to the same time was $27,663,964 60. The annual sales since that time are given below in detail.

Year.	Quantity of Public Land sold.	Amount paid by Purchasers.
	Acres.	
From 1787 to 30th June 1820	13,649,641 10	$27,663,964 60
From 1st July to 31st Dec.	303,404 09	424,962 26
1821 - - -	781,213 32	1,169,224 98
1822 - - - -	801,226 18	1,023,267 83
1823 - - -	653,319 52	850,136 26
1824 - - -	749,323 04	953,799 03
1825 - - -	893,461 59	1,205,068 37
1826 - - -	848,082 26	1,128,617 27
1827 - - -	926,727 76	1,318,105 36
1828 - - -	965,600 36	1,221,357 99
1829 - - -	1,244,860 01	1,572,863 54
1830 - - - -	1,929,733 79	2,433,432 94
1831 - - -	2,777,856 88	3,557,023 76
1832 - - -	2,462,342 16	3,115,376 09
1833 - - -	3,856,227 56	4,972,284 84
1834 - - -	4,658,218 71	6,099,981 04
1835 - - -	12,564,478 85	15,999,804 11
1836 - - -	20,074,870 92	25,167,833 06
to Sept. 30. 1837 - -	4,805,462 97	6,127,418 39
Total	74,946,051 17	106,004,521 72

QUANTITY of Public Land sold in each State and Territory, from the earliest Period of the Sales to the 30th September, 1837.

State or Territory.	Quantity of Public Lands sold.	Amount paid by Purchasers.
	Acres.	
Ohio - - -	12,373,247 58	$21,777,692 95
Louisiana - -	2,010,426 45	2,714,805 78
Indiana - -	13,754,370 12	17,569,450 39
Mississippi - -	9,235,945 26	12,538,606 13
Illinois - -	9,273,256 99	11,610,024 72
Alabama - -	10,088,687 75	16,466,849 08
Missouri - - -	5,531,954 81	7,435,881 96
Arkansas - -	2,127,695 53	2,686,775 86
Michigan - -	8,894,224 68	11,186,537 41
Florida - -	683,324 39	895,236 36
Wisconsin - .	1,051,921 94	1,363,796 24
Total - -	75,025,055 50	$106,245,656 88

The totals in this and in the preceding account differ slightly in amount; but from what cause does not appear.

The whole territory ceded to the general government is estimated at about 319½ millions of acres: so that 244½ millions of acres remain unsold.

H.

COMMERCE OF THE UNITED STATES.

ACCOUNTS of the exports of the United States have been kept since the adoption of the present constitution, but it was not till the year 1802 that any distinction was made between articles which were the growth, produce, or manufacture of the United States, and such as were originally imported from foreign countries, and afterwards re-exported; since that time the accounts have been kept with great accuracy, and the above two classes of exports are not only distinguished, but have been further subdivided in a manner that presents many interesting statistical details.

The exports of domestic origin are in the first instance divided into such as are,

1st. The produce of the sea, viz. fish, oil, &c.

2d. The produce of the forest, viz. timber, ashes, furs, pitch, &c.

3d. The produce of agriculture.

4th. Manufactures, and articles which do not come under the above classes.

From 1803 to 1830 the produce of agriculture constituted rather less than three quarters of the value of the whole exports; but since that time, owing to the increased production of cotton, this most important branch has considerably exceeded that proportion.

The produce of the sea constitutes about $\frac{1}{30}$ of the whole; the produce of the forest about $\frac{1}{18}$, and manufactures the remainder; but the latter division, from including the exports of gold and silver coin, ought hardly to be estimated so high.

The produce of agriculture is further subdivided into,

1st. Articles which constitute vegetable food, such as wheat, flour, rice, Indian corn, &c.

2d. The products of animals, such as beef and pork, tallow, hides, butter, and cheese, and the animals themselves when exported.

3d. Tobacco.

4th. Cotton.

5th. Other productions of minor importance, such as indigo, flax, &c.

It would occupy too much space and be unnecessary to republish details which may be found in various statistical publications*, but in table No. 1. details are given of the the general exports of the United States from the year 1800; distinguishing, after 1802, between such as were of domestic, and such as were of foreign origin.

The value of the various articles imported into the United States since 1816 is added, and a general list of the shipping of the United States from 1800. No correct official documents exist in respect to imports before 1816, owing to the value of those articles only which paid an *ad valorem* duty being returned, prior to that time, to the treasury department. The imports are likewise classed and subdivided; but the divisions are less significant than in the case of the exports, being into such as are free of duty, such as pay an *ad valorem* duty, and such as pay specific duties. The first of these comprises gold and silver, and most metals in a state fit only to be manufactured; also tea, coffee, manufactures of silk and worsted, worsted stuffs, linen, &c., besides various articles connected with science and literature. The merchandise paying an *ad valorem* duty consists chiefly of other manufactures than those of silk and worsted, viz. manufactures of wool and

* See particularly Pitkin's Statistical View of the Commerce of the United States; also the Financial Register, and Hazard's United States' Commercial and Statistical Register.

cotton, flaxen and hempen goods, implements of iron, glass, earthenware, saddlery, &c. The articles which pay a fixed duty consist chiefly of wines and spirits, molasses, oil, sugar, salt, &c. In table No. 2. a statement is given of the proportion in which each state contributed to the commerce of the country in 1838, and in No 3. an enumeration is given of the several countries with which the United States were engaged in commerce during that year, with the value of the exports to and imports from each.

Of the domestic produce exported in 1838, there appears to have been obtained

From the sea - - - -	$ 3,175,576
From the forest - - - -	5,200,499
From agriculture, (comprised in the two first divisions) - - - -	9,105,514
Tobacco - - -	7,392,029
Cotton - - - -	61,556,811
Sugar, flax, indigo, &c. - -	140,093
Manufactures (including cotton goods) $3,758,755, and gold and silver coin $472,941 - -	8,483,321
Sundries - - - -	979,978
	$96,033,821

Of the imports,

Those admitted free of duty (including $17,747,116 in gold and silver) amounted to - -	- $60,860,005
Those paying an *ad valorem* duty, to - -	27,090,480
Those paying specific duties, to - -	25,766,919
	$113,717,404

The remaining tables show in detail the extent of the commerce of those states which have been most engaged in foreign trade from the year 1821 to the present time.

If the details of these several tables be examined, they will be found to abound in instructive matter. If the amounts of bullion imported and exported be deducted from the respective values of the general imports and exports of the United States, it will be seen that the imports in 1838 fell short of the exports. In the year 1836, and for some years before, the imports had greatly exceeded the exports, to which circumstance is to be attributed the large supply of states' stocks and other public securities sent to Europe, whence the imports were chiefly derived, in settlement of the balance. The simultaneous introduction into the market of so large an amount of securities of a class little known to the European public (but which it has been the object of the preceding pages to explain so far as regards the state securities), has had the effect of throwing such general discredit on the whole, as to have rendered them in a great measure unavailable for this purpose. Importers in the United States being forced in consequence to find in the productions of the country a more legitimate means of paying for the supplies they obtain from Europe, are now limited by the amount of these in their operations, and hence the diminished amount of imports without any corresponding reduction in the exports. The healthy influence of this has been very great, not only in preventing a further transmission of state securities to Europe, but in checking a further creation in America; for the English market at first not only absorbed all that appeared, but, by the demand, stimulated the production of more than the real interests of the states required; a state of things which, it may be hoped, has now been effectually put a stop to.*

* The improvident increase in the amount of imports is rendered more remarkable by the circumstance, that the increase of late years in the amount of exports has arisen more from the great increase that has taken place in prices, than from an increase in the quantities produced. As a remarkable proof of this, it appears that the total quantities of the products coming to market by the New York canals had increased only 16 per cent. from 1834 to 1838, although the aggregate value had in-

Comparing the years 1838 and 1836, the chief falling off in imports was in the following articles: —

	1836.	1838.
Cotton goods	$17,876,087	$6,599,330
Woollen goods	12,758,430	6,967,530
Silk goods	22,862,177	9,812,338
Linen	8,271,213	3,583,540
Iron and steel	12,892,648	7,418,504
Sugar	12,514,718	7,586,825
Teas	5,342,811	3,497,156
Wines	4,332,034	2,318,202

In the exports, the chief falling off was in cotton, tobacco, and rice. In some articles of export there was an increase, as will be seen by the following statement: —

	1836.	1838.
Cotton	$71,284,925	$61,556,811
Tobacco	10,058,640	7,392,029
Rice	2,548,750	1,721,819
Flour	3,572,599	3,603,299
Lumber	2,860,691	3,116,196
Manufactures	6,107,528	8,397,078

The following statement exhibits the imports and exports, during those years, of the states which were most deeply engaged in the foreign trade : —

	Imports.	
	1836.	1838.
Massachusetts	$ 25,681,462	$13,300,925
New York	118,253,416	68,453,206
Pennsylvania	15,068,233	9,360,731
Maryland	7,131,867	5,701,869

creased 77 per cent. In the articles of wheat and flour the increase of quantity in this period was only 2 per cent., while the total value of these products had increased nearly 73 per cent. There can scarcely be a greater proof of the extravagance of the speculation that must have been going forward.

	Imports.	
	1836.	1838.
Virginia - -	$1,106,814	$577,142
South Carolina -	2,801,361	2,318,791
Georgia - -	573,222	776,068
Alabama -	651,618	524,548
Louisiana - -	15,117,649	9,496,808

	Exports.	
	1836.	1838.
Massachusetts -	$10,380,346	$9,104,862
New York -	28,920,438	23,008,471
Pennsylvania -	3,971,555	3,477,151
Maryland - -	3,675,475	4,524,575
Virginia - -	6,192,040	3,986,228
South Carolina -	13,684,376	11,042,070
Georgia - -	10,722,200	8,803,839
Alabama - -	11,184,166	9,688,244
Louisiana - -	37,179,828	31,502,248

It remains only to be stated in reference to these tables
that the exports are valued at their cost or real value at
the place of exportation, and the imports at their cost
or worth at the foreign ports, from whence they were
exported for importation into the United States. In
respect, however, to imports subject to *ad valorem* duties,
Congress in 1823 directed the duties to be added to their
actual cost, and in 1832 again varied the rule, and ordered
the charges only (insurance excepted) to be added.

No. 1.

COMMERCE of the UNITED STATES from 1800 to 1838.

Years.	EXPORTS. Domestic.	EXPORTS. Foreign.	EXPORTS. Total.	Imports.	Tonnage of every Description.
1800			$70,971,780		$972,492
1801			94,115,925		1,033,219
1802			72,483,160		892,101
1803	$42,205,961	$13,594,072	55,800,033		949,147
1804	41,467,477	36,231,597	77,699,074		1,042,404
1805	42,387,002	53,179,019	95,566,021		1,140,369
1806	41,253,727	60,283,236	101,536,963		1,208,735
1807	48,699,592	59,643,558	108,343,150		1,268,548
1808	9,433,546	12,997,414	22,430,960		1,242,595
1809	31,405,700	20,797,531	52,203,231		1,350,281
1810	42,366,679	24,391,295	66,757,974		1,424,783
1811	45,294,041	16,022,790	61,316,831		1,232,502
1812	30,032,109	8,495,127	38,527,236		1,269,997
1813	25,008,152	2,847,845	27,855,997		1,166,628
1814	6,782,272	145,169	6,927,441		1,159,209
1815	45,974,403	6,583,350	52,557,753	$113,041,274	1,368,127
1816	64,781,896	17,138,556	81,920,452	147,103,000	1,372,218
1817	68,313,500	19,358,069	87,671,569	99,250,000	1,399,911
1818	73,854,437	19,426,696	93,281,133	121,750,000	1,225,184
1819	50,976,838	19,165,683	70,142,521	87,125,000	1,260,751
1820	51,683,640	18,008,029	69,691,669	74,450,000	1,280,166
1821	43,671,894	21,302,488	64,974,382	62,585,724	1,298,958
1822	49,874,079	22,286,202	72,160,281	83,241,541	1,324,699
1823	47,155,408	27,543,622	74,699,030	77,579,267	1,336,565
1824	50,649,500	25,337,157	75,986,657	80,549,007	1,389,163
1825	66,944,745	32,590,643	99,535,388	96,340,075	1,423,112
1826	53,055,710	24,539,612	77,595,322	84,974,477	1,534,190
1827	58,921,691	23,403,136	82,324,827	79,484,068	1,620,608
1828	50,669,669	21,595,017	72,264,686	88,509,824	1,741,392
1829	55,700,193	16,658,478	72,358,671	74,492,527	1,260,978
1830	59,462,029	14,387,479	73,849,508	70,876,920	1,191,776
1831	61,277,057	20,038,526	81,310,583	103,191,134	1,267,846
1832	63,137,470	24,039,473	87,176,943	101,029,266	1,439,450
1833	70,317,698	19,822,735	90,140,433	108,118,311	1,601,150
1834	81,024,162	23,312,811	104,336,973	126,521,332	1,758,907
1835	101,189,082	20,504,495	121,693,577	149,895,742	1,824,940
1836	106,916,680	21,746,360	128,663,040	189,980,035	1,892,102
1837	95,564,414	21,854,962	117,419,376	140,989,217	1,896,685
1838	96,033,821	12,452,795	108,486,616	113,717,406	1,995,639 80

No. 2.

IMPORTS AND EXPORTS OF EACH STATE.

STATEMENT of the Commerce of each State and Territory, commencing on the 1st of October, 1837, and ending on the 30th of September, 1838.*

States and Territories.	VALUE OF EXPORTS.			VALUE OF IMPORTS.		
	Domestic Produce.	Foreign Produce.	Total.	In American Vessels.	In Foreign Vessels.	Total.
Maine - -	$915,076	$20,456	$935,532	$773,643	$125,499	$899,142
N. Hampshire	56,103	18,567	74,670	168,585	1,400	169,985
Vermont - -	132,650	- -	132,650	258,417	- -	258,417
Massachusetts	6,158,529	2,946,333	9,104,862	12,857,816	443,109	13,300,925
Rhode Island	270,065	21,192	291,257	648,363	8,250	656,613
Connecticut -	543,610	- -	543,610	333,752	9,579	343,331
New York -	16,432,333	6,576,138	23,008,471	62,722,855	5,730,351	68,453,206
Pennsylvania	2,481,543	995,608	3,477,151	8,974,118	386,613	9,360,731
New Jersey -	28,010	- -	28,010	1,700	- -	1,700
Delaware - -	36,844	- -	36,844	- -	1,348	1,348
Maryland - -	4,165,168	359,407	4,524,575	4,968,119	733,750	5,701,869
D.of Columbia	366,760	6,353	373,113	87,399	35,349	122,748
Virginia - -	3,977,895	8,333	3,986,228	443,518	133,624	577,142
N. Carolina -	544,952	271	545,223	223,687	66,718	290,405
S. Carolina -	11,017,391	24,679	11,042,070	1,842,484	476,307	2,318,791
Georgia - -	8,803,839	- -	8,803,839	673,415	102,653	776,068
Florida ter. -	71,983	50,549	122,532	126,177	42,513	168,690
Alabama - -	9,688,049	195	9,688,244	355,019	169,529	524,548
Louisiana - -	30,077,534	1,424,714	31,502 248	7,342,614	2,154,194	9,496,808
Tennessee - -	- -	- -	- -	527	- -	527
Kentucky	- -	- -	- -	8,932	- -	8,932
Missouri - -	- -	- -	- -	15,921	- -	15,921
Ohio - -	139,827	- -	139,827	6,460	6,435	12,895
Michigan -	125,660	- -	125,660	253,927	2,735	256,662
	96,033,821	12,452,795	108,486,616	103,087,448	10,629,956	113,717,404

* In this table, and in that showing the condition of the banks in the several states, the classification hitherto adopted has been exchanged for one in which the states are arranged in their geographical order, as affording a better comparison of the condition of the states in these several respects. There are some trifling errors in the details which I have not the means of correcting.

No. 3.

TABLE exhibiting the VALUE of EXPORTS to, and IMPORTS from, each Foreign Country during the Year ending 30th of September, 1838.

Countries.	Exports.	Imports.
Russia - - -	$1,048,289	$1,898,396
Prussia - - -	84,944	6,629
Sweden - - -	277,431	854,771
Swedish West Indies -	78,421	46,019
Denmark - - -	122,831	27,118
Danish West Indies - -	1,177,096	1,617,747
Netherlands - - -	2,954,248	1,180,897
Dutch East Indies - -	495,961	576,396
Dutch.West Indies - -	251,149	382,591
Dutch Guiana - - -	70,848	54,354
Belgium - - -	1,614,951	239,928
England - - -	50,445,076	44,191,851
Scotland - - -	1,695,979	594,665
Ireland - - -	38,555	75,162
Gibraltar - - -	762,189	25,624
Malta - - - -	86,033	16,866
British East Indies - -	578,907	675,531
Cape of Good Hope - -	22,718	12,034
Australia - - -	34,362	30,538
British West Indies - -	2,200,852	1,635,848
British America - -	2,723,491	1,555,570
British Honduras - -	109,196	201,488
British Guiana - - -	146,054	36,043
Hanse Towns - - -	3,291,645	2,847,358
France (on the Atlantic) -	14,066,616	16,823,112
France (on the Mediterranean)	1,716,900	948,685
French West Indies - -	468,897	310,050
French Guiana - - -	- -	5,302
Spain (on the Atlantic) -	149,875	234,200
Spain (on the Mediterranean) -	339,499	868,336
Canaries - - -	53,305	151,366

Countries.	Exports.	Imports.
Manilla and Philippines -	$242,517	$386,528
Cuba - - - -	6,175,758	11,694,812
Other Spanish West Indies -	723,052	2,636,152
Portugal - - -	76,063	296,864
Madeira - - -	400,957	366,274
Azores - - -	9,237	32,746
Cape de Verds - - -	105,874	29,174
Italy - - - -	459,893	944,238
Sicily - - - -	47,345	345,362
Sardinia - - -	- -	851
Trieste - - -	768,963	372,378
Turkey - - -	257,909	296,533
Greece - - -	9,030	
Morocco - - -	- -	10,174
Hayti - - - -	910,255	1,275,762
Texas - - - -	1,247,880	165,718
Mexico - - -	2,164,097	3,500,709
Central America - -	243,040	155,614
Colombia - - -	724,739	1,615,249
Brazil - - - -	2,657,194	3,191,238
Argentine Republic - -	236,665	1,010,908
Cisplatine Republic - -	60,329	18,631
Chili - - - -	1,370,264	942,095
Peru - - - -	203,399	633,437
Other parts of South America -	1,875	
China - - - -	1,516,602	4,764,536
Other parts of Europe - -	31,759	
Ditto Asia - - -	181,831	212,091
Ditto Africa - -	491,902	541,931
Other West Indies - -	339,052	217
South Sea Islands - -	82,837	55,561
Uncertain places - -	- -	97,186
Total - -	108,486,616	113,717,404

No. 4.

COMMERCE of MASSACHUSETTS from 1821 to 1838.

Years.	EXPORTS.			Imports.	Registered Tonnage.
	Domestic.	Foreign.	Total.		
1821	$3,698,517	$8,846,174	$12,484,691	$14,826,732	196,975 45
1822	4,072,166	8,526,359	12,598,525	18,337,320	197,512 16
1823	3,944,985	9,738,254	13,683,239	17,607,160	165,393 15
1824	4,038,972	6,395,356	10,434,328	15,378,758	172,817 66
1825	4,262,104	7,170,883	11,432,987	15,845,141	173,344 71
1826	3,888,138	6,210,724	10,098,862	17,063,482	183,177 20
1827	3,820,349	6,604,034	10,424,383	13,370,564	225,111 40
1828	4,096,025	4,929,760	9,025,785	15,070,444	247,369 92
1829	3,949,751	4,305,186	8,254,937	12,520,744	227,067 92
1830	3,599,952	3,613,242	7,213,194	10,453,544	215,463 18
1831	4,027,201	3,706,562	7,733,763	14,269,056	225,226 15
1832	4,656,635	7,337,133	11,993,768	18,118,900	254,508 58
1833	5,150,584	4,532,538	9,683,122	19,940,911	276,723 86
1834	4,672,746	5,476,074	10,148,820	17,672,129	307,490 22
1835	5,564,499	5,479,291	10 043,790	19,800,373	331,173 47
1836	5,113,196	5,267,150	10,380,346	25,681,462	316,998 50
1837	4,781,901	4,856,289	9,728,190	19,975,667	288,346 47
1838	6,158,529	2,946,333	9,104,862	13,300,925	296,110 84

COMMERCE of NEW YORK from 1821 to 1838.

Years.	EXPORTS			Imports.	Registered Tonnage.
	Domestic.	Foreign.	Total.		
1821	$7,898,604	$5,264,313	$13,162,917	$23,629,246	118,750 65
1822	10,987,167	6,113,315	17,100,482	35,445,628	126,797 89
1823	11,362,995	7,675,995	19,058,990	29,421,349	133,085 75
1824	13,528,654	9,368,480	22,897,134	36,113,723	146,620 67
1825	20,651,558	14,607,703	35,259,261	49,639,174	159,327 32
1826	11,496,719	10,451,072	21,947,791	38,115,630	163,574 11
1827	13,920,627	9,913,510	23,834,137	38,719,644	171,835 56
1828	12,362,015	10,415,634	22,777,649	41,927,792	165,898 26
1829	12,036,561	8,082,450	20,119,011	34,743,307	117,585 06
1830	13,618,278	6,079,705	19,697,983	35,624,070	110,163 08
1831	15,726,118	9,809,026	25,535,144	57,077,417	130,933 26
1832	15,057,250	10,943,695	26,000,945	53,214,402	137,960 25
1833	15,411,296	9,983,821	25,395,117	55,918,449	159,554 03
1834	13,849,469	11,662,545	25,512,014	73,188,594	186,365 73
1835	21,707,867	8,637,397	30,345,264	88,191,305	200,780 47
1836	19,816,520	9,104,118	28,920,438	118,253,416	202,118 83
1837	16,083,969	11,254,450	27,338,419	79,301,722	202,370 55
1838	16,432,333	6,576,138	23,008,471	68,453,206	181,031 39

COMMERCE of PENNSYLVANIA from 1821 to 1838.

Years.	EXPORTS.			Imports.	Registered Tonnage.
	Domestic.	Foreign.	Total.		
1821	$2,832,387	$4,559,380	$7,391,767	$8,158,922	59,296 24
1822	3,575,147	5,472,655	9,047,802	11,874,170	61,237 02
1823	3,139,809	6,477,383	9,617,192	13,696,770	61,408 73
1824	3,182,694	6,182,199	9,364,893	11,865,531	62,771 18
1825	3,936,133	7,333,848	11,269,981	15,041,797	65,589 54
1826	3,158,711	5,173,011	8,331,722	13,551,779	63,443 34
1827	3,391,296	4,184,537	7,575,833	11,212,935	61,699 90
1828	3,116,001	2,935,479	6,051,480	12,884,408	66,839 50
1829	2,617,152	1,472,783	4,089,935	10,100,152	50,234 94
1830	2,924,452	1,367,341	4,291,793	8,702,122	47,979 32
1831	3,594,302	1,919,411	5,513,713	12,124,083	51,293 79
1832	2,008,991	1,507,075	3,516,066	10,678,358	45,956 32
1833	2,671,300	1,407,651	4,078,951	10,451,250	49,021 84
1834	2,031,803	1,957,943	3,989,746	10,479,268	51,441 02
1835	2,416,099	1,323,176	3,739,275	12,389,937	51,587 81
1836	2,627,651	1,343,904	3,971,555	15,068,233	51,034 73
1837	2,565,712	1,275,887	3,841,599	11,680,111	39,156 17
1838	2,481,543	995,608	3,477,151	9,360,731	42,266 21

COMMERCE of MARYLAND from 1821 to 1838.

Years.	EXPORTS.			Imports.	Registered Tonnage.
	Domestic.	Foreign.	Total.		
1821	$2,714,850	$1,135,544	$3,850,394	$4,070,842	46,613 24
1822	3,496,993	1,039,803	4,536,796	4,792,486	50,429 52
1823	3,173,112	1,857,116	5,030,228	4,946,179	51,546 09
1824	3,549,957	1,313,276	4,863,233	4,551,442	33,412 80
1825	3,092,365	1,408,939	4,501,304	4,751,815	59,499 38
1826	2,947,352	1,063,396	4,010,748	4,928,569	62,127 28
1827	3,457,691	1,058,715	4,516,406	4,405,708	60,627 14
1828	3,107,819	1,226,603	4,334,422	5,629,694	66,640 49
1829	3,662,273	1,142,192	4,804,465	4,804,135	31,194 29
1830	3,075,985	715,497	3,791,482	4,523,866	24,430 24
1831	3,730,506	578,141	4,308,647	4,826,577	25,959 51
1832	3,015,873	1,484,045	4,499,918	4,629,303	27,401 44
1833	3,301,014	761,453	4,062,467	5,437,057	27,685 88
1834	3,012,708	1,155,537	4,168,245	4,647,483	33,811 72
1835	3,176,866	748,368	3,925,234	5,647,153	33,806 54
1836	3,028,916	646,559	3,675,475	7,131,867	33,245 51
1837	3,365,173	424,744	3,789,917	7,857,033	35,340 02
1838	4,165,168	359,407	4,524,575	5,701,869	25,563 87

COMMERCE of VIRGINIA from 1821 to 1838.

Years.	EXPORTS.			Imports.	Registered Tonnage.
	Domestic.	Foreign.	Total.		
1821	$3,026,169	$53,040	$3,079,209	$1,078,490	12,216 06
1822	3,209,852	7,537	3,217,389	864,162	8,960 93
1823	4,000,914	5,874	4,006,788	681,810	11,139 86
1824	3,276,478	1,086	3,277,564	639,787	10,759 39
1825	4,122,340	7,180	4,129,520	553,562	10,572 80
1826	4,596,077	655	4,596,732	635,438	13,724 29
1827	4,646,737	11,201	4,657,938	431,765	14,239 58
1828	3,324,616	15,569	3,340;185	375,238	15,627 08
1829	3,783,493	3,938	3,787,431	395,352	14,505 79
1830	4,788,804	2,480	4,791,644	405,739	10,061 43
1831	4,149,986	1,489	4,150,475	488,522	12,400 13
1832	4,493,916	16,734	4,510,650	553,639	13,784 79
1833	4,459,534	8,053	4,467,587	690,391	17,038 30
1834	5,469,240	13,858	5,483,098	837,325	18,966 70
1835	6,054,445	9,618	6,064,063	691,255	19,737 62
1836	6,044,028	148,012	6,192,040	1,106,814	16,501 37
1837	3,699,110	3,604	3,702,714	813,823	8,299 64
1838	3,977,895	8,333	3,986,228	577,142	7,405 82

COMMERCE of SOUTH CAROLINA from 1821 to 1838.

Years.	EXPORTS.			Imports.	Registered Tonnage.
	Domestic.	Foreign.	Total.		
1821	$6,867,515	$332,996	$7,200,511	$3,007,113	16,249 32
1822	7,136,366	123,954	7,260,320	2,283,586	12,842 65
1823	6,671,998	226,816	6,898,814	2,419,101	12,275 68
1824	7,833,713	200,369	8,034,082	2,166,185	12,176 51
1825	10,876,475	180,267	11,056,742	1,892,297	10,712 07
1826	7,468,966	85,070	7,554,036	1,534,483	12,066 50
1827	8,189,496	133,065	8,322,561	1,434,106	12,694 82
1828	6,508,570	42,142	6,550,712	1,242,048	12,871 44
1829	8,134,676	40,910	8,175,586	1,139,618	7,842 03
1830	7,580,821	46,210	7,627,031	1,054,619	7,043 48
1831	6,528,605	46,596	6,575,201	1,238,163	5,802 88
1832	7,685,833	66,898	7,752,731	1,213,725	5,837 21
1833	8,337,512	96,813	8,434,325	1,517,705	6,038 19
1834	11,119,565	88,213	11,207,778	1,787,267	6,200 37
1835	11,224,298	113,718	11,338,016	1,891,805	9,314 12
1836	13,482,757	201,619	13,684,376	2,801,361	9,260 32
1837	11,138,992	81,169	11,220,161	2,510,860	8,413 53
1838	11,017,391	24,679	11,042,070	2,318,791	11,848 24

COMMERCE of GEORGIA from 1821 to 1838.

Years.	EXPORTS.			Imports.	Registered Tonnage.
	Domestic.	Foreign.	Total.		
1821	$5,979,995	$34,315	$6,014,310	$1,002,684	8,226 11
1822	5,483,219	1,650	5,484,869	989,591	6,079 57
1823	4,279,885	13,781	4,293,666	670,705	4,643 23
1824	4,619,753	4,229	4,623,982	551,888	4,635 36
1825	4,220,939	1,894	4,222,833	343,356	4,829 38
1826	4,366,630	1,874	4,368,504	330,993	5,763 55
1827	4,260,864	691	4,261,555	312,609	5,461 55
1828	3,104,425	- -	3,104,425	308,669	7,570 77
1829	4,980,642	734	4,981,376	380,293	7,494 07
1830	5,336,626	- -	5,336,626	282,436	4,359 09
1831	3,957,245	2,568	3,959,813	399,940	4,899 27
1832	5,514,681	1,202	5,515,883	253,417	4,462 08
1833	6,270,040	- -	6,270,040	318,990	7,387 12
1834	7,567,337	- -	7,567,337	546,802	9,208 03
1835	8,890,674	- -	8,890,674	393,049	6,528 19
1836	10,721,700	500	10,722,200	573,222	8,752 15
1837	8,935,041	- -	8,935,041	774,349	7,875 13
1838	8,803,839	- -	8,803,839	776,068	10,611 51

COMMERCE of ALABAMA from 1821 to 1838.

Years.	EXPORTS.			Imports.	Registered Tonnage.
	Domestic.	Foreign.	Total.		
1821	$108,960	- -	$108,960	- -	$1,088 68
1822	209,748	- -	209,748	$36,421	619 60
1823	200,387	- -	200,387	125,770	140 68
1824	457,725	$3,002	460,727	91,604	829 62
1825	691,897	738	692,635	113,411	821 57
1826	1,518,701	8,411	1,527,112	179,554	1,494 18
1827	1,330,770	45,594	1,376,364	201,909	1,462 37
1828	1,174,737	7,822	1,182,559	171,909	3,526 07
1829	1,679,385	14,573	1,693,958	233,720	4,625 20
1830	2,291,825	3,129	2,294,594	144,823	1,585 79
1831	2,412,862	1,032	2,413,894	224,435	2,137 56
1832	2,733,554	2,833	2,736,387	107,787	2,330 83
1833	4,522,221	5,740	4,527,961	265,918	1,920 21
1834	5,664,047	6,750	5,670,797	395,361	4,180 61
1835	7,572,128	2,564	7,574,692	525,955	4,556 34
1836	11,183,788	378	11,184,166	651,618	1,741 16
1837	9,652,910	18,491	9,671,401	609,385	2,733 69
1838	9,688,049	195	9,688,244	524,548	8,203 22

COMMERCE of LOUISIANA from 1821 to 1838.

Years.	EXPORTS.			Imports.	Registered Tonnage.
	Domestic.	Foreign.	Total.		
1821	$6,907,599	$364,573	$7,272,172	$3,379,717	$16,244 45
1822	7,303,461	675,184	7,978,645	3,817,238	13,922 52
1823	6,769,410	1,009,662	7,779,072	4,283,125	11,634 61
1824	6,442,946	1,485,874	7,928,820	4,539,769	11,270 84
1825	10,965,234	1,617,690	12,582,924	4,290,034	11,797 31
1826	9,048,506	1,235,874	10,284,380	4,167,521	15,357 27
1827	10,602,832	1,126,165	11,728,997	4,531,645	13,562 16
1828	10,163,342	1,784,058	11,947,400	6,217,881	19,447 72
1829	10,898,183	1,487,877	12,386,060	6,857,209	18,737 25
1830	13,042,740	2,445,952	15,488,692	7,599,083	13,234 27
1831	12,835,531	3,926,458	16,761,989	9,766,693	16,408 57
1832	14,106,118	2,425,812	16,530,930	8,871,653	21,888 88
1833	16,133,457	2,807,916	18,941,373	9,590,505	18,350 44
1834	23,759,607	2,797,917	26,557 524	13,781,809	25,241 35
1835	31,265,015	5,005,808	36,270,823	17,519,814	28,244 93
1836	32,226,565	4,953,263	37,179,828	15,117,649	26,744 92
1837	31,546,275	3,792,422	35,338,697	14,020,012	31,383 83
1838	30,077,534	1,424,714	31,502,248	9,496,808	39,593 08

I.

NUMBER and CONDITION of the STATE BANKS in the UNITED STATES,

	State or Territory.	No. of Banks.	No. of Branches.	Capital.	Loans and Discount.	Stocks.	Real Estate.	Other Investments.
1	Maine - -	55	-	$5,458,750	$7,552,938	- -	$136,260	- -
2	New Hampshire	27	-	2,839,500	4,200,245	- -	82,250	- -
3	Vermont - -	19	-	1,274,970	2,405,249	$10,000	33,728	$70,682
4	Massachusetts -	124	-	37,080,000	56,398,121	- -	1,117,883	- -
5	Rhode Island -	62	-	9,849,853	13,250,296	74,860	301,945	- -
6	Connecticut -	31	3	8,744,697	13,246,945	416,016	175,883	56,019
7	New York - -	95	2	36,611,460	60,999,770	2,795,207	2,356,249	38,256
8	Pennsylvania -	49	-	24,944,435	38,237,566	1,407,803	1,833,326	3,658,404
9	New Jersey -	28	-	4,997,012	8,029,700	2,438,001	307,738	380,117
10	Delaware - -	4	4	990,653	1,550,221	187,990	88,131	- -
11	Maryland - -	22	2	11,971,876	15,813,006	1,505,641	541,677	91,946
12	Dist. of Colombia	7	-	2,175,970	3,109,814	272,752	311,636	169,793
13	Virginia - -	5	18	7,005,356	15,900,987	439,781	636,404	123,305
14	North Carolina -	3	7	2,980,640	4,571,328	- -	127,424	34,495
15	South Carolina -	10	2	7,947,419	16,657,217	1,162,630	211,759	98,325
16	Georgia - -	20	16	11,790,573	15,937,526	1,215,501	1,830,430	324,715
17	Florida - -	6	2	2,387,585	3,207,015	5,000	466,134	105,540
18	Alabama - -	3	4	10,150,538	26,087,750	600,000	158,499	213,380
19	Mississippi - -	11	15	19,231,123	28,999,984	367,633	1,618,676	4,731,925
20	Louisiana - -	16	31	39,943,832	55,593,371	995,076	4,235,476	1,791,030
21	Arkansas - -	1	2	413,105	374,791	- -	- -	100,657
22	Tennessee - -	3	8	5,309,454	11,249,170	59,750	84,021	345,792
23	Kentucky - -	4	10	8,499,094	10,346,152	2,256,000	208,562	324,301
24	Missouri - -	1	2	607,398	1,034,852	- -	50,101	67,335
25	Illinois - -	2	6	4,673,050	4,416,577	2,690,000	27,533	4,944
26	Indiana - -	1	10	1,900,687	3,556,341	- -	97,301	298,658
27	Ohio - -	33	1	11,331,618	17,212,694	- -	387,427	- -
28	Michigan - -	18	2	1,918,365	3,773,370	- -	123,113	253,681
29	Wisconsin - -	2	-	119,625	152,676	- -	3,179	- -
30	Bank of U. States	1	19	35,000,000	45,181,854	14,862,108	1,504,772	10,809,774
		663	166	318,148,643	489,110,526	33,761,749	19,057,517	24,093,074

The above table is taken from the Financial Register. The details and the according to the Returns dated nearest to the 1st of January, 1838.

	Specie.	Specie Funds.	Notes of other Banks.	Due by other Banks.	Circulation.	Deposits.	Due to other Banks.	Other Liabilities.
1	$ 246,720	- -	$ 163,145	$ 640,696	$ 1,690,023	$ 763,741	$ 351,260	$ 315,656
2	148,793	- -	109,308	531,638	1,111,074	466,092		
3	97,333	$ 85,029	53,793	431,693	1,457,441	282,283	44,112	1,135
4	1,474,743	- -	2,954,804	5,662,780	9,964,110	8,231,580	5,498,012	5,318,484
5	399,944	- -	420,196	537,350	2,164,344	799,306	788,680	764,115
6	415,386	-	296,725	941,314	3,998,325	1,484,966₈	639,824	288,130
7	4,139,732	618,277	3,616,918	18,297,899	12,432,478	15,895,684	15,221,478	6,142,047
8	3,674,194	- -	3,148,184	9,254,641	11,330,474	10,363,562	8,862,928	2,972,846
9	418,992	.-	324,396	645,909	1,345,241	820,805	495,993	4,140,111
10	126,007	- -	163,543	310,877	756,148	444,020	49,766	
11	1,259,908	- -	1,452,574	3,076,511	3,002,085	3,253,683	3,036,772	1,395,714
12	318,354	- -	394,925	342,560	764,822	1,222,052	553,511	
13	1,366,582	- -	473,895	1,477,542	7,178,776	3,028,954	342,568	1,600,386
14	705,389	- -	177,763	878,308	2,267,793	756,591	187,774	
15	1,436,315	- -	622,571	923,161	5,011,656	3,383,468	698,675	1,610,411
16	2,475,788	- -	1,345,808	1,057,866	5,077,273	2,121,617	1,954,361	93,409
17	161,310	16,872	107,392	316,527	621,393	417,191	173,404	637,376
18	796,151	- -	117,625	1,081,412	7,535,475	5,220,346	2,395,062	1,293,351
19	766,360	- -	1,058,274	2,563,783	7,472,334	4,638,669	3,039,201	3,505,364
20	2,729,983	- -	4,508,761	1,395,737	7,558,465	7,426,468	9,131,466	3,748,343
21	96,455	40,395	2,450	3,678	8,100	87,242	- -	102,095
22	595,667	- -	327,817	581,711	2,620,185	1,502,271	660,513	2,370,481
23	1,716,489	- -	673,852	1,279,274	3,600,570	2,159,700	872,112	1,245,005
24	628,167	- -	223,930	45,271	94,000	748,655	312,760	297,808
25	684,487	- -	70,718	234,145	1,990,993	789,652	348,995	188,836
26	1,221,181	- -	209,185	281,393	2,308,130	952,009	136,647	5,720
27	2,674,212	- -	864,597	1,340,338	6,221,136	4,071,975	481,344	1,509,459
28	435,073	- -	233,031	569,011	1,724,409	1,313,286	196,366	113,959
29	83,494	- -	27,432	45,908	141,363	43,228	163	9,435
30	3,770,842	- -	866,597	3,657,251	6,768,067	2,617,253	4,957,291	20,524,568
	35,064,051	760,573	25,010,209	58,406,184	118,216,683	85,306,349	61,431,038	60,194,244

the totals in many of the columns do not agree : the errors appear to be in details.

INCREASE and DECREASE of ASSETS and LIABILITIES of the STATE BANKS between 1st of January, 1837, and 1st of January, 1838.

	1837.	1838.	Increase or Decrease.
Number of Banks	634	663	29 inc.
Number of Branches	154	166	12 inc.
Whole number of Banks and branches	788	829	41 inc.
Capital paid in	$ 290,772,091	318,148,643	27,376,552 inc.
Loans and discounts	525,115,702	489,110,526	36,005,176 dec.
Stocks	12,407,112	33,761,749	21,354,637 inc.
Real estate	19,064,451	19,057,517	6,934 dec.
Other investments	10,423,630	24,093,074	13,669,444 inc.
Total of investments supposed to yield income	567,010,895	566,022,866	988,029 dec.
Specie	37,915,340	35,064,051	2,851,289 dec.
Specie funds	5,366,500	760,573	4,605,927 dec.
Notes of other banks	36,533,527	25,010,209	11,523,318 dec.
Due from other banks	59,663,910	58,406,184	1,257,726 dec.
Total of the immediate means	139,479,227	119,241,017	20,238,260 dec.
Circulation	149,185,890	118,216,683	30,969,207 dec.
Deposits	127,397,185	85,306,349	42,090,836 dec.
Due to other Banks	62,421,118	61,431,038	990,080 dec.
Total of immediate liabilities	339,004,193	264,954,070	74,050,123 dec.
Other liabilities	36,560,289	60,194,244	23,633,955 inc.
Total liabilities	375,564,482	325,148,314	50,416,168 dec.
Nett circulation	112,652,363	93,206,474	19,445,889 dec.
Excess of investments supposed to yield income above capital paid in	276,238,804	257,874,223	28,364,581 dec.

K.

POPULATION of the UNITED STATES, according to Five Enumerations.

States.	1790.	1800.	1810.	1820.	1830.
New Hampshire -	141,899	183,762	214,360	244,161	269,328
Massachusetts -	378,717	423,245	472,040	523,287	610,408
Rhode Island -	69,110	69,122	77,031	83,059	97,199
Connecticut - -	238,141	251,002	262,042	275,202	297,675
New York - -	340,120	586,756	959,949	1,372,812	1,918,608
Pennsylvania -	434,373	602,365	810,091	1,049,458	1,348,233
New Jersey -	184,139	211,949	249,555	277,575	320,823
Delaware - -	59,096	64,273	72,674	72,749	76,748
Maryland - -	319,728	341,548	380,546	407,350	447,040
District of Colombia	- -	14,093	24,023	33,039	39,834
Virginia - -	748,308	880,200	974,622	1,065,379	1,211,405
North Carolina -	393,751	478,103	555,500	638,829	737,987
South Carolina -	249,073	345,591	415,115	502,741	581,185
Georgia - -	82,548	162,101	252,433	340,987	516,823
Vermont - -	85,416	154,465	217,713	235,764	280,652
Kentucky - -	73,077	220,955	406,511	564,317	687,917
Tennessee - -	- -	105,602	261,727	422,813	681,904
Ohio - -	35,791	45,365	230,760	581,434	937,903
Louisiana - -	- -	.. -	76,556	153,407	215,739
Indiana - -	- -	4,875	24,520	147,178	343,031
Mississippi - -	- -	8,850	40,352	75,448	136,621
Illinois - -	- -	- -	12,282	55,211	157,455
Alabama - -	- -	- ..	20,845	127,901	309,527
Maine - -	96,540	151,719	228,705	298,335	399,455
Missouri - -	- -	- -	20,845	66,586	140,455
Arkansas - -	- -	- -	- -	14,273	30,388
Michigan - -	- -	- -	4,762	8,896	31,639
Florida Territory -	- -	- ..	- -	- -	34,730
Total - -	3,929,827	5,305,925	7,239,814	9,638,131	12,860,702

The last of these columns is taken from Pitkin : if to the number there shown 5,318 persons, belonging to the navy, be added, it will make the total population 12,866,020. The other columns are taken from the American Almanac. The tables of population in different works vary considerably; and the details and the total in the same table seldom correspond : the last column may, I think, be depended upon as correct.

POPULATION in 1830, showing the Number of the Free
and the Slave Population.

States.	Free.	Slaves.	Total.
New Hampshire -	269,325	3	269,328
Massachusetts - -	610,407	1	610,408
Rhode Island - -	97,182	17	97,199
Connecticut - -	297,650	25	297,675
New York - -	1,918,533	75	1,918,608
Pennsylvania - -	1,347,830	403	1,348,233
New Jersey - -	318,569	2,254	320,823
Delaware - -	73,456	3,292	76,748
Maryland - -	344,046	102,994	447,040
District of Colombia	33,715	6,119	39,834
Virginia - -	741,648	469,757	1,211,405
North Carolina -	492,386	245,601	737,987
South Carolina -	265,784	315,401	581,185
Georgia- - -	299,292	217,531	516,823
Vermont - -	280,652	- -	280,652
Kentucky - -	522,704	165,213	687,917
Tennessee - -	540,301	141,603	681,904
Ohio - -	937,897	6	937,903
Louisiana - -	106,151	109,588	215,739
Indiana - -	343,028	3	343,031
Mississippi - -	70,962	65,659	136,621
Illinois - -	156,698	747	157,445
Alabama - -	191,978	117,549	309,527
Maine - -	399,953	2	399,455
Missouri - -	115,364	25,091	140,455
Arkansas - -	25,812	4,576	30,388
Michigan - -	31,607	32	31,639
Territory of Florida -	19,229	15,501	34,730
Total - -	10,851,659	2,009,043	12,860,702

L.

STATISTICS OF COTTON.

As the cotton crop is one of the principal sources of the wealth of the United States, and furnishes the chief means by which the inhabitants pay for the imports they receive from Europe, and are enabled to meet their other foreign engagements, the progress which has been made and is still making in the production of this great staple of the country is worthy of attentive consideration.

The rapid increase that has taken place in the quantity of cotton exported since the invention of Mr. Whitney's machine in 1793 is very remarkable. In 1792, the cotton of all sorts exported from the United States amounted only to 138,328 pounds; in 1794, the quantity had reached 1,601,760 pounds:

In 1795	6,276,300 lbs.		In 1800	17,789,803 lbs.
1796	6,106,729		1801	20,911,201
1797	3,788,429		1802	27,501,075
1798	9,360,005		1803	41,105,623
1799	9,532,263		1804	38,118,011

From about this time to 1814, owing to commercial restrictions and to the war, the increase in the quantity exported was inconsiderable; and, indeed, towards the close of the period, the quantity had much fallen off, although the quantity grown, owing to the increased consumption at home, had, on the whole, considerably increased : since that period, the extension of the growth, and the increase in the quantity exported, have been extremely rapid, though occasionally fluctuating much from one year to another.*

* During the period of commercial restriction, the quantities exported also varied much from one year to another : in 1810, the quantity exported was 93⅓ millions of pounds.

The following table shows the estimated quantities grown, and the official quantities and values exported, in each year from 1814 to 1833 inclusive, distinguishing the description of cotton.

Years.	Estimated Quantity grown.	EXPORTS.		Value.
		Sea Island.	Upland.	
1814	70,000,000	2,520,238	15,268,669	$ 2,683,000
1815	100,000,000	8,449,951	74,548,796	17,529,000
1816	124,000,000	9,900,326	72,046,790	24,106,000
1817	130,000,000	8,101,880	77,547,448	22,628,000
1818	125,000,000	6,457,335	86,013,843	31,334,000
1819	167,000,000	7,448,775	80,508,270	21,082,000
1820	160,000,000	11,569,015	116,291,137	22,309,000
1821	180,000,000	11,344,066	113,549,339	20,157,484
1822	210,000,000	11,250,635	133,424,460	24,035,058
1823	185,000,000	12,136,688	161,586,582	20,445,520
1824	215,000,000	9,525,722	132,843,941	21,947,401
1825	255,000,000	9,665,278	166,784,629	36,846,649
1826	350,000,000	5,972,852	198,562,563	25,025,214
1827	270,000,000	15,140,798	279,169,317	29,359,545
1828	325,000,000	11,288,449	199,302,044	22,487,229
1829	365,000,000	12,833,307	252,003,879	26,575,311
1830	350,000,000	8,147,165	290,311,937	29,674,883
1831	385,000,000	8,311,762	268,668,022	25,289,492
1832	390,000,000	8,743,373	313,471,749	31,724,682
1833	445,000,000	11,142,987	313,553,617	36,191,105

After this time I cannot furnish the same accurate accounts; but, in 1834, the quantity produced was estimated at 460 millions, and the quantity exported of both descriptions amounted in round numbers to 384,750,000, of the value of $ 49,500,000.

No official returns are made of the quantity of cotton grown in the several states, but it is computed that the crop of 1834 was produced as follows, which will afford some idea of the comparative quantities furnished by each of the principal cotton-growing states: —

Mississippi	-	-	- 85,000,000 lbs.
Alabama	-	-	- 85,000,000
Georgia	-	-	- 75,000,000

South Carolina	-	-	- 65,500,000 lbs.
Louisiana	-	-	- 62,000,000
Tennessee	-	-	- 45,000,000
Florida	-	-	- 20,000,000
Virginia	-	-	- 10,000,000
North Carolina	-	-	- 9,500,000
The other states	-	-	- 3,000,000
			460,000,000

The exports were shipped from ports in the following states : —

Louisiana	-	-	- 164,000,000 lbs.
South Carolina	-	-	- 67,750,000
Georgia	-	-	- 56,500,000
Alabama	-	-	- 51,500,000
New York	-	-	- 30,250,000
North Carolina and Virginia		-	11,500,000
Rest of the United States		-	3,250,000
			384,750,000

No great dependence can, however, be placed, in the above accounts, on the accuracy of the estimates of the quantities grown in the United States. Mr. Mc Culloch, in his Dictionary, has given an estimate of the quantities grown in North America from 1821 to 1832, which is considerably lower — viz.

In 1821	110,940,000 lbs.	In 1827	285,120,000 lbs.
1822	121,485,000	1828	213,840,000
1823	136,125,000	1829	255,780,000
1824	152,880,000	1830	292,040,000
1825	169,860,000	1831	311,655,000
1826	211,680,000	1832	296,245,000

The following table gives a third estimate from 1826 to the present time, and is further useful in showing the destination of the cotton crop during these years.

| Years. | Crops of the United States. | EXPORTS. | | | | Consumption of the United States. |
		Great Britain.	Average Weight of Bales imported in Great Britain.	France.	Other Ports.	
	Bales.	Bales.	lbs. per Bale.	Bales.	Bales.	Bales.
1826–7	957,281	605,685	320	- -	- -	103,483
1827–8	727,593	424,743	326	148,519	26,738	120,593
1828–9	870,415	498,001	326	184,823	66,178	118,853
1829–30	976,845	595,713	328	200,791	42,212	126,512
1830–1	1,008,847	618,718	334	127,029	27,036	182,142
1831–2	987,475	638,148	343	207,209	46,371	173,800
1832–3	1,070,438	630,145	357	207,517	29,793	194,412
1833–4	1,204,394	756,291	360	216,224	54,914	196,413
1834–5	1,254,328	722,718	363	252,470	48,311	216,888
1835–6	1,361,628	771,148	370	266,188	79,267	236,733
1836–7	1,422,963	850,786	374	260,722	56,917	223,540
1837–8	1,801,497	1,165,155	372	321,480	88,994	246,063
1838–9	1,360,532	798,418	not ascertained; probably 375 per bale	242,243	34,028	276,018

The following table shows the quantities exported by the different states in 1838, as well as the countries to which the exports from each were sent.

From	To Great Britain.	To France.	To the North of Europe.	Other Foreign Ports.	Total.
	Bales.	Bales.	Bales.	Bales.	Bales.
New Orleans - -	481,501	127,828	7,580	14,528	631,437
Mississippi (Natchez)	15,246	- -	- -	- -	15,246
South Carolina -	158,212	55,685	28,853	3,717	246,467
Georgia (Savannah and Darien)	201,582	27,024	560	632	229,798
Alabama - -	158,029	61,123	3,988	1,910	225,050
Florida - -	31,902	2,240	- -	12	34,154
New York - -	97,005	42,929	18,196	3,820	161,950
North Carolina -	4,279	- -	- -	- -	4,279
Virginia - -	12,205	4,136	2,446	651	19,438
Baltimore - -	2,240	- -	78	- -	2,318
Philadelphia - -	2,954	465	905	282	4,606
Boston - -	- -	50	493	343	886
Grand Total -	1,165,155	321,480	63,099	25,895	1,575,629

It appears by the first of these tables, that in the year 1838 the quantity exported and consumed at home exceeded the crop, large as it was; the quantity on hand at the different ports, which, on the 1st October, 1837, was 75,820, having been reduced on the 1st of October, 1828, to 40,305: 15,601 bales were either burnt or lost at New Orleans and other places. Among the exports were included 281 bales of foreign cotton previously imported. The stock on hand at the outports on the 1st October, 1839, was 52,244 bales. The great variation in the relative quantities exported by the several states, as shown by the second table and that before given, in which the exports of 1834 are detailed, is very remarkable.

The statistical facts respecting the crop of the latter year are taken from extracts of a letter from the secretary of the treasury, inserted in the American almanac for 1837. An estimate of the quantities of cotton produced in that year in the whole world is given on the same authority; and although estimates of this nature must be liable to great errors, seeing how little even the accounts respecting the produce of the United States are to be relied upon, it is interesting as furnishing some idea of the relative importance of the cotton trade of America and that of other countries.

By this estimate, the quantity grown in the whole world in 1834 amounted to 900 millions of pounds, of which there were grown —

In the United States -	- 460	millions of pounds.
In the Brazils - -	- 30	ditto.
In Mexico and the rest of South		
America - -	- 35	ditto.
In the West Indies -	- 8	ditto.
In Egypt - -	- $25\frac{1}{2}$	ditto.
In the west of Africa -	- 34	ditto.
In India - -	- 185	ditto.
In the rest of Asia -	- 110	ditto.
Elsewhere - -	- $12\frac{1}{2}$	ditto.
	900	

Of this amount, the United States exported $284\frac{3}{4}$ millions, as above stated; India about eighty millions, and the Brazils and Egypt nearly all they produced.

M.

TRADE OF THE AMERICAN COLONIES BEFORE THE REVOLUTIONARY WAR.

UNDER the head of Virginia, an account is given of the imports of several of the American colonies in the year 1769; but on comparing this statement with an account of the trade of these colonies with the mother-country from 1697 to 1776, lately published, in the United States' Commercial and Statistical Register, it appears that this solitary instance does not present an accurate view of the relative commercial importance of the several colonies during a course of years; it ought to be remarked, too, that in the exports of Virginia those of Maryland are included, and in those of South Carolina are comprised those of both the provinces of North and South Carolina.

The instance given of the year 1769 is interesting, however, as furnishing some data respecting the extent of the commerce of the colonies at that time with other countries as well as with Great Britain. The following table shows the countries from which the imports were received : —

	New England.	New York.	Pennsylvania.	Virginia and Maryland.	Carolina.
From Great Britain -	£223,695	£75,931	£204,979	£714,944	£327,084
From the South of Europe	25,409	14,927	14,249	14,125	7,099
From the West Indies -	314,741	97,420	180,592	109,651	76,270
From Africa - -	180	698		12,420	125,261
	£564,025	£188,976	£399,820	£851,140	£535,714

The account for this year of the trade with Great Britain differs, however, materially from that given for the same year in the United States' Commercial and Statistical Register.

The following is an account of the trade with Great Britain according to the latter authority, from 1760 to 1774. That for the year 1769 is from Macpherson's Annals of Commerce. The account under the head of Virginia, being taken from an American publication, differs slightly from this.

EXPORTS.

Years.	New England.	New York.	Pennsylvania.	Virginia and Maryland.	Carolina.	Georgia.
1760	£37,802	£21,425	£22,754	£504,451	£162,769	£12,198
1761	46,225	48,648	39,170	455,083	253,002	5,764
1762	41,733	58,882	38,091	415,709	181,695	6,522
1763	74,815	53,998	38,228	642,294	282,366	14,469
1764	88,157	53,697	36,258	559,508	341,727	31,325
1765	145,819	54,959	25,148	505,671	385,918	34,183
1766	141,733	67,020	26,851	461,693	293,587	53,074
1767	128,207	61,422	37,641	437,926	395,027	35,856
1768	148,375	87,115	59,406	406,048	508,108	42,402
1769	129,353	73,466	26,111	361,892	387,114	82,270
1770	148,011	69,882	28,109	435,094	278,907	55,532
1771	150,381	95,875	31,615	577,848	420,311	63,810
1772	126,265	82,707	29,133	528,404	425,923	66,083
1773	124,624	76,246	36,652	589,803	456,513	85,391
1774	112,248	80,008	69,611	612,030	432,302	67,647

IMPORTS.

Years.	New England.	New York.	Pennsylvania.	Virginia and Maryland.	Carolina.	Georgia.
1760	£599,647	£480,106	£707,998	£605,880	£218,131	
1761	334,225	289,570	204,067	545,350	254,587	£24,279
1762	247,385	288,046	206,199	418,599	194,170	23,761
1763	258,854	238,560	284,152	555,391	250,132	44,908
1764	459,765	515,416	436,191	515,192	305,808	18,338
1765	451,299	382,349	363,368	383,224	334,709	29,165
1766	409,642	330,829	327,314	372,548	296,732	67,268
1767	406,081	417,957	371,830	437,628	244,093	23,334
1768	419,797	482,930	432,107	475,984	289,868	56,562
1769	207,993	74,918	199,906	488,362	306,600	58,340
1770	394,451	475,991	134,881	717,782	146,273	56,193
1771	1,420,119	653,621	728,744	920,326	409,169	70,493
1772	824,830	343,970	507,909	793,910	449,610	92,406
1773	527,055	289,214	426,448	328,904	344,859	62,932
1774	562,476	437,937	625,652	528,738	378,116	57,518

N.

DEBTS OF THE SEPARATE STATES.

ALTHOUGH the amount of the debts of the several states cannot be stated with certainty, the following summary may be given of the amounts of stock issued, and authorised to be issued, by each: —

Massachusetts	$4,943,197 92
New York	13,394,018 19
Pennsylvania	27,665,003 32
Maryland	16,407,001 39
Virginia	6,662,089 17
South Carolina	5,753,770 12
Georgia	1,500,000 00
Kentucky	7,369,000 00
Tennessee	1,789,166 66
Ohio	10,030,162 71
Louisiana	23,139,000 00
Indiana	14,717,000 00
Mississippi	7,000,000 00
Illinois	11,600,000 00
Alabama	15,700,000 00
Maine	554,976 00
Missouri	2,500,000 00
Arkansas	3,100,000 00
Michigan	5,340,000 00
Florida	3,900,000 00
	$183,064,385 48

The above table, however, is necessarily incomplete, owing to several of the states having authorised issues of which the amounts, though limited, are dependent on contingent circumstances, and cannot, therefore, be exactly estimated: many instances of this are recorded in the course of the preceding chapter.

AA to KK.

THE following tables exhibit the condition at various times of such of the banks as are connected with the states in which they are situated, by the capital being wholly, or in part, raised by means of an issue of state bonds.

The accounts are chiefly taken or made up from documents which have been submitted to Congress, or to the legislatures of the respective states. Some of the items are occasionally not very intelligible, and distinctions are often made between different descriptions of bills discounted, which it is difficult to understand. This may be a necessary result of different modes of business being adopted in the two countries. Some errors of detail have been corrected, but others, from want of the means of correcting them, have of necessity been allowed to stand. As the discrepancies of this sort are too numerous to be specially alluded to, the existence of the errors are simply pointed out by asterisks in the margins of the accounts.

AA

Condition of the Bank of Kentucky and

LIABILITIES.

Capital stock - - - - -	*$*4,679,404 00
Notes in circulation - - - -	2,781,812 00
Individual deposits - - - -	695,450 88
Due to other banks - - - -	618,135 78
Due to treasurer of state - - -	69,598 28
Due to treasurer of United States -	27,263 34
Due to commissioners of sinking fund	9,805 22
Due to treasurer of internal improvements	245,744 84
Contingent fund and profit and loss -	100,000 00
Discounts and premiums - - -	230,614 87
Bank of the United States - - -	275,000 00
Board of education - - - -	21,945 02
Dividends unclaimed - - -	12,865 95
District court United States -	2,220 00
James Clark, Governor - - -	100,000 00
Real estate - - - - -	2,500 00
Total	*$*9,872,360 18

AA

Condition of the Northern Bank of Kentucky

LIABILITIES.

Capital stock - - - - -	*$*2,895,685 00
Notes in circulation - - - -	2,167,994 00
Due to other banks - - - -	333,820 88
Due to treasurer of United States -	32,409 32
Individual depositors - - - -	512,677 86
Bank of the United States - - -	184,380 90
Contingent fund and profit and loss -	211,289 95
Dividends unclaimed - - - -	5,793 02
Due to state government's officers -	32,124 94
Total	*$*6,376,175 87

1.

its Branches on the 31st December, 1838.

RESOURCES.

Bills discounted - - - -	- $4,567,110 70
Bills of exchange - - - -	- 1,785,168 19
Suspended debt - - - - -	61,745 16
Real estate - - - - - -	55,311 74
Due by other banks - - - - -	721,765 83
Specie on hand - - - - -	642,776 36
Notes of other banks - - - - -	317,686 54
State and city bonds - - - - -	1,675,000 00
Bank checks unpaid - - - - -	13,222 85
Treasurer of the state - - - -	451 48
Interest account - - - - -	31,000 00
Costs of suit - - - - - -	111 54
Suspense account - - - - -	1,009 79

Total $9,872,360 18

2.

and its Branches on the 31st December, 1838.

RESOURCES.

Bills discounted - - - -	- $2,049,760 44
Bills of exchange - - - -	- 1,835,537 02
Suspended debt - - - - -	43,443 71
State bonds - - - - -	755,000 00
Due from other banks - - - -	565,677 45
Real estate - - - - - -	100,857 88
Specie on hand - - - - -	698,302 37
Notes of other banks - - - - -	302,597 00
State of Kentucky - - - - -	25,000 00

Total $6,376,175 87

AA

Condition of the Banks of Kentucky before

BANK OF KENTUCKY.

LIABILITIES.	31st Dec. 1836.	31st Aug. 1837.
Capital - - -	$3,667,331	$4,588,770
Circulation - - -	1,771,675	1,293,670
Deposits - - -	1,017,800	1,333,693
Due to other banks - -	708,556	573,719
Other liabilities - -	1,100,000	1,069,131
Contingent fund - -	74,000	} 174,170
Profit and loss - -	180,127	
	$8,519,489	$9,033,153

RESOURCES.		
Loans and discounts - -	$5,742,958	$5,571,751
Stocks - - -	1,060,000	1,370,000
Real estate - - -	42,708	54,349
Other investments - -		
Specie - - -	487,739	767,799
Notes of other banks - -	435,178	308,869
Due by other banks - -	750,906	960,385
	$8,519,489	$9,033,153

3.

and after the Suspension of Specie Payments.

NORTHERN BANK OF KENTUCKY.

LIABILITIES.	31st Dec. 1836.	16th Sept. 1837.
Capital - - -	$2,227,995	$2,572,155
Circulation - - -	1,696,155	1,101,485
Deposits - - -	1,974,649	493,497
Due to other banks - -	563,351	346,216
Other liabilities - -	553,142	553,142
Contingent fund - -	45,000	} 115,600
Profit and loss - -	119,583	
	$7,179,875	$5,182,095

RESOURCES.		
Loans and discounts - -	$3,844,980	$2,792,541
Stocks - - -	1,006,000	756,000
Real estate - - -	54,856	83,945
Other investments - "	25,000	
Specie - - -	755,029	760,600
Notes of other banks - -	562,365	169,331
Due by other banks - -	931,645	619,678
	$7,179,875	$5,182,095

BB

Condition of the Union Bank of Tennessee

LIABILITIES.

Capital stock paid in - - - - -			$2,553,739 00
Post notes on time - - - - - -			426,834 74
Circulation; viz.			
Payable at Nashville -	-	$799,605 00	
at offices -	-	19,050 00	
at Philadelphia and New			
York -	- -	43,255 00	
at New Orleans -	-	411,125 00	
			1,273,035 00
Due to offices - - - - - -			18,938 13
Due to banks - - - - - -			439,037 94
Treasurer of Tennessee -	-	43,129 31	
State officers and agents -	-	2,589 37	
			45,718 68
State of Tennessee, special deposit -		- -	707,353 00
Treasurer of United States -	-	94,547 17	
Pension agents - - -	-	18,675 66	
Disbursing officers and agents -	-	10,005 2½	
			123,228 07
Unclaimed dividends - - -		- -	2,412 52
Contingent fund, 1st of January, 1837		124,894 03	
Profit and loss - - -	-	351,089 29	
			475,983 32
Profits since 1st of January last -		- -	43,631 08
Certificates of deposit -	-	36,115 63	
Individual depositors -	-	227,046 13	
			263,161 76
			$6,373,073 24

1.

and Branches on the 3d of March, 1838.

RESOURCES.

Notes under discount - - - $4,106,440 62		
Domestic bills of exchange - . 1,015,880 60		
	5,122,321	22
Suspended debt - - - - - -	25,877	05
Banking houses and lots - - - -	59,039	38
Due from banks and agents - - - -	356,607	62
State of Tennessee for interest on bonds - - - - - - -	15,285	40
Expenses since 1st of January - - -	5,624	94
Cash funds on hand ; viz.		
State and city bank notes - 89,185 00		
Distant bank notes - " 422,815 00		
Gold and silver - - " 276,317 63		
	788,317	63

$6,373,073 24

BB

Condition of the Union Bank of Tennessee and

(on the 2d of

LIABILITIES.

Capital stock paid in - - - -	$2,425,560 00	
Ditto (new state stock) - - -	68,543 75	
		$2,494,103 75
Circulation payable to bearer; viz.		
at New Orleans - - -	1,730,400 00	
at Philadelphia and New York	154,395 00	
at Nashville - - - -	39,870 00	
at Jackson - - - -	12,750 00	
at Knoxville - - -	17,320 00	
		1,954,735 00
Post notes on time payable at New Orleans - -		164,856 27
Treasurer of the United States - -	864,635 60	
United States' disbursing officers and agents	43,183 05	
		907,818 65
Treasurer of Tennessee at Nashville -	8,620 10	
at Jackson -	612 84	
State officers and institutions - - -	22,416 50	
		31,649 44
Due to offices - - - - -	29,029 57	
Due to other banks - - - -	200,244 29	
		229,273 86
Due to individual depositors at Nashville -	139,387 36	
at Jackson -	30,838 04	
at Columbia -	40,163 35	
at Knoxville	40,775 66	
		251,164 41
Dividend declared this day - - -	114,253 17	
Former dividend unclaimed - - -	2,612 15	
State dividend - - - - -	34,112 58	
State bonus - - - - - -	8,259 68	
		159,237 58
Contingent fund , - - - -	124,894 03	
Profit and loss - - - - -	2,017 87	
		126,911 90
		$6,319,750 86

2.

Branches before the Suspension of Specie Payments
January, 1837).

RESOURCES.

Notes under discount at Nashville -	- $736,846 02	
at Jackson -	- 106,994 29	
at Columbia -	- 240,403 31	
at Knoxville	- 201,194 20	
		$1,285,437 82
Domestic bills of exchange at Nashville -	2,516,185 53	
at Jackson -	799,375 96	
at Columbia -	694,886 75	
at Knoxville -	58,564 40	
		4,069,012 64
Loan to the state of Tennessee at 6 per cent. interest - - - - - -	- -	84,092 53
Suspended debt, Nashville - - -	1,730 88	
Jackson - - - -	4,346 79	
Knoxville - - -	400 00	
		6,477 67
Banking house and lot, Nashville - -	31,497 06	
Jackson - -	2,152 44	
Knoxville - -	6,600 00	
		40,249 50
Due from other banks - - - - -	- -	602,719 19
Cash on hand ; viz.	48,130 00	
State and city bank notes - - -	67,700 00	
Distant bank notes - - - -	6,195 00	
United States' bank notes - -	109,736 51	
Gold and silver - - - -		231,761 51

$6,319,750 86

BB

Condition of the Union Bank of Tennessee and
on the 1st

LIABILITIES.

Capital stock paid in - - - - -		$2,553,179 00
Notes in circulation (to bearer)		
Payable at Nashville - -	$156,135 00	
at New Orleans - -	576,345 00	
at Philadelphia and New		
York - - -	55,860 00	
ʋt offices - - ··	20,900 00	
		809,240 00
Post notes on time (payable to order) - -		598,336 48
State of Tennessee, special (on time		
and interest) - - - - - -		707,353 00
Due to banks in current account -	437,298 71	
to offices - - - -	13,369 98	
to treasurer of Tennessee -	61,085 77	
to treasurer of the United States	104,424 57	
to sundry public officers and		
agents - - - -	58,050 83	
to individual depositors - -	301,983 21	
		976,213 07
Contingent fund, and profit and loss - -		451,878 32
		$6,096,199 87

BB

Condition of the Bank of Tennessee and

LIABILITIES.

Capital stock, state bonds - -	$1,000,000 00	
Ditto school fund - -	90,893 71	
		$1,090,893 71
Sinking or contingent fund - - - -		35,387 48
Due to banks - - - - - -		22,759 15
Treasurer of Tennessee - - - -		26,565 59
Exchange account - - -	47,005 72	
Discounts received - - -	23,979 22	
		70,984 94
Circulation - - - - - -		757,667 18
Individual depositors - - - - -		97,096 67
		$2,101,354 82 *

2.

Branches, after the Suspension of Specie Payments, October, 1837.

RESOURCES.

Notes under discount - · -	$4,035,593 46	
Bills of exchange - - -	909,824 01	
Ditto protested (not yet liquidated)	157,653 20	
		$5,103,070 67
Suspended debt (in suit) - -	- -	22,291 28
State of Tennessee (interest on bonds)	12,500 00	
Paymaster of United States' army -	160 89	
		12,660 89
Real estate (banking houses and lots) - - - - -	- -	44,844 54
Due by banks in current account -	- -	307,055 00
Expenses since 1st of July - -	- -	6,749 36
Cash funds, viz. : —		
State and city bank notes -	69,700 00	
Foreign bank notes - -	222,640 00	
Checks on Philadelphia -	76,500 00	
Gold and silver - - -	230,688 13	
		599,528 13
		$6,096,199 87

3.

Branches on the 1st *Day of October,* 1838.

RESOURCES.

State bonds - - - - - -		$ 400,000 00
Discounted notes - - -	$962,617 59	
Domestic bills - - -	204,536 69	
		1,167,154 28
Expences - - - - - - -		23,004 97
Due from other banks · - - -		104,653 92
Branch balances - - - - -		25,179 86
Specie and bank notes - - - ·.		381,361 79
		$2,101,354 82

CC

Condition of the Banks of Louisiana

Names of the Banks.	Capital.		Real Estate and other Investments.
	Nominal.	Paid up.	
Bank of Louisiana	$4,000,000	$3,997,560	$96,446
Mechanics' and Traders' Bank	2,000,000	1,998,390	56,216
Consolidated Association	1,951,000	1,951,000	80,928
Union Bank of Louisiana	7,000,000	7,000,000	437,395
Citizens' Bank of Louisiana	12,000,000	6,344,444	234,584

Names of the Banks.	Domestic Bills and Bank Notes of other States held by the Banks.		Balances due to or from Banks in other States, including Checks and Post Notes.	
	Bills.	Bank Notes.	Dr.	Cr.
Bank of Louisiana	- -	$37,680	$162,422	
Mechanics' and Traders' Bank	- -	- -	102,159	$45,555
Consolidated Association	- -	2,650	- -	3,234
Union Bank of Louisiana	- -	59,060	358,472	349,660
Citizens' Bank of Louisiana	- -	1,090	54,066	292,936

Names of the Banks.	Circulation.	Local Bank Notes on Hand.	Specie in the Vaults.
Bank of Louisiana	$162,052	$470,940	$307,948
Mechanics' and Traders' Bank	612,275	23,150	185,750
Consolidated Association	216,225	68,575	76,353
Union Bank of Louisiana	1,293,230	29,600	696,430
Citizens' Bank of Louisiana	68,545	495,430	339,711

1.

on the 1st October, 1839.

On Pledge of Bank Stock.	Discounts and Loans.			Balances due to from Foreign Bankers.	
	On Stock by Property Banks as required by their Charter.	On Real Estate and Bills and Notes, including the Capital of Branches.		Dr.	Cr.
$211,600	- -	$4,827,761		- -	$13,890
259,916	- -	2,547,485		- -	10,731
- -	$1,168,219	1,539,156		- -	198,168
- -	2,902,694	6,710,001		$73,547	367,513
- -	3,917,585	5,019,903		329,884	4,094

Liabilities other than those expressed, Bills payable, Bonds, &c., and Dividends unpaid.	Assets other than those expressed, Municipality Notes, &c.	Balances due to or from Local Banks.		Deposits.	
		Dr.	Cr.	By Individuals or Corporations.	By Public Officers.
$15,713	$296	- -	- -	$ 485,736	
47,097	1,870	- -	- -	96,446	
2,347	486	$ 30	1,560	537,895	
21,137	2,688	54,528	14,528	747,769	$78,554
13,500	- -	- -	50,000	1,251,443	

Capital gained, and Profits undivided.	Post Notes issued, bearing Interest at 5½ per Cent. per Annum, and guaranteed by an equal Amount of Louisiana State 5 per Cents., payable in		
	1841.	1842.	1843.
$1,123,513			
265,628			
431,338			
1,967,019			
494,656	$423,000	$422,500	$423,000

CC

Condition of the Banks of Louisiana before the

	Capital.		
Names of Banks.	Nominal.	Paid up.	Real Estate and other Investments.
Bank of Louisiana - -	$4,000,000	$3,997,480	$ 86,210
Mechanics and Traders' Bank	2,000,000	1,998,355	46,397
Consolidated Association -	2,054,000	2,054,000	72,401
Union Bank - - -	7,000,000	7,000,000	150,345
Citizens' Bank - -	12,000,000	3,000,000	117,759

Names of Banks.	Bank Notes of other States.	Balances due to or from Banks in other States.	
		Dr.	Cr.
Bank of Louisiana - -	$710	$1,004,209	$56,511
Mechanics and Traders' Bank	- -	615,970	42,316
Consolidated Association -	- -	- -	87,919
Union Bank - - -	25,868	1,884,800	441,099
Citizens' Bank - -	7,975	551,891	6,466

2.

Suspension of Specie Payments, 23d January, 1837.

	Loans and Discounts.			Balances due to and from foreign Bankers.		
On Pledge of Bank Stock.	On Stock by Property Banks as required by their Charters.	On real Estate and Bills originating in this State.	On Bills originating out of the State.	Dr.	Cr.	Domestic Bills held by the Banks.
$178,100	- -	$4,748,362	$549,306	- -	$47,566	$1,154,572
230,361	- -	1,782,177	531,315	- -	1,296	1,106,272
- -	$1,042,131	1,733,750	92,577	$242,085	50,707	9,561
- -	3,059,627	5,769,981	1,103,941	73,498	241,487	4,240,889
- -	396,625	2,879,740	123,110	95,858	76,878	736,394

Balances due to or from Local Banks.		Deposits.	Circulation.	Local Bank Notes.	Specie.
Dr.	Cr.				
$270,150	$249,434	$513,682	$841,190	$209,030	$261,721
149,096	39,193	313,870	919,395	193,885	96,343
44,963	67,079	675,564	385,605	177,770	325,846
169,624	390,053	3,872,726	1,476,445	304,505	353,637
- -	180,533	729,497	372,110	89,035	293,595

CC

Condition of the Banks of Louisiana

Name of Bank.	Date.	Capital.
	1837.	
Bank of Louisiana - - -	July 25th	$4,021,805
Mechanics and Traders' Bank -	June 30th	1,998,390
Consolidated Association - -	Aug. 5th	2,254,000
Union Bank - - - -	July 31st	7,820,000
Citizens' Bank - - - -	July 31st	4,500,000

Name of Bank.	Notes of other Banks.	Specie.
Bank of Louisiana - - -	$194,655	$50,841
Mechanics and Traders' Bank -	28,655	111,414
Consolidated Association - -	174,065	200,684
Union Bank - - - -	246,217	80,577
Citizens' Bank - - - -	146,765	442,876

3.

after the Suspension of Specie Payments.

Real Estate.	Loans and Discounts.	Stocks.	Other Investments.	Due from other Banks.
$70,504	$4,333,091	$5,000	$1,344,343	$315,125
46,426	2,441,390	- -	500,000	73,556
64,676	2,895,640	17,530	112,237	38,129
148,845	9,395,991	220,830	2,149,082	689,247
154,814	4,948,151	- -	825,646	77,466

Circulation.	Deposits.	Due from other Banks.	Other Liabilities.	Suspended Debt.
$519,390	$566,361	$120,853	- -	$370,570
545,455	303,000	159,213	$723	15,348
89,890	737,213	45,938	4,695	170,887
1,205,470	1,526,084	861,656	359,053	1,068,205
44,650	1,090,533	144,144	598,811	281,547

DD

Condition of the State Bank of

LIABILITIES.

Capital stock paid in - - - -	$1,585,481 51
Notes in circulation - - - -	1,927,050 00
Treasurer of the United States - - -	2,267,489 68
Pension agent of Indiana - - -	8,868 08
Due to branch banks - - - -	832,199 90
Other banks - - - - - -	66,867 08
Dividends due to stockholders - - -	30,345 44
State bank of Indiana - - - -	157,984 50
Commissioners of the sinking fund - -	37,324 00
Commissioners of the canal fund - -	27,253 87
School fund - - - - - -	4,200 00
Surplus fund - - - - - -	129,312 56
Individual depositors - - - -	431,703 16
Profit since last dividend - - - -	30,003 44
	$7,536,083 22

1.

Indiana, 26th November, 1836.

RESOURCES.

Bills discounted and notes purchased - -	$2,292,724 69
Bills of exchange - - - - -	883,888 41
Suspended debt - - - - -	2,650 00
Real estate — Banking house - - -	48,901 32
Furniture - - - - - -	6,001 72
Due from branch banks - - - -	886,025 98
Other banks - - - - - -	1,457,204 65
Remittances - - - - - -	131,568 72
State bank of Indiana - - - -	22,925 62
Commissioners of the sinking fund - -	40,165 13
Commissioners of canal fund - - -	69,536 00
Bank notes of other states' banks - -	489,753 39
Gold and silver - - - - -	1,204,737 59
	$7,536,083 22

DD

Condition of the State Bank of

LIABILITIES.

Capital stock paid in - - - -	$1,847,125 00
Notes in circulation - - - - -	2,205,810 00
Treasurer of the United States - - -	639,611 50
Pension agent - - - - - -	7,475 21
Late dividend - - - - - -	90,050 00
Former unpaid - - - - - -	5,007 34
Sinking fund - - - - - -	15,250 84
Cumberland road - - - - -	6,395 28
Due to other banks - - - - -	69,725 18
School fund - - - - - -	6,400 00
Surplus fund (after deducting interest to United States $20,283 75) - - -	292,143 92
Due to individual depositors - - -	328,159 27
	$5,513,153 54

DD

Table showing the Capital, Discounts, Circulation, and

Date.	Capital.	Discounts.	Circulation.	Specie.
Jan. 1. 1835	$800,000 00	$529,843 75	$456,065 00	$751,083 29
April 4. 1835	800,000 00	1,085,261 87	879,000 00	632,800 80
July 11. 1835	800,000 00	1,228,224 82	1,186,795 00	723,584 47
Oct. 3. 1835	800,000 00	1,496,638 24	1,361,430 00	700,201 85
Jan. 9. 1836	1,279,857 78	2,304,683 19	1,981,650 00	874,340 25
April 2. 1836	1,279,935 90	2,768,384 56	2,101,065 00	995,463 09
July 9. 1836	1,279,921 88	2,776,905 87	2,057,300 00	1,096,820 28

2.

Indiana, 31st October, 1837.

RESOURCES.

Notes discounted - - - - -	$2,976,879 10
Bills of exchange - - - - -	390,388 31
Banking house and furniture - - -	97,854 93
Branch balances - - - - -	20,341 55
Due from other banks - - - -	589,372 52
Remittances and other cash items - -	188,602 41
Notes of other banks - - - -	201,000 00
Specie - - - - - - -	1,048,714 72

$5,513,153 54

3.

Specie of the State Bank of Indiana at different Periods.

Date.	Capital.	Discounts.	Circulation.	Specie.
Oct. 3. 1836	$1,310,000 00	$2,747,155 57	$1,834,310 00	$997,118 00
Jan. 7. 1837	1,782,813 50	3,914,933 53	2,157,595 00	1,236,164 35
April 1. 1837	1,824,921 88	4,314,825 13	2,498,960 00	1,177,776 96
July 8. 1837	1,845,000 00	3,821,561 12	2,475,385 00	1,112,719 44
Sept. 30. 1837	1,845,000 00	3,562,491 67	2,378,075 00	1,158,887 72
Dec. 23. 1837	1,900,687 50	3,520,163 35	2,288,458 00	1,291,265 42

EE

Condition of the Planters' Bank of

LIABILITIES.

Capital stock - - - - - -	$4,203,740 00
Circulation - - - - - -	1,583,897 13
Treasurer of the United States - - -	1,035 504 88
Public officers - - - - - -	29,084 13
Deposits - - - - - -	345,362 00
Due to banks - - - - - -	707,413 32
Other liabilities - - - - - -	918,441 23
Profit and loss - - - - - -	928,857 90

$9,752,280 59*

1.

Mississippi, on the 27th April, 1837.

RESOURCES.

Loans and discounts - - - - -	$3,733,106 55
Bills of exchange - - - - -	2,880,084 29
Suspended debt - - - - -	2,307,228 46
Stocks - - - - - - -	42,200 00
Real estate - - - - - -	184,678 65
Other investments - - - - -	87,867 90
Due from other banks - - - -	66,685 73
Notes of other banks - - - -	48,908 00
Specie - - - - - - -	401,521 01
	$9,752,280 59

EE

Condition of the Planters' Bank of

LIABILITIES.

Capital stock paid in - - - - -	$4,260,200	00
Discounts - - - - - - -	140,047	92
Profit and loss - - - - - -	1,321,351	24
Treasurer of the United States - - -	323,367	96
Do. for post-office department - -	5,384	25
Suspense account - - - - -	24,407	96
Unclaimed dividends - - - - -	22,339	99
Circulation, notes on demand $330,143 21		
12-month post-notes 213,963 19		
	544,106	40
Individual deposits - - - - -	135,516	88
Deposit — certificates - - - -	25,782	99
Bills payable - - - - - -	447,559	94
Checks payable - - - - - -	510,089	05
Literary fund - - - - - -	68	00
Three per cent. fund - - - - -	3,958	30
Sinking fund - - - - - -	36,857	01
Seminary lands - - - - - -	2,520	00
Council of Natchez - - - - -	1,683	76
Bonds payable - - - - - -	2,233,333	33
Due to banks - - - - - -	283,396	40
Pension agents - - - - - -	11,080	13
	$10,333,052	24 *

2.

Mississippi, on 18*th April,* 1839.

RESOURCES.

Bills discounted - - - - - - -			$7,105,781 53
In suit - - - -			643,368 39
Bills of exchange - - - - -			280,350 75
Real estate - - - - - -			228,951 92
Cotton account - - - - - -			624,876 39
Expense account - - - - -			28,700 78
Bank stock - - -	$396,869	16	
State bonds - - -	140,000	00	
			536,869 16
Interest - - - - - - -			14,388 99
Due from banks - - - - -			242,790 92
Notes of other banks - - - -			422,727 95
Brown, Brothers, and Co., New York - -			227 13
Deferred interest - - - - -			7,959 84
Natchez insurance company stock - -			675 00
A. M. Feltus, agent - - - - -			2,000 00
Specie - - - - - - -			193,383 49

$10,333,052 24

FF

Condition of the State Bank

LIABILITIES.

Capital stock owned by the state - -	- $2,100,000 00
Do. by individuals -	- 1,415,000 00
Real estate fund - - - - -	- 500,000 00
Notes in circulation - - - -	- 1,838,325 00
State bank and branches - - -	- 2,842,601 34
Other banks - - - - -	- 347,077 05
Unclaimed dividends - - - -	- 1,350 00
Retained dividends - - - -	- 87,130 00
State of Illinois (canal fund) -	- - 420,000 00
Fund commissioners - - - -	- 4,473 55
Individual depositors - - - -	- 177,085 07
Discount, exchange, and interest -	- - 51,601 33
Surplus fund - - - - -	- 54,556 78
Profit and loss - - - - -	- 17,652 50

$9,856,852 62

FF

Condition of the Bank of Illinois

LIABILITIES.

Capital stock owned by the state of Illinois	- $100,000 00
Do. by individuals -	- 157,550 00
Notes in circulation - - - -	- 146,273 00
Treasurer of United States - - -	- 28,142 47
Fund commissioners - - - -	- 63,500 00
Unclaimed dividends - - - -	- 229 61
Individual depositors - - - -	- 31,710 64
Due to other banks - - - -	- 80,920 10
Surplus fund - - - - -	- 18,320 77

626,646 59

1.

of Illinois, 8th January, 1838.

RESOURCES.

Bills discounted - - - -	$2,929,325 05
Bills of exchange - - - -	593,154 90
Loans on real estate - - - -	484,740 50
Illinois bank and internal improvement stock	1,765,000 00
Illinois and Michigan canal stock - -	525,000 00
Real estate - - - - -	25,806 96
Personal property - - - -	4,944 62
Incidental expenses - - - -	5,099 20
State of Illinois - - - -	23,200 09
State bank and branches - - -	2,740,983 06
Other banks - - - -	144,529 96
Board of commissioners of Illinois and Michigan canal - - - - -	43,631 44
Notes of other banks - - -	46,433 00
Gold and silver coin - - -	524,992 34
	$9,856,852 62*

2.

at Shawneetown, 1st January, 1838.

RESOURCES.

Bills discounted - - - -	$327,202 24
Bills of exchange - - - -	13,648 58
Real estate - - - - -	1,727 00
Due from other banks - - -	94,783 44
Notes of other banks - - - -	29,760 00
Specie - - - - -	159,525 33
	$626,646 59

FF

Condition of the Banks of Illinois before

STATE BANK OF ILLINOIS.

LIABILITIES.		2d Jan. 1837.	5th Sep. 1837.
Capital	- - -	$1,863,060	$2,250,600
Circulation	- - -	1,459,810	1,561,920
Deposits	- - -	718,848	439,813
Due to other banks	- -	18,678	104,496
Other liabilities	- -	1,681	31,712
Profit and loss	- -	152,383	110,454
		$4,214,460	$4,498,995
RESOURCES.			
Loans and discounts	-	$2,849,470	$3,529,389
Stocks	- - -	- -	105,000
Real estate	- - -	13,204	21,351
Other investments	- -	11,070	15,358
Specie	- - -	553,998	508,950
Notes of other banks	- -	203,833	31,419
Due by other banks	- -	582,885	287,528
		$4,214,460	$4,498,995

3.

and after the Suspension of Specie Payments.

BANK OF ILLINOIS AT SHAWNEETOWN.

LIABILITIES.			21st Jan. 1837.	2d Sep. 1837.
Capital	-	-	$151,700	$257,550
Circulation	-	-	105,563	75,196
Deposits	-	-	109,796	159,530
Due to other banks	-	-	18,664	2,851
Profit and loss	-	-	4,054	10,525
			$389,777	$505,652
RESOURCES.				
Loans and discounts	-	-	$249,281	$266,071
Real estate	-	-	975	400
Other investments	-	-	-	575
Specie	-	-	36,796	158,610
Notes of other banks	-	-	64,820	17,505
Due by other banks	-	-	37,905	62,491
			$389,777	$505,652

GG

Condition of the Bank of the State

LIABILITIES.

Capital Stock *	-	$1,217,248 45
Circulation account	-	2,483,411 00
Individual deposits	-	495,499 84
Common school fund	-	151,448 40
Partial payments	-	64,750 67
Sinking fund	-	289,287 00
Discount received	-	4,105 51
Premium ditto	-	64 96
Interest ditto	-	704 67
Branch state bank at Montgomery	-	21,961 76
Branch state bank at Decatur	-	6,890 66
Office bank of Columbus, Mississippi	-	649 84
Bank of Louisiana, New Orleans	-	499 02
Bank of America, New York	-	7,705 46
United States' surplus revenue	-	133,817 79

$4,878,045 03

* Composed of		
Revenue fund	-	$404,156 55
University fund	-	282,016 34
3 per cent. fund	-	431,075 56
6 per cent. Loan	-	100,000 00

$1,217,248 45

1.

of Alabama, November 7. 1837.

RESOURCES.

Notes discounted - - -	$3,135,833 35
Bills of exchange - - -	766,386 60
Real estate - - - -	12,040 53
Permanent expense - - -	827 62
Branch of state bank at Mobile - -	183,900 83
Branch of state bank at Huntsville -	5,435 31
Office bank United States, Mobile - -	379 62
Commercial bank, Columbus, Mississippi -	4 00
Planter's and Merchant's bank, Mobile -	53,389 85
Bank of Virginia, Richmond - -	8,780 00
Bank of Mobile - - -	25,762 41
Profit and loss - - - -	35 25

Cash

Foreign notes - -	$ 27,780 00	
Circulation - -	- 434,357 00	
Specie - -	- 223,132 66	
		685,269 66
		$4,878,045 03

GG

Condition of the Branch of the Bank of the

LIABILITIES.

State bonds paid in - - $2,300,000 00		
Sinking fund - - - 577,944 00		
		$2,877,944 00
Profit and loss - - - - -		272,918 34
Treasurer of the United States - - -		905,393 33
Treasurer of the state of Alabama - - -		133,817 35
Sundry persons - - - - -		148,824 06
Suspense account - - - - -		133,334 11
Due to banks - - - - - -		704,623 60
Circulation - - - - - -		1,748,231 00
Deposits - - - - - -		1,526,378 59
A. M. Nathan, New Orleans, as collateral security - - - - -		21,954 05
J. N. Gossler, special deposit - - -		15,000 00
Commissioners of 16th section as principal - - - -	1,585 41	
Commissioners of 16th section as interest - - - -	210 01	
		1,795 42
City of Mobile special account - - - -		4,342 78
Treasurer of the United States, service of Post Office Department - - -		25,791 46

$8,520,348 09

2.

State of Alabama at Mobile, 9th October, 1837.

RESOURCES.

Bills discounted	-	- $4,011,099 72	
Bills discounted under protest	-	- 1,375,450 07	
			$5,386,549 79
Domestic bills of exchange			
On Tuscaloosa	- - -	3,326 89	
On Montgomery	- - -	3,111 11	
On New Orleans	- - -	121,678 29	
On New York	- - -	118,364 83	
On Columbus, Miss. -	- -	18,000 00	
On Decatur -	- - -	5,000 00	
			269,481 12
On London -	- - - - -		39,563 74
Premium of exchange on London	- - -		9,574 60
Exchange on London protested	- - -		46,056 07
Thomas Wilson and Co., London	- - -		9,087 69
Suspended debt	- - - - -		1,000 00
Do. on bonds and mortgages	- - -		76 59
Real estate—banking house and lot	-	76,611 19	
bank furniture	- -	3,478 06	
			80,089 25
Protest account	- - -	7,571 00	
Exchange account protested	- -	2,162,887 81	
			2,170,458 81
Thomas Eastin, navy agent, over draft	- -		120 41
A. Pope, agent at Liverpool	- - - -		110,956 99
Due from banks	- - - - -		192,039 07
Bills receivable	- - - - ..		22,103 86
Bank notes on hand	- - - - -		183,190 10
			$8,520,348 09

GG

Condition of the Branch of the Bank of the State

LIABILITIES.

Capital stock - - - -	-	$882,000 00
Notes in circulation - - -	-	1,423,519 00
Individual depositors - - -	-	179,315 47
Due to other banks - - -	-	87,256 27
Common school fund - - -	-	115,049 49
Treasurer of the United States for services of post office department - - -	-	2,091 71
Treasurer of state of Alabama -	-	133,817 36
Partial payments, costs on suits, and fund to pay expenses on mortgages under bond system	-	31,998 92
Damages liable to be remitted -	-	34,056 15
Assets over and above liabilities, being the amount of nett profits on sinking fund to 1st October, 1836 - - $213,869 65		
Nett profits accruing from 1st October, 1836, to 1st October, 1837, carried to the credit of the sinking fund - - 91,003 05		
		304,872 70
		$3,193,977 07

3.

of Alabama at Montgomery, 10th October, 1837.

RESOURCES.

Banking-house, lot, and furniture	- -	$16,189 76
Notes discounted at twelve months from 1st February, 1837 - - - - -		999,961 00
Notes discounted under the 21st section of act of June, 1837 - - -		891,900 00
Notes discounted under the 2d section of act of June, 1837	- -	213,825 77
Notes discounted under the 20th section of act of June, 1837 - - -		74,211 91
Bills of exchange - - - -		750,940 09
Notes protested - - - -		36,941 00
Due from other banks - - - -		116,151 63
Suspended debt - - - -		2,178 88
Specie - - - - -		91,677 03

$3,193,977 07

GG

Condition of the Branch of the Bank of the State

LIABILITIES.

Capital stock - ·· - -	$1,500,000 00
Sinking fund - - - -	356,812 52
Profit and loss - - - -	42,639 49
Sixteenth section school fund - -	98,562 31
Individual depositors - - -	343,972 73
Discount account - - - -	29,091 78
Exchange account - - - -	190 23
Treasurer of the State of Alabama - ··	133,817 36
Damages on protested bills - - -	4,736 07
Interest account - - ·· -	6,530 53
Amount due to banks within the State of	
Alabama - - - ·· -	77,553 58
Amount due to other banks - - -	340,327 66
Notes in circulation - - - -	1,300,503 00
	$4,234,737 26

4.

of Alabama at Decatur, 31st October, 1837.

RESOURCES.

Internal improvement fund - - -	$812 15
Notes discounted at 6 per cent. interest -	518,314 14
Notes discounted at 7 per cent. interest -	800,002 67
Notes on interest at 8 per cent. - -	1,557,151 30
Banking house and lot - - -	11,943 59
Bank furniture account - - -	2,327 20
Protest account - - - -	1,152 42
Expense account - - - -	266 53
Bills of exchange - - - -	564,538 79
Inland bills - - - -	707,915 29
Amount due from banks within the State of Alabama - - - -	35,939 83
Amount due from other banks - -	21,434 86
Notes of other banks - - -	3,078 00
Specie - - - - -	9,810 48
	$4,234,737 26*

GG

Condition of the Branch of the Bank of the State

LIABILITIES.

Capital stock - -	- $1,000,000	00
Interest expended - -	- 107,126	81
Damages on bills protested -	- 1,796	40
Profit and loss - -	- 10,369	30
Sinking fund - -	- 58,852	71
Sixteenth section school fund -	- 32,019	51
Individual depositors - -	- 152,828	59
Building committee - -	- 6,599	40
Treasurer of the state of Alabama -	- 133,817	26
Treasurer of the United States for the post-office department -	- 3,328	07
Secretary of the treasury of the United States - -	- 12,500	00
Amounts due, sundry banks -	- 151,145	61
Notes in circulation payable at counter - - - $75,975 00		
Post notes in circulation payable at the bank of Louisiana - 93,960 00		
Post notes in circulation payable at the branch bank of Mobile 140,210 00		
	310,145	00
	$1,980,528	76*

5.

of Alabama at Huntsville, 31st October, 1837.

RESOURCES.

Notes discounted	-	-	-	$674,315 21
Domestic bills	-	-	-	135,460 33
Notes and bills extended	-	-	-	812,780 60
Suspended debt	-	-	-	65,776 88
Banking house and lot	-	-	-	19,795 25
Bank furniture	-	-	-	723 73
Amounts due from sundry banks	-	-	189,897 29
Cash, viz.				
Specie	-	-	$76,739 47	
United States' notes	-	-	5,040 00	
				81,779 47

$1,980,528 76

GG

Condition of the Bank of

LIABILITIES.

Real estate - - - - -		$21,921 50
Bills and notes discounted -	$1,183,658 58	
Bills receivable - -	778,484 09	
Loans secured by bank stock -	134,400 00	
		2,046,543 66 *
Domestic exchange - -	468,441 82	
Williams, Deacon, and Co., London - - - -	65,847 75	
		534,289 55 *
Specie in vault - - - - -		260,683 67
Due from banks in New York and New Orleans - - -	287,291 36	
Due from other banks - -	328,875 18	
		616,166 54
Notes of the different banks in this state - - - -	- -	319,095 00
State of Alabama - - - -		3,000 00
Suspense account · - - - -		18,565 78
Expenses - - - - -		4,983 51
Notes in transitu - - - -		7,075 00
		$3,832,325 21 *

3.

Mobile, March 28. 1838.

RESOURCES.

Capital stock` - - - - -		$1,500,000 00
Bills payable, viz. two notes to the Bank of the United States, due 1839 and 1840 - -	- -	547,723 39
Profit and loss - - -	$213,310 40	
Discount, exchange, and interest -	44,523 33	
Interest on extensions to 1839 -	24,966 76	
Interest on extensions to 1840 -	23,748 78	
		306,549 37*
Unclaimed dividends - - - -		2,856 27
Due to banks (special) - - - -		435,023 86
Corporation orders - - - -		1,471 95
Post office department - - - -		711 00
Individual depositors - - - -		650,595 37
Notes in circulation - - - -		397,394 00

$3,832,325 21*

GG

Condition of the Banks of Alabama before and

Banks and Branches,	Capital stock.	Notes discounted and Bills purchased.	Due from other Banks.
On 1st November, 1836.			
Bank of the State of Alabama -	$1,169,636	$1,922,956	$238,252
Branch at Mobile - -	2,000,000	5,953,621	1,156,226
Branch at Montgomery -	800,000	2,303,140	197,102
Branch at Decatur - -	1,000,000	2,845,855	118,220
Branch at Huntsville - -	500,000	1,059,448	233,056
Bank of Mobile - -	1,500,000	3,265,545	139,392
On 1st June, 1837.			
Bank of the State of Alabama -	1,207,886	2,186,245	377,510
Branch at Mobile - -	2,300,000	8,175,581	349,113
Branch at Montgomery -	882,000	2,025,011	104,563
Branch at Decatur - -	1,500,000	3,720,258	57,754
Branch at Huntsville - -	1,000,000	1,586,888	252,131
Bank of Mobile - -	1,500,000	2,951,269	58,224

HH.

Condition of the Bank of the State of

LIABILITIES.

Capital	-	-	-	-	-	$607,398 00
Circulation	-	-	-	-	-	94,000 00
Deposits	-	-	-	-	-	584,384 00
Due to other banks	-	-	-	-	198,614 00
Other liabilities	-	-	-	-	297,808 00

$1,782,204 00

7.

after the Suspension of Specie Payments.

Specie.	Notes in circulation.	Individual deposits.	Due to other Banks.	Sinking Fund.	Profit since.
$197,810	$664,472	$231,126	- -	$146,928	
282,236	2,060,565	1,664,516	945,685	577,944	
195,032	1,399,476	137,093	183,386	213,869	
137,107	1,140,904	282,342	139,392	306,812	
97,945	565,400	165,892	38,050	40,969	
355,388	1,031,717	333,299	382,397		
229,499	780,094	253,726	21,831	146,928	$85,889
79,794	1,684,763	2,547,940	1,126,806	577,944	318,867
96,950	822,000	88,699	20,254	213,869	149,000
10,777	751,885	410,192	646,687	306,812	108,280
75,355	538,010	2 07,992	87,117	40,969	68,063
159,212	691,909	264,621	381,406	- -	204,752

Missouri and Branches, 30th December, 1837.

RESOURCES.

Loans and discounts	- - - -	$825,080 00
Real estate	- - - -	50,101 00
Other investments	- - -	65,000 00
Specie	- - - -	622,945 00
Notes of other banks	- - -	174,350 00
Due by other banks	- - -	44,674 00
		$1,782,204 00*

II.

Condition of the Bank of the State of

LIABILITIES.

Amount of capital received from sale
 of 5 per cent. state bonds - -$100,000 00
200 5 per cent. bonds contracted for
 (payable in specie) by the Secretary
 of War on account of the Chickasaw
 orphan fund - - - 200,000 00
Received on account of surplus revenue
 of the United States - - 286,156 49
Received on account 5 per cent. on
 sale of public lands - - 26,725 00
Received on account of seminary and
 saline funds - - - 222 80
          ————— $613,105 29*
Amount due to depositors, in specie - 25,552 95
Amount due in post and other current
 bank notes - - - 61,689 51
          ————— 87,242 46

Amount on notes in circulation, viz:—
   Payable on demand - - 8,100 00
   Payable 8th August, 1838 - 85,785 00
   Payable 1st January, 1839 - 16,310 00
         ————— 110,195 00
Balance of profit and loss account as
 last rendered to the legislature - 8,460 28
Discount and premium since received - 3,361 83
          ————— 11,822 11

          $822,364 86*

Arkansas on the 1st *January,* 1838.

RESOURCES.

Amount of bills and notes discounted - -		$374,791 98
Amount of specie furnished the two branches - - - - - -		100,000 00
Amount of specie on hand per cash book	$96,455 41	
Amount due by treasurer of the United States for balance account -	11,000 00	
Amount due by Secretary of War for 200 state bonds - - -	200,000 00	
Treasury warrants on St. Louis payable in specie - - - -	24,795 89	
Treasury warrants on Natchez payable in specie - - - -	4,600 00	
		336,851 30
In bank notes of Kentucky, New Orleans, &c. - - - -	2,450 00	
Due by banks in Philadelphia and New Orleans - - - -	3,678 00	
Due by our own branches - -	657 80	
		6,786 43
Amount of interest paid on $100,000 of 5 per cent. state bonds to 1st January, 1838. - - -	2,404 11	
Amount of incidental and other expense accounts - - - -	1,531 04	
		3,935 15
		$822,364 86

KK

Condition of the Union Bank

LIABILITIES.

Stock - - - - -	$1,000,000 00		
Cash stock - - - -	2,900 00		
		$1,002,900 00
Due to other banks - - - - -		14,372 11
Individual deposits - - - - -		113,937 19
Bank bonds - - - - - -		484,000 00
Bank notes in circulation - - - - -		185,517 00
Profit and losses - - -	87,973 16	
Discount premium, &c. - - $94,012 67		
Deduct interest on territorial bonds $60,000 00		
Bank bonds - 932 36		
Expenses here and at the agency - 20,528 57		
————$81,460 93		
	12,551 74	
		100,524 90
		$1,901,251 20

1.

of Florida, 1*st January,* 1838.

RESOURCES.

Stock notes discounted	- - -	$605,427 99	
Stock notes in suit	- - -	50,503 00	
			$665,730 99*
Bonds and notes	- - -	535,159 19	
Bonds and notes in suit	- - -	19,270 25	
			554,429 44
Bills of exchange	- - -	96,080 65	
Bills of exchange under protest	- -	334,822 93	
			430,903 58
Agency at St. Joseph	- - - - -		56,832 70
Due by other banks	- - - - -		115,750 04
Claims on the United States	- -	1,117 39	
Seminole expedition	- - -	1,046 93	
			2,162 32*
Protests and damages	- - - - -		4,845 04
Cash balances, viz. : —			
In specie	- - -	47,179 09	
In notes of other banks	- -	33,416 00	
			80,595 09
			$1,901,251 20*

KK

Condition of the Southern Life Insurance

LIABILITIES.

Capital stock paid in	-	-	-	- $500,150	74
Dividends unpaid	-	-	-	315	60
Notes in circulation	-	-	-	151,608	70
Deposits in trust at interest	-	-	-	11,338	00
Due to other banks	-	-	-	27,461	00
Bills payable in January, February, March, and April	-	-	-	99,442	84
Deposits, partial payments on discounts, bills part due	-	-	-	17,292	53
Private deposits	-	-	-	48,067	09
Profits, discount account	-	$31,957 48			
interest account	-	11,725 37			
exchange account	-	4,595 51			
Profit and loss	-	-	11,757 42		
				60,035	78
				915,711	05*

KK

Condition of the Bank of

LIABILITIES.

Capital stock	-	-	-	- $470,875	00
Notes in circulation	-	-	-	161,655	00
Deposits	-	-	-	81,556	56
Bank United States	-	-	-	84,303	35
Other banks	-	-	-	34,502	38
Individuals for collection	-	-	-	9,141	33
Profits	-	-	-	33,889	87
				$875,923	49

2.

and Trust Company, 26th December, 1837.

RESOURCES.

Stocks owned by the company, worth at least - - - -		$5,000 00
Amounts due from other solvent banks - - - - -		127,922 21
Discounted bills, notes, mortgages, and loans of all kinds- - - -		702,736 69
Personal property - - - -		5,170 36
Expense accounts - - - -		15,649 46
Cash, viz.		
Notes of other solvent banks, and United States' treasury notes and drafts - -	$46,192 59	
Specie - - - -	13,039 74	
		59,232 33
		$915,711 05*

3.

Pensacola, 30th December, 1837.

RESOURCES.

Credits for Alabama, Florida and Georgia railroad - - -		$449,840 33
Amount due from other banks - -		46,236 10
Gold and silver - -	$18,792 50	
Notes of other banks -	- 22,211 00	
		41,003 50
Bank property - - - -		3,973 12
Notes discounted - - -		179,179 44
Bills receivable - - - -		87,519 50
Bills and notes protested - - -		55,544 47
Interest account - - - -		7,182 77
Contingent expenses - - -		4,444 26
		$875,923 49*

THE END.

ERRATA.

Page 27. line 9. for " Chactan " read " Chocktaw."
28. line 12. and page 30. note, for " Quassaws " read " Quapaws."
49. line 3. from the bottom, for " August last " read " August, 1838."
63. note, for " Appendix Letter A." read " Letter K."
70. note, line 1. from the bottom, for "cost" read " at."
72. line 6. for " have " read " has."
75. line 7. for " are " read " is."
92. line 13. after " power " insert " arising out of their connection with the government."
114. line 12. for " August last " read " August, 1838."
162. line 12. for " 1st November," read " 1st August."
190. line 21. for " Kennaway " read " Kanawha."
256. lines 10, 11, 12, and 13. for "$1,250,000 00" read "$125,000 00."
256. line 19. for " New York Company " read " American Company."
318. line 31. for " Ganesville " read " Zanesville."